Customizing macOS

Fantastic Tricks, Tweaks, Hacks, Secret Commands, & Hidden Features to Customize Your macOS User Experience

High Sierra Edition

Tom Magrini

Created & Printed in the United States of America.

ISBN-13: 978-1979631389
ISBN-10: 1979631387

Terms & Conditions of Use

Some of the customizations contained in this book allow access to hidden preference settings not visible in the macOS System Preferences application. These customizations do not add to or change any part of the macOS High Sierra operating system. They are additional preference settings defined by Apple and built into macOS High Sierra. All of the customizations are reversible and can be reset to the system default. The customizations were tested in the macOS High Sierra version 10.13.3. There is always the possibility that future updates to macOS could cause some of the customizations to no longer work as expected.

While the author has taken every precaution in the preparation of this book, the author assumes no responsibility whatsoever for errors or omissions, or for damages resulting from the use of the information contained herein. The information contained in this book is used at your own risk. Any use of the information contained in this book constitutes your agreement to be bound by these terms and conditions.

Table of Contents

1

macOS High Sierra

Customizing macOS

 Like previous releases, macOS High Sierra lets you completely customize your user experience until your Mac has a look and feel different from everyone else's Mac. You can completely personalize your Mac, fine-tuning various aspects of the operating system to transform how you interact with it. Besides changing the look and feel, the customizations I'll show you will allow you to be more productive and efficient by making macOS more closely match your personal style and the way you work.

Why customize macOS? Because you can. It's that simple. The default macOS settings that come out of the box make your Mac incredibly easy and efficient to use. And for most people the defaults are all they'll ever need. But if you are reading this book, then you are not like most people. You want to tinker and tweak macOS to personalize it to the way you use your Mac. Besides, who wants their Mac to look, feel, and operate just like every other Mac? And of course, its always cool to impress your friends when they notice your Mac does things theirs does not. This book will turn you into a macOS geek, showing you how to bend macOS to your every will.

You don't need to be an Apple genius to customize your user experience. Anyone with a little bit of familiarity with macOS can safely customize their user experience. Some customizations require a basic knowledge of how to use an application called Terminal. I'll teach you enough about Terminal in the next few pages to become truly dangerous (just kidding). My goal is not to turn you into a Terminal expert, but to give you a basic foundation so you can execute simple commands to customize your user experience. Once you have learned the basics of Terminal, you will be able to configure all of the macOS customizations, hacks, and tweaks in this book to unlock macOS' hidden features.

Each chapter focuses on customizing a particular aspect of macOS. We'll start first with a short introduction to macOS High Sierra and the basics of macOS customization in Chapter 1. I'll introduce you to the System Preferences application and the command line interface of Terminal.

Next up are Gestures in Chapter 2. Starting with the 2015 models, Apple's Force Touch technology became available in its MacBook and MacBook Pro laptops. Even Apple's iMac, Mac Mini, and Mac Pro desktops are Force Touch capable with the addition of

Apple's Magic Trackpad 2. I'll show you how to take advantage of the additional Force Touch functionality available in macOS. If you are new to Macs and macOS, Chapter 2 will make you an expert on gestures. And once we have covered the standard macOS gestures, I'll teach you how to create your own personal, custom trackpad and mouse gestures. Creating your own unique set of gestures is guaranteed to increase your efficiency and productivity.

Once you've mastered these skills, we'll focus on the customization of each aspect of macOS starting first with the Desktop in Chapter 3. You'll learn how to customize the Desktop, personalize it, and make it more efficient and presentable.

In Chapter 4, we'll tweak Mission Control, which provides a view of everything on your Mac – windows, apps in Full-Screen and Split-View mode, Desktops, and the Dashboard. You'll learn how to increase your desktop real estate, declutter your desktop, and efficiently manage window clutter.

We'll customize various options available in the Menu Bar, a component of the macOS Desktop in Chapter 5. I'll show you a few Menu Bar apps available in the Mac App Store to help squeeze a little more out of the Menu Bar.

Next up in Chapter 6 is the Dock, one of the most recognizable features of macOS, where I'll teach you how to fine-tune the default macOS Dock to make it your own personal, highly productive Dock. You'll learn how to add shortcuts to the Dock including iCloud Drive, System Preference Panes, Applications, and Siri.

Then we move on to Chapter 7 where you'll learn about Stacks, a cool feature of the Dock. You'll learn a dozen different tweaks guaranteed to increase your productivity including how to create App Stacks and Recent Items stacks.

Better searching is the topic of Chapter 8, where we'll customize Spotlight. I'll show you some tips and tricks for more accurate searches.

Next up is Siri, Apple's intelligent virtual assistant application, in Chapter 9. I'll show you how to add the "Hey Siri" function missing from macOS and how to configure type to Siri, a new feature in macOS High Sierra.

Next up is the Notification Center. In Chapter 10, I'll teach you how to fine tune this one-stop shop that consolidates alerts from a variety of sources. You'll learn how to completely customize Notification Center with Apple's and third party widgets.

I'll show you a number of customizations for the Dashboard in Chapter 11 to make this feature a little more useful. I'll even show you how to completely disable it.

In Chapter 12, we'll explore some tweaks to Launchpad, a macOS feature that blurs the line between macOS and iOS.

In Chapter 13, we'll focus on Finder, the macOS file manager application, which provides a user interface to manage files, disk drives, network drives, and to launch applications. We'll customize Finder to make it more useful and more efficient. And you'll learn about the seamless integration of iCloud, making online storage a part of the macOS operating system instead of an add-on app.

Window snapping and management is the focus of Chapter 14. I'll help those former Microsoft Windows users who miss Windows' snapping feature. Everything is better on a Mac including window snapping. I'll show two different apps that will give you some cool window snapping options.

The keyboard is the topic of Chapter 15. I know what you are thinking. "Why a chapter on the keyboard?" "Everyone knows how to use the keyboard." I'll show you a few keyboard customization tricks. macOS let's you change the behavior of the keys and allows you to create custom keyboard shortcuts.

In Chapter 16, we'll learn how to customize the Touch Bar, a dynamic input device with a strip of vitual keys that automatically change based on the running application and what you're doing.

Next, we'll focus on customizing applications starting with Safari in Chapter 17 and will move on to Mail in Chapter 18. I'll show you how to customize these apps to make them perform more efficiently and add to your productivity.

The Internet can be a dangerous place. Security & Privacy is the focus of Chapter 19, where I'll show you some tweaks to make your Mac a little more secure and to keep your data safe.

Finally, Chapter 20 is a giant grab bag containing a huge line up of tricks, tweaks, and hacks to customize macOS and a number of applications.

How to Use This Book

There is no one way to use this book. If you want impress your friends and make them think you are an Apple genius, read it cover to cover, trying out each of the tweaks, hacks, secret commands, and hidden features. Or you could start by focusing on a specific chapter that interests you, say like the Dock, which by the way, was the first chapter I wrote. The Dock chapter was originally Chapter 2 when I wrote the draft of the first book in this series, *Taming the Pride: Customizing macOS Mountain Lion*, back in 2013. Another option is to review the Table of Contents and go directly to a tweak, hack, secret command, or hidden feature that interests you. No matter how you use this book, I hope that the tweaks, hacks, secret commands, and hidden features will make you a more efficient and productive Mac user.

Before we get started, let's review some of the conventions used in this book.

Keyboard Shortcuts

This book uses keyboard shortcuts extensively. A keyboard shortcut allows you to do actions that would normally require selecting a command from a menu or executing a gesture on a mouse or trackpad. Keyboard shortcuts require the use of one or more of the modifier keys listed below. These modifier keys will always be bolded in the text.

fn	Function	**^**	Control	**⌥**	Option
⌘	Command	**⇧**	Shift	**F**	F key

Keyboard shortcuts will also be listed in parenthesis, for example, ⇧⌘G will be followed by (shift+command+G). To use a keyboard shortcut, you will need to hold down the listed modifier key(s) while pressing the last key of the shortcut. For ⇧⌘G, you will hold down the shift and command keys while pressing the letter "G."

Note that when I refer to an **F** key, I am not referring to the key for the letter "F." I am referring to the 12 function keys at the top of your keyboard that are labeled **F1** to **F12**. You should also note that Macs are a little different than Windows PCs. On a Mac, each of the function keys is pre-configured to execute a specific action, such as increasing or decreasing the volume, launching Mission Control, or pausing and playing your music. If you want to use a function key as a plain old **F** key, you will need to hold down the **fn** (function) key to avoid executing the assigned key command. This is the opposite of how **F** keys work on a Windows PC.

Command Typeface

When a tweak, hack, secret command, or hidden feature requires you to type a command into the Terminal or Finder, I will use a different typeface. When you see this typeface, these are commands that you will need to enter in the specified app.

```
defaults write com.apple.dock workspaces-edge-delay -float 0.5
```

```
killall Dock
```

By the way, don't let the "killall" command scare you. I'm not really asking you to kill your Dock. I wouldn't do that. I like the Dock. It is one of my favorite features. The "killall Dock" command simply restarts the Dock so the previous command can take effect.

When a button needs to be clicked, the button name will be bolded, as in click the **Trackpad Options...** button.

Menus

Some commands in this book are executed using the **Apple Menu**. So when you see this symbol: I'm referring to the Apple Menu on the Menu Bar in the upper left hand corner of your desktop. I bet you are wondering why "Apple Menu" is bolded in the first sentence of this paragraph. Whenever I introduce a new feature, I bold it so you will know that I'm introducing a new feature or concept.

Now back to menus, when I ask you to execute a command using a menu, it will look like this: **> System Preferences... > Dock**. This is shorthand asking you to first select the Apple Menu, then System Preferences... and finally, to select the Dock preference pane from the drop-down menu. Whenever you see this symbol: **>** I'm asking you to make a selection from a menu.

In addition to the Apple Menu, I will ask you to make selections from other drop-down menus. In this example, **Finder > Preferences...,** I am asking you to select the Finder menu, then select Preferences. The Finder menu will appear to the right of the Apple menu, but only when Finder is the active application.

Graphical Controls

macOS uses a number of graphical controls to enable, disable, tweak, and configure various features as shown in the image of the Dock preference pane below.

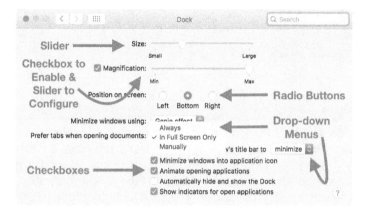

A slider allows you to choose any value between pre-defined minimum and maximum values by dragging it anywhere within the range. Most sliders allow you to select any value within the range, however some sliders are "stepped," meaning you can only select pre-defined values within the range.

A checkbox turns a feature on or off. I also use the terms enable and disable, for on and off, respectively. Checking the checkbox enables or turns the feature on while unchecking disables, or turns it off. Sometimes a checkbox is combined with a slider as shown in the image above. If the checkbox is not checked, the feature is disabled and the slider will be grayed out. To use the slider, the feature must be enabled by first checking the associated checkbox.

Drop-down menus are denoted by the white up and down arrows on a blue background (the default colors) at far right of a configuration field. Clicking the arrows or anywhere in the field drops down a menu of configuration options from which to choose, thus the name "drop-down" menu.

Radio buttons are sometimes used instead of drop-down menus, particularly when the available options are few. Selecting one radio button simultaneously deselects another as only one option can be selected.

Finally, a configuration sheet appears to drop down from underneath the title bar. It is typically used to select and configure additional options. The image above shows the configuration sheet that appears after clicking the **Trackpad Options...** button in the Accessibility preference pane.

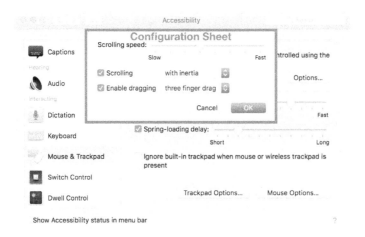

System Preferences

 We'll do a lot of customization work using the preference panes in the **System Preferences** application. macOS provides an extensive set of customization capabilities in System Preferences to modify many system-wide settings and behavior. Most of these customization options are accomplished using the macOS graphical user interface (GUI) using sliders, checkboxes, drop-down menus, radio buttons, and configuration sheets accessible from various preference panes.

Throughout this book I'll ask you to launch the **System Preferences** application in order to customize a specific macOS parameter. In macOS, there are often multiple ways of doing the same thing and there are a number of different ways to launch Systems Preferences. You can launch the System Preferences application by any one of the following methods:

1. Click on the System Preferences icon in the **Dock**,
2. Launch System Preferences using **Launchpad**,
3. Select > **System Preferences…** from the Apple menu,
4. Open **Spotlight**, search for System Preferences, and press the **return** key,
5. Launch **Finder**, open the **Applications** folder, and double-click on System Preferences, or
6. Launch Siri and ask it to, "Launch System Preferences."

System Preferences will display a default set of 29 icons, called **Preference Panes**, organized into rows of four or five categories from top to bottom. The preference panes contain a tremendous amount of customization power to safely tweak your macOS user experience.

In versions of macOS prior to OS X Yosemite, Apple labeled the rows from top to bottom in this order: Personal, Hardware, Internet & Wireless, System, and Other. Even though Apple has since dropped the categories, the organization of the preference panes still follows the same categorization scheme of earlier versions of macOS.

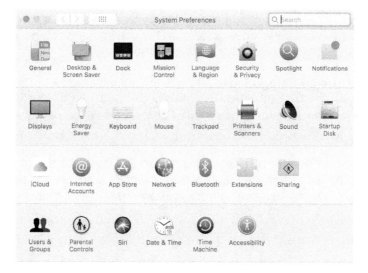

The first row, formerly labeled the "Personal" category, contains a collection of eight system preference panes to customize the basic look and feel of macOS. Eight preference panes relating to hardware are located in the second row. The third row contains seven preference panes that allow you to customize various Internet & Wireless preferences such as iCloud, Wi-Fi, and Bluetooth. Six preference panes grouped into the fourth row are used to customize various system preferences such as Users & Groups, Siri, Date & Time, and Accessibility preferences. A fifth category, formerly labeled "Other," is used for third party preference panes and is only visible if you have a third party application installed, like Adobe Flash Player. Clicking on any preference icon launches the associated preference pane, in which you can modify various customization options.

Organize the Preference Panes Alphabetically

The organization of the preference panes in System Preferences is our very first customization. By default, the panes are organized by category. macOS allows you to change the display to alphabetical order. Select **View > Organize Alphabetically**.

There are a couple of advantages to organizing the preference panes alphabetically. The System Preferences window takes up less room on the desktop and you no longer have to know in which category or row a particular pane is located

Select **View > Organize by Categories** to return to the default display.

The **View** menu also provides a drop down list of all the preference panes in alphabetical order, allowing you to make a quick selection.

A secondary click on the **System Preferences** icon in the Dock will also display a menu with the preference panes in alphabetical order. If you have a preference pane open, it is displayed at the top of the list and a checkmark is shown next to its name.

At the very top of the System Preferences window is a toolbar with four controls: window controls, navigation buttons, a **Show All button**, and a **Search** field. The back button is grayed out until you navigate to a preference pane since is nothing to go back to until then. The forward button is grayed out until you click on a preference pane and then return to the main display. Essentially these navigation buttons serve the same purpose as they do in Safari, allowing you to navigate forward and backward through the preference panes.

Clicking and holding the **Show All** button, the button with a grid of 12 squares located to the right of the navigation buttons, displays an alphabetical list of the preference panes. If you know what preference pane you want, this option will get you there quickly. When viewing a preference pane, clicking the back button returns you to the main System Preferences display as does clicking the Show All button.

Search System Preferences

Sometimes finding the preference pane containing the specific setting you want to modify is not always intuitive. The **Search field** comes in handy when you know which particular setting you want to modify, but don't know where to find it.

As you type in the Search field, macOS highlights the preference panes that are most likely related to your search and displays a list of suggested items in the Spotlight menu below the search field. Eventually, macOS will zero in on the applicable preference pane.

If you don't know exactly what the macOS setting is called, Spotlight offers suggestions to help you find the right preference pane. Click the highlighted preference pane or one of the items listed under the Search field to open the associated preference pane.

Find a Preference Pane Using Spotlight

Spotlight is the macOS search feature that allows you to search for items on your Mac and the Internet. To open **Spotlight**, click on the magnifying glass in the upper right corner of the Menu Bar or press ⌘**space** (command+space).

If you don't know which Preference Pane contains the specific setting you want to modify, open **Spotlight** and start typing in the **Spotlight Search** field. As you type, Spotlight will offer results it thinks are likely matches, refining them as you type and organizing them into categories directly below the search field. Results are displayed in categories, with the **Top Hit**, the result Spotlight determined to be the most likely, highlighted at the top of the list. If you press **return**, macOS will launch the **Top Hit**.

Spotlight organizes search results into categories. In the example above, when I searched for "Scrolling," Spotlight suggested two Preference Panes, Trackpad and Mouse, under the **System Preferences** category. To open the desired preference pane, highlight it and press the **return** key or double-click on it.

Hide Preference Panes

Clicking and holding the **Show All** button reveals an alphabetical list of the preference panes and offers a **Customize...** option at the bottom of the list. Selecting **Customize...**

puts little checkboxes at the lower right of each preference pane icon. Unchecking the checkbox hides the associated preference pane. You can also access this feature from **View > Customize...** under the System Preferences View menu.

Why hide a preference pane? There are a few preference panes that you may never use or you've made changes in one or more and have no desire to make additional changes. Hiding preference panes removes superfluous clutter that distracts you from the panes you actually need. For example, if you don't own a mouse, why do you need the Mouse preference pane?

When you are finished hiding preference panes, click the **Done** button, which is located where the **Show All** button was. Note that unchecking a preference pane simply hides it from view. It does not delete it. And don't worry, a hidden preference pane can always be unhidden by selecting **Show All > Customize...** and checking its checkbox.

Delete Preference Panes

As you use your Mac, you'll likely install and try apps, uninstalling them if they don't fit your needs. Sometimes third party apps come with their own preference pane to modify various application preferences. Third party preference panes are shown in the bottom row of System Preferences when organized by categories. If you want to delete a third party preference pane for software you no longer use, secondary click on the preference pane to display an option to remove it.

macOS will remove the preference pane icon from System Preferences and move the preference pane to the Trash.

Note that macOS only allows you to remove third party preference panes. macOS does not allow you to remove Apple preference panes as they are needed by macOS.

System Preferences is extremely powerful, providing you the power to customize a multitude of system-wide settings. In each of the coming chapters, we'll focus on specific aspects of the macOS user experience, learning options available to tweak. Even if you find System Preferences a little intimidating, I'll show you just how easy it is to customize your macOS user experience. It's your Mac, so feel free to customize, hack, and tweak it.

Terminal

 Apple offers a number of customizations to change the behavior of macOS that are not accessible from the macOS GUI. There is nothing really hidden or secret about these features other than the fact they are not directly accessible using System Preferences. These hidden features require you to enter commands into an application called **Terminal**. Terminal provides a command line interface for you to directly interact with macOS, allowing you to take your macOS customization to an entirely new level not achievable using System Preferences alone.

If entering commands into a command line interface sounds intimidating, it isn't. First, I'll show you how to use the Terminal application. Once you have learned the basics of Terminal, you will be able to configure all of the macOS customizations, hacks, and tweaks in this book and unlock macOS's hidden or secret features. I have tested each of the commands shown in this book on my own MacBook Pro. Many are my personal favorites.

The average Mac user may never know of the existence of the **Terminal** application, which is tucked away in the **Utilities** folder in **Applications**. Almost everything the average Mac user needs to do can be accomplished through the macOS GUI. Those who know of Terminal's existence may avoid it because they find its archaic command line interface strange and intimidating. The modern computer user sees Terminal as a throwback to the old days of computing before GUIs became the norm. Terminal reminds us of a time when geeky computer scientists with thick glasses sat hunched over their keyboards, pounding away in a strange language more familiar to a computer than a human. As you'll see in the next few pages, Terminal may seem archaic, but it certainly isn't very intimidating.

Why bother using Terminal in the first place? While Terminal appears at first glance to be a relic more appropriate for a museum then your modern, beautiful, and elegant macOS GUI, it is one of the most powerful, versatile, and useful applications in macOS. It has many uses beyond just customization of your macOS user experience. However, our focus is customization and personalization of macOS, so I won't cover Terminal's other uses in this book.

Terminal can be used by users of all skill levels, even a novice Mac user who is learning about Terminal for the first time. We'll take some baby steps to build your confidence and learn the basics, enough so that you will be able to configure any of the macOS customizations, hacks, and tweaks in this book.

What is Terminal?

Terminal is Apple's implementation of a Unix command line interface, commonly called a shell or command line interpreter. The macOS operating system, as well as their precursor NeXTSTEP, are based on Unix, an operating system first developed by AT&T in the 1970s. Apple macOS represents the largest installed base of Unix.

Essentially, Terminal gives you text-based access to macOS, allowing you to enter Unix commands which let you configure various attributes that are not presented via the GUI. Other than its function as a command line interpreter, Terminal is like any other application.

Before You Begin

Some of the customizations require you to use Terminal to change preference settings which are not visible in the macOS System Preferences. These preference settings do not add or change any part of the macOS operating system. The preference settings described in this book are defined by Apple as part of macOS. All of the customizations are reversible.

While the Terminal commands in this book are safe to use and I have tested them on my MacBook Pro, you must enter the commands exactly as shown. In Terminal, every character is important including the spaces. Since I cannot be there looking over your shoulder to correct you if you fat finger a command, it is always good practice to have a current **Time Machine** backup in case you have to restore your Mac. To create a Time Machine backup, select **Back Up Now** from the **Time Machine** Menu Extra in the Menu Bar at the top of your desktop to back up to an external disk drive. Readers of the ebook edition are encouraged to copy and paste the commands from this book into Terminal.

Launching Terminal

Let's launch the **Terminal** application. Similar to System Preferences, there are multiple, ways to launch the Terminal application. You can launch Terminal by any one of the following methods:

1. Launch Terminal using **Launchpad** by typing "Terminal" in the Launchpad search field,
2. Open **Spotlight**, search for Terminal, and press the **return** key,
3. Launch **Finder**, open the **Applications** folder, open the **Utilities** folder, and double-click on Terminal, or
4. Launch Siri and ask it to, "Launch Terminal."

Terminal provides a text-based user interface showing the name of your computer and your location in its file system (normally your Home directory) followed by a **$** sign. A gray rectangular pointer, called the **prompt**, waits patiently for your commands. The default view is shown in the picture above. Note that the name of the current user, the type of shell (macOS uses a shell called bash), and the size of the window (80 characters by 24 lines) is shown on the window's Title Bar. The home icon to the left of to my name in the Title Bar indicates that I am working in my home directory.

Terminal Basics

The first thing you'll notice about Terminal is the **prompt**. The prompt is where we will enter all of the commands shown in this book. When you open Terminal, the first two lines will look something like this.

```
Last login: Tue Sep 20 22:07:26 on console
Toms-MacBook-Pro:~ Tom$ |
```

The first line tells you when you last logged in via the Terminal application. The second line contains the prompt. The beginning of the prompt tells you the machine you're logged into and your location in its file system. The cursor appears after the **$** sign. Depending on your selections in Terminal preferences, accessible by entering **⌘,** (command+comma), the cursor may or may not be blinking and could appear as a block, an underline, or a vertical bar.

Commands are entered at the **prompt**. You do not have to use your mouse or trackpad as anything you type will appear at the prompt. Once a command has been completely entered, you will press the **return** key to execute it.

A behavior first time users often find odd is that Terminal provides no feedback when a command is entered correctly. Feedback is typically provided only when an invalid command is entered. And don't worry, macOS will not make any changes if the command is not valid. If a command is entered correctly, an error will be displayed and a new prompt will appear on the next line awaiting your next command.

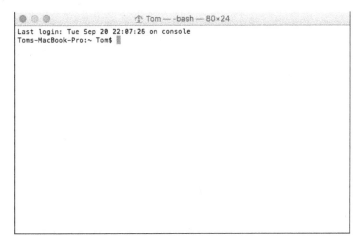

You will enter one command at a time into Terminal, pressing the **return** key after each to execute it. Note that commands shown in this book are case sensitive, therefore, you must enter each one exactly as shown. Remember, every character is important in Terminal, including the spaces.

If you purchased the e-book edition, I recommend that you copy and paste the commands into a text editor like **Notes**. Once in text editor, check the command to make sure you copied the entire command, then copy and paste it over to Terminal. Why use a text editor and not paste the command directly into Terminal? Many ebook readers also copy the source – the title, author, and page number – none of which Terminal will understand.

So far it sounds pretty simple doesn't it? The customizations that require the use of Terminal simply require you to type a few commands exactly as you see them in this book, pressing the **return** key after each command. Yes, it is that simple. Let's try a Dock customization to help you learn and gain more confidence using Terminal.

Your First Customization Using Terminal

macOS offers two standard animations when minimizing windows, the **Genie** and **Scale** effects, with the default being Genie. Unless you have changed the window minimization effect in the Dock preference pane in System Preferences, you are using the default, Genie. Let's launch the Terminal application and check. Once Terminal has launched, enter the following command.

```
defaults read com.apple.dock mineffect
```

The command you just entered is a **read** command, which you just used to find out the current setting of the **mineffect**, short for minimization effect. If the output looks like the following, telling you that com.apple.dock mineffect does not exist, that is okay. All it means is that you have never changed the minimization effect in System Preferences. Therefore, you are using the default, Genie.

```
Toms-MacBook-Pro:~ Tom$ defaults read com.apple.dock mineffect
2016-09-21 13:48:02.477 defaults[20630:1037086]
The domain/default pair of (com.apple.dock, mineffect) does not
exist
```

Now let's change the minimization effect using Terminal. First, minimize the Terminal window or any open window so you can view the animation. If you minimized the Terminal window, click on it in the Dock to reopen it. This time you will enter a **write** command, which is used to change a setting. Enter the following two commands and press the **return** key after you enter each command. Be sure to capitalize the **D** in **D**ock.

```
defaults write com.apple.dock mineffect -string scale
```

```
killall Dock
```

Now minimize the Terminal window and note the change to the minimization animation. It is no longer set to the default of Genie. You can check this by entering the following command.

```
defaults read com.apple.dock mineffect
```

The output should look like the following and indicates that the mineffect is now set to **Scale** instead of the default of Genie.

```
Toms-MacBook-Pro:~ Tom$ defaults read com.apple.dock mineffect
scale
```

You can also check this setting using the System Preferences application. Launch System Preferences, then click on the **Dock** preference pane. Check out the setting next to **Minimize windows using:**.

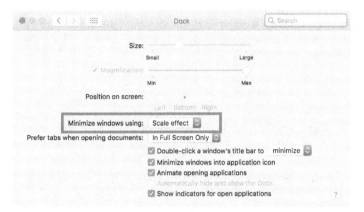

Wasn't that way cool? You just changed a macOS system parameter using the command line interface in Terminal.

If you want to change the window minimization effect back to Genie, you could simply select **Genie effect** from the drop-down menu next to **Minimize windows using:** in the Dock preference pane. But let's do it using Terminal instead. First, close the Dock preference pane then enter the following commands in the Terminal application.

defaults write com.apple.dock mineffect -string genie

killall Dock

Now try your read command again. This time the Terminal will return **Genie**. Check the effect by minimizing the Terminal window or any other open window. You can also check the setting in the Dock preference pane in System Preferences. Note that if you didn't follow my directions (shame on you) and left the Dock preference pane open when changing back to the Genie effect, the change will not be reflected properly. Close and reopen the Dock preference pane to see the change.

defaults read com.apple.dock mineffect

You could have also reverted to the default Genie animation using a **delete** command as shown below. When you delete a setting, macOS will revert to the system default, in this case, the Genie effect.

defaults delete com.apple.dock mineffect

killall Dock

Congratulations! You just completed your first customization using the Terminal command line and then you reverted back to the macOS system default. I told you it was that easy!

Wait a minute. Why would you use Terminal to change the window minimization animation when it is so much easier to change it using System Preferences? That is because some settings are not available in System Preferences, like the third animation, the **suck** effect. System Preferences allows you to switch between the Genie and Scale effects, but macOS has a third, hidden animation called **suck** that is not accessible in System Preferences. It can only be changed using a command in the Terminal app. Check it out in the chapter on the Dock.

History Command

Before we finish our basic lesson on Terminal, I'll show you a few commands that will come in handy. The first command provides a history of all the commands you have entered. **History** comes in handy when you want to see what you did or you want to reuse a command. Copy and paste is supported in Terminal. Using the history command allows you to not only see the commands you entered, but to copy a command you wish to reuse. Remember to copy only the command.

```
history
```

Now is probably a good time to remind you about the typeface. All Terminal commands will be shown in the typeface shown above. When you see this typeface, it is your signal that these are commands you will enter into Terminal.

Up and Down Arrows

The **up** arrow key will display the last command you entered in Terminal. This lets you rerun the command by pressing the **return** key again or to backspace over part of the command to make changes. After you have entered a number of commands, pressing the **up** arrow lists each command in reverse order, essentially going backwards through your history. Terminal will beep to let you know when you reach the end of your history.

Conversely, the **down** arrow will move you forward through your history of commands. The up and down arrows come in handy when you need to enter a previous command again. Once you have found the command you want and it is displayed in Terminal, simply press the **return** key to execute it.

Clear

After entering a number of commands, the prompt will be at the bottom of the window and the Terminal window will be full of commands. If you want to clear the window, enter this command. Don't forget to hit the **return** key.

```
clear
```

Note that using the clear command will not delete your command history. All the clear command does is clean up your interface.

Entering Long Commands

Some of the commands in this book are too long to fit on a single line in Terminal. A long command will simply flow onto the next line. A really long command can take two, three, or even four lines. Even though the command appears on multiple lines, it is still a single command and will not be executed until you press the **return** key. For example, note that the following command appears on one line in the book:

`defaults write com.apple.screencapture disable-shadow -bool TRUE`

However, when entered into Terminal it appears on two lines as shown in the image below. Remember, a command is executed when you press the **return** key, so do not press **return** when you reach the end of a line in Terminal. Press **return** only after you have entered the entire command and want to execute it.

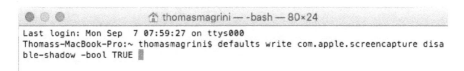

Let's Start Customizing macOS

You can quit the Terminal application by selecting **Terminal > Quit Terminal** or by entering ⌘**Q** (command+Q).

Now that you have learned the basics of the System Preferences and Terminal apps, you now have the basic knowledge necessary to configure any of the customizations in this book. I told you it was that easy!

So, let's get started with Gestures.

2

Gestures

Hands down Apple has the best multitouch trackpad and mouse in the industry. No other computer manufacturer comes close. In this chapter, we'll review the standard gestures for both the trackpad and mouse as well as various attributes such as tracking speed, double-click speed, and Force Touch. Since this book is about customizing and personalizing your macOS user experience, once we have covered the standard gestures, I'll teach you how to create your own personal, custom trackpad and mouse gestures. Creating your own unique set of gestures is guaranteed to increase your efficiency and productivity, giving you precise and completely natural control over your Mac.

A built-in trackpad is standard on the MacBook, MacBook Air, and MacBook Pro series of laptops. If you have an iMac, Mac Mini, or Mac Pro desktop computer I highly recommend that you indulge yourself and spend $129 for an Apple Magic Trackpad 2 so you can take advantage of the full set of standard and custom gestures in macOS. It will look great next to your Apple Wireless Keyboard! If you are using an Apple Magic Mouse, you have access to a smaller number of gestures. macOS offers a total of six standard gestures for the Magic Mouse while the Magic Trackpad supports a total of fifteen. While creating custom gestures can help alleviate this limitation, I find that I am far more productive using a trackpad than a mouse. And once you have mastered trackpad gestures, it's hard to go back to a mouse.

Those switching from a Windows PC typically find gestures to be strange and foreign. Where is the right mouse button? Nevermind that, where is the left one?! However, with just a little practice macOS gestures become completely natural. In fact, macOS gestures will become so natural that eventually you'll no longer need to think about which gesture does what. You'll rely on muscle memory, performing trackpad and mouse gestures without any conscious effort. Once you have mastered the built-in macOS gestures and have created a few custom gestures, you'll never want to go back to a Windows PC! And with macOS you'll never have to move your fingers far from the keyboard or get greasy fingerprints on your screen.

If you're an experienced Mac user you may be thinking about skipping this chapter since you may already be familiar with gestures. If that's the case, I suggest you skim through this chapter as I will introduce a few features that are not configured in either the Trackpad or Mouse preference panes or you may want to skip directly to the section titled "Create Custom Gestures."

Trackpad Gestures

Apple enables twelve trackpad gestures, leaving three disabled by default. I suggest you turn on all trackpad gestures and spend about a half an hour or so in the **Trackpad** preference pane learning them. Apple provides handy videos to demonstrate each gesture in the Trackpad preference pane. After a few days of practice, you'll find the gestures will become completely natural and you will no longer have to think which gesture accomplishes what task.

Besides enabling and disabling gestures, the Trackpad preference pane also allows you to customize six of the gestures, letting you to decide how many fingers you will use for the gesture. The Trackpad preference pane also allows you to adjust the pointer tracking speed and Force Touch options. And if you need to set up a new Bluetooth trackpad, you'll do so in the Trackpad preference pane.

To open the **Trackpad** preference pane, launch the System Preferences application from the Dock or Launchpad and select **Trackpad**. You can also launch the Trackpad preference pane from the Apple menu by selecting > **System Preferences... > Trackpad**. Another option is to enter ⌘**space** (command+space) to activate **Spotlight** and use it as an application launcher. Type "trackpad" in the Spotlight search window. The Trackpad preference pane will be displayed under **Top Hits** by the time you type the "c" in "trackpad." Press **return** to launch it. Or give Siri a try. Hold down ⌘**space** (command+space) and tell Siri to "Launch System Preferences."

Set Up a New Bluetooth Trackpad

To set up a new Bluetooth trackpad, first ensure your new trackpad is on. Launch the **Trackpad** preference pane and click **Set Up Bluetooth Trackpad...** at the lower right.

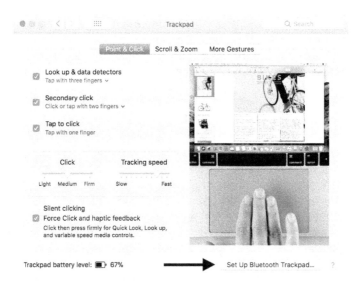

Your Mac will search for your new trackpad. If Bluetooth is off, macOS will display a **Turn On Bluetooth** button at the lower right of the discovery window, which you will need to click to enable Bluetooth. Once your trackpad is discovered, click **Done**.

Configure Trackpad Gestures

The standard macOS trackpad gestures are enabled, disabled, and configured in the **Trackpad** preference pane. When you launch the Trackpad preference pane, you'll notice three tabs at the top for each of the gesture categories – **Point & Click**, **Scroll & Zoom**, and **More Gestures**. The currently selected tab is highlighted in blue.

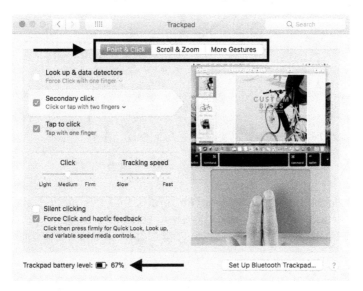

If you connected an Apple Magic Trackpad or Magic Trackpad 2 over Bluetooth, you can see its battery level at the lower left of the preference pane.

The left side of the Trackpad preference pane lists the available trackpad gestures with checkboxes next to each. To enable a gesture, simply check the checkbox. Unchecking the checkbox disables the gesture. The videos on the right side of the pane demonstrate how to perform each gesture and what action the gesture does. Hover over any of the gestures with the pointer and the video will automatically change to demonstrate the highlighted gesture and its associated action.

Look Up & Data Detectors

The **Look Up & Data Detectors** gesture gives you the option of using a three-finger tap or a one-finger Force Click. Using either gesture on a word will look it up in the dictionary, thesaurus, Wikipedia, or Siri. Depending on the word, you'll see other options such as apps, sports, TV, and movies. Note that you'll need a trackpad that supports Force Touch for the one-finger option to appear.

The **Data Detector** feature recognizes the type of data such as dates and addresses. This is an extremely handy feature allowing you to quickly add a new event to Calendar or a contact to the Contacts app.

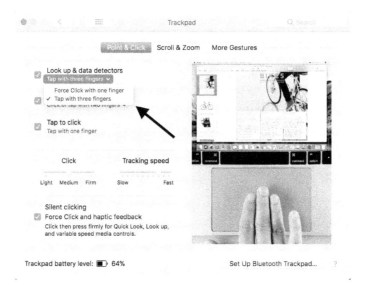

An advantage of selecting **Tap with three fingers** is that this setting also enables the three-finger tap Quick Look. With Quick Look, you can use a three-finger tap on a file in Finder to preview it. You can also use a three-finger tap to preview a web link in Safari.

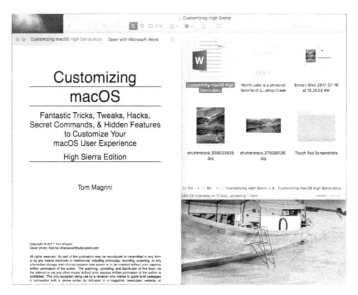

Configure the Dictionary

By default, macOS uses the language you chose when you first set up your Mac. If you would like to change or add additional languages for the dictionary, use the Look up & data detectors gesture on any word in Safari, Mail, or another Apple application. Click on the tiny gear next to **Configure Dictionaries** in the results. This reveals a preference pane where you can change or add languages, select a dictionary and thesaurus, and enable or disable Wikipedia.

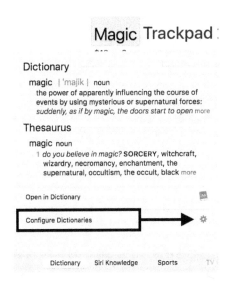

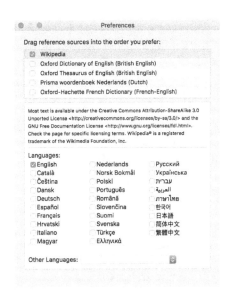

The options shown at the very bottom of the results pane allow you to see other categories pertinent to the word you looked up. These could include the dictionary, thesaurus, Siri, sports scores, TV shows, movies, web videos, music, or results from the App Store.

Secondary Click

A secondary click is used to reveal context sensitive menus, and for those you familiar with Windows PCs, is similar to a right button mouse click in the Windows world. Secondary click has three options – **Click or tap with two fingers**, **Click in the bottom right corner**, or **Click in the bottom left corner**.

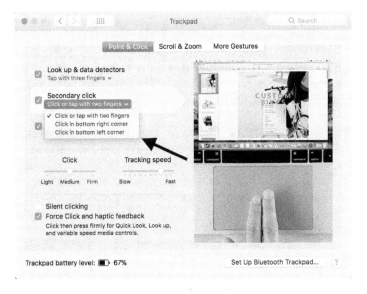

I prefer tapping with two fingers over using one of the corners. This allows me to perform a secondary click regardless of where my fingers are on the trackpad. I find the corner options to be a little restrictive, but this is a personal choice. Another reason I don't use the corner options for a secondary click is because I have created a custom gesture that utilizes the corners. I'll show you how you can create your own custom gestures later in this chapter.

Note that in order to tap with two fingers, you will first have to enable the **Tap to click** gesture. Otherwise you will have to click with two fingers to accomplish a secondary click. Enabling a two-finger tap for the secondary click does not replace the option of pressing down on the trackpad with two fingers. Both options are supported. You can also perform a secondary click by holding down the ⌘ (command) key while clicking or tapping.

Tap To Click

The **Tap to click** gesture is disabled by default, which forces you to press down on the trackpad to click. Selecting this option allows you to tap the trackpad with one finger to click. Tap to click does not replace pressing down on the trackpad to click, as both options are supported when tap to click is enabled.

Pressing down on the trackpad is still required to perform a click and hold in order to drag, move, or lasso items although you can accomplish these actions using three fingers when **three finger drag** is enabled. See "Enable Three Finger Dragging" later in this chapter.

Enabling tap to click also adds the ability to enable two-finger tap for a secondary click. When tap to click is disabled, you will have to press down on the trackpad to click or to perform a two-finger secondary click.

Scroll Direction: Natural

Natural scrolling was much derided when it first appeared in OS X Lion. This was because this gesture is opposite how most of us learned how to scroll using scrollbars or how we learned how to scroll on a Windows PC. With a scrollbar you scroll up to move your content down and scroll down to move your content up. Natural scrolling works exactly opposite – your content moves in the same direction as your fingers, which, by the way, is exactly how scrolling works on an iPhone or iPad. So in reality, you probably have been scrolling naturally for years without even realizing it.

With natural scrolling, you move your fingers in the direction you want to move your content. If you want to move your content up, scroll up with two fingers. If you want to move your content down, scroll down with two fingers. While I'll admit I was initially turned off, once I got my head around the fact that natural scrolling works exactly the same on my iPhone and iPad and I had been doing it for years, it made perfect sense.

Scrollbars only appear along the right edge of a window when scrolling. This, of course, is customizable. I'll show you several scrollbar customizations in a later chapter.

A neat scrolling trick is to flick your fingers at the beginning or end of your scroll. This will engage a feature called inertia scrolling, which causes your content to continue to scroll a little further until it slowly stops.

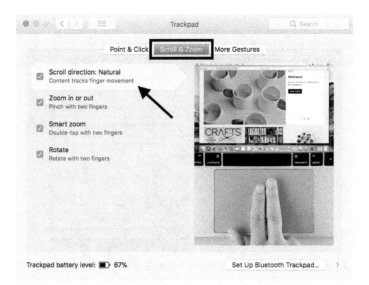

Rubberband scrolling lets you scroll a little further past the end of a file or webpage and bounces back to the end of the content. This rubberband animation lets you know you've reached the end. This is the same animation used by iOS on the iPhone and iPad.

Zoom In or Out

Similar to the two-finger pinch zoom of an iPhone or iPad, macOS allows you to spread two fingers to zoom in. Be sure to maintain continuous contact with the trackpad while spreading your fingers apart. To stop zooming, stop moving your fingers and lift them off the trackpad. A rubberband animation lets you know when you have reached the maximum limit of a zoom. To zoom out, pinch your two fingers together until you have reached your desired zoom. Rubberband animation will let you know when you have fully zoomed out.

When you have multiple tabs open in Safari, a two-finger pinch zoom on a webpage will execute the **Show All Tabs** command, displaying all of the webpage as a set of tabs. This is similar to entering ⇧⌘\ (shift+command+\). To take a tab back to full size, click on it or hover over it with the pointer and zoom in by spreading two fingers apart on the trackpad.

Smart Zoom

Smart Zoom is another feature macOS borrows from iOS. When you want to zoom in on an area of a webpage, double tap with two fingers. Double tap again to zoom out.

Rotate

Rotate is another handy feature I often use in the Photos application and when working with PDF documents. You can rotate a picture or a page in a PDF document by placing your thumb and forefinger on the trackpad and rotating in a clockwise or counterclockwise direction while maintaining continuous contact with the trackpad.

Swipe Between Pages

Swiping between pages is very much like thumbing through pages in a book. This gesture is used to move forward and backward through webpages in Safari by swiping right and left, respectively.

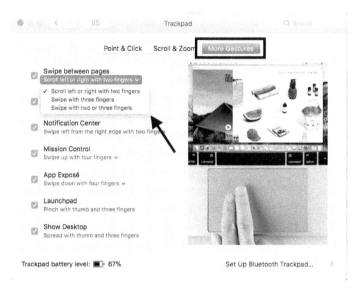

This gesture can often be used in other applications and can also be used to scroll horizontally in documents. There are three options – **Scroll left or right with two fingers**, **Swipe with three fingers**, or an option to **Swipe with two or three fingers**.

Swipe Between Full Screen Apps

If you use Full Screen apps or Desktop Spaces, both of which I will introduce in Chapter 4, this gesture lets you swipe between them. This gesture can be configured to use either three or four fingers.

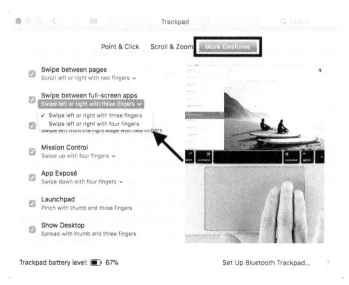

Swiping left moves the current Desktop Space left to reveal its neighboring Space located to its right. Similarly, swiping right moves the current desktop right, revealing its neighboring Space located to its left. A rubberband animation signifies that you have reached the last space or Full Screen app.

Notification Center

This gesture seems a little odd at first because you actually start off the right edge of your trackpad. Starting off the right edge, swipe left with two fingers to reveal **Notification Center**. Swipe in the opposite direction to hide it. I'll show you how to personalize your Notification Center in Chapter 10.

Mission Control

 Mission Control is a handy feature that provides a view of every window running in every Desktop Space as well as applications in Full Screen or Split View mode. It also allows you to create, delete, manage, navigate, and rearrange Desktop Spaces. I will cover Desktop Spaces in Chapter 4. Using Mission Control, you can quickly jump to another application window, Desktop Space, Full Screen app, or Split View app. Mission Control also allows you to move a window from one Desktop Space to another by dragging it to its destination.

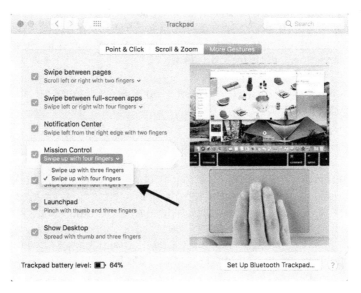

You can configure the Mission Control gesture to **Swipe up with three fingers** or **Swipe up with four fingers**. You can also access Misson Control by pressing the **F3** key, **^up** (control+up arrow), or clicking the Mission Control icon in Launchpad, the Dock, or in the Applications folder.

To close Mission Control, swipe down with the same number of fingers as the swipe up gesture, press the **F3** key, or enter **^up** (control+up arrow) or click on one of the windows or a Desktop Space.

App Exposé

App Exposé lets you see all the windows of an open application regardless in which Desktop Space the window resides. You can quickly jump to a window by clicking on it.

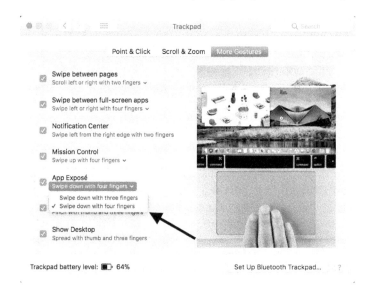

App Exposé differs from Mission Control which allows you to see windows of open applications active a single Desktop Space at a time. With App Exposé, you can see all the windows of a single application. This gesture can be configured to **Swipe down with three fingers** or **Swipe down with four fingers**.

To close App Exposé, swipe up with the same number of fingers as the swipe down gesture or click one of the windows.

Launchpad

 Launchpad is another feature macOS borrows from iOS. Launchpad allows you to see, launch, and organize the applications on your Mac in a very iOS-looking screen. The Launchpad gesture is to pinch with your thumb and three fingers. You can also access Launchpad by pressing the **F4** key, clicking the Launchpad icon in the Dock, or launching it from the Applications folder. To exit Launchpad, press the **esc** key or use the **Show Desktop** gesture. We will cover Launchpad in Chapter 12.

Show Desktop

Show Desktop is used to completely clear all windows from your desktop. This gesture is the opposite of the Launchpad gesture. Starting with your thumb and three fingers placed close together on the trackpad, spread them apart to show the desktop.

This gesture can also be used to exit Launchpad and return to the previous application. You should also note that as of this writing, you can use your thumb with either three or four fingers even though a four-finger option does not exist in the Trackpad preferences.

Enable Three-Finger Dragging

One of my favorite macOS gestures is missing from the Trackpad preference pane – the three-finger drag. The three-finger drag gesture is extremely useful since it essentially accomplishes what a click, hold, and drag does in a single gesture, allowing you to drag, move, highlight, or lasso multiple items.

To enable three-finger dragging, open the **Accessibility** preference pane from System Preferences and select **Mouse & Trackpad** from the column on the left side of the pane. Next, click **Trackpad Options...** to reveal a drop-down configuration sheet.   Check **Enable dragging** if not already checked and select **three finger drag** from the drop-down menu. Click **OK** to finish.

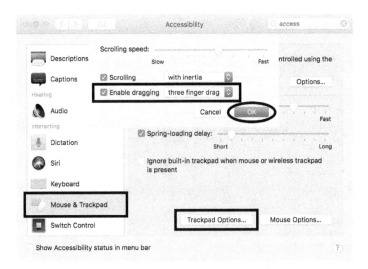

To use a three-finger drag to move a window, position your pointer over the title bar, place three fingers on your trackpad, and move the window anywhere on the desktop or to another Desktop Space. Lift your fingers off the trackpad to end the drag. This gesture can be used to move files in Finder by positioning your pointer over a file (or folder) and using a three-finger drag to move it to another folder or to the Trash. If you hold down the ⌥ (option) key, the file will be copied to the new location. A three-finger drag can also be used to lasso a group of files in Finder.

If you see an image on a webpage that you want to download, position your pointer over the picture and use a three-finger drag to download it to a Finder folder. The three-finger drag is also handy for selecting text. Position the pointer in your document and use the three-finger drag gesture either forward or backward to select the text. You can also use the gesture to lasso a group of emails in Mail.

Coast with a Three-Finger Drag

Place your pointer on a window title bar and use the three finger drag to move it. Leaving two adjacent fingers on the trackpad, flick your third finger left or right. The window will coast and slowly come to a stop. Coasting can also be used to select files, text, or items in a list, and to window snap, although it does require some practice.

Enable Double-Tap Dragging with Drag Lock

Another option to drag an item, say a file to another folder for example, is to double-tap the item without lifting your finger off the trackpad after the second tap. Keep your finger on the trackpad to drag the item to its new location. Exactly when the drag ends is configurable.

By default, dragging ends when you remove your finger from the trackpad. By enabling the **Drag Lock** feature you can change this behavior so that the drag ends when you tap the trackpad upon reaching the destination. This advantage of drag lock is that if you accidentally lift your finger off the trackpad, the drag will not prematurely end nor will the item be mistakenly moved or copied into the wrong folder. Drag Lock comes in handy when you're dragging an item from one side of the screen to another as you often run out of trackpad space before completing the drag.

To enable Drag Lock, open the **Accessibility** preference pane from System Preferences. Next, scroll down and select **Mouse & Trackpad** in the list at the left. Click the **Trackpad Options...** button. Next, verify the checkbox next to **Enable dragging** is checked and then select **with Drag Lock** from the pull-down menu. Click **OK** to finish.

Similar to the three-finger drag, double-tap dragging with or without drag lock can be combined with the ⌥ (option) key to copy an item to its new location.

An added benefit of enabling Drag Lock is that it makes using spring-loaded folders easier. For more information on spring-loaded folders, see the chapter on Finder.

Adjust the Tracking Speed

If you are using your trackpad for the first time, you may notice that the pointer moves pretty slowly. If you want the pointer to move more or less quickly, you can adjust the tracking speed from the **Point & Click** tab in the **Trackpad** preference pane.

Move the Tracking speed slider to select your desired tracking speed. Changes take effect immediately so you can try out your new tracking speed and adjust if necessary.

Ignore the Built-in Trackpad

I often use my external Bluetooth trackpad when I'm using my MacBook Pro. However, I find it annoying when I accidentally brush against the built-in trackpad and the pointer flies off into left field. There is a simple solution for this annoyance – configure macOS to ignore the built-in trackpad when a Bluetooth trackpad is connected.

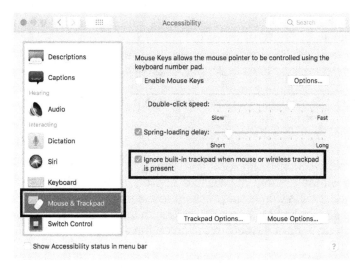

To ignore the built-in trackpad, open the **Accessibility** preference pane and scroll down to select **Mouse & Trackpad** in the left-hand column. Check the checkbox next to **Ignore built-in trackpad when mouse or wireless trackpad is present**. Uncheck the checkbox to disable this feature.

Adjust the Double-Click Speed

To change the double-click speed, launch the **Accessibility** preference pane and select **Mouse & Trackpad** in the left column. Use the slider in the right-hand pane to adjust the **Double-click speed**.

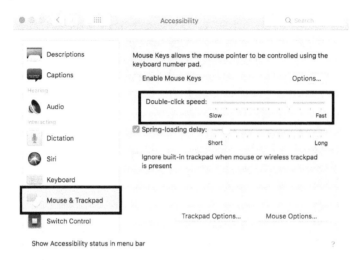

Force Touch Gestures

Force Touch is a pressure sensitive multi-touch technology developed by Apple that first became available in its MacBook and MacBook Pro laptops starting with the 2015 models. Apple also released a new Force Touch version of its Bluetooth trackpad, the Magic Trackpad 2, to bring Force Touch technology to its iMac, Mac Mini, and Mac Pro series of desktops.

Force Touch trackpads feature sensors underneath the trackpad surface that can distinguish the amount of pressure being applied. This allows you to take advantage of additional functionality available in many applications and in the macOS operating system.

A trackpad with Force Touch technology can distinguish between a tap, a click and a **Force Click** based on the amount of pressure applied to the trackpad surface. A Force Click is accomplished by applying more pressure to the trackpad than a standard click. To view a video demonstrating how to Force Click, launch the **Trackpad** preference pane and hover over the **Look up & data detectors** option on the **Point & Click** tab.

Here are some of the things you can do with a Force Click: Quick Look, App Exposé, rename a file, see Reminder details, see iMessage details, preview a web link, perform a look up in Dictionary, Thesaurus, or Wikipedia, add an event to Calendar, see event details, preview an address in Maps, empty the trash, access Dock preferences, drop a location pin in Maps, increase the fast forward rate in videos, track a package, and annotate a PDF or image in Mail. And with the custom gestures I will show you at the end of this chapter, you can do even more.

Adjust Force Click Pressure

The amount of pressure needed to perform a Force Click is adjustable in the Trackpad preference pane. By default, this setting is set to **medium**. Launch the Trackpad preference pane and select the **Point & Click** tab at the top of the pane. A slider located just below Tap to Click provides options that let you adjust the pressure needed for a Force Click. Select your desired pressure from **Light**, **Medium**, or **Firm**.

If you are having a hard time engaging Force Click, set it to **Light**, which requires less pressure and makes it easier to perform a Force Click. If you adjust the pressure to **Firm**, a Force Click will require more muscle on your part, but ensures that you will not accidentally trigger a Force Click when you wanted to do a standard click.

Note that the sound associated with a Force Click changes as you change the pressure setting, becoming louder as you move the slider from **Light** to **Firm**.

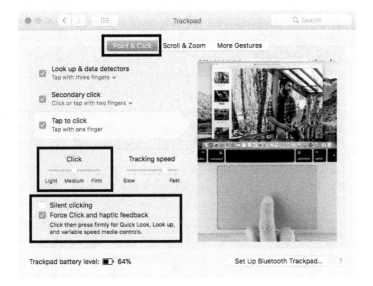

Silence Trackpad Clicking

Force Touch trackpads provide auditory feedback with clicking or Force Clicking. A standard trackpad click will produce a single clicking sound while a Force Click produces two clicking sounds in rapid succession. If you prefer your trackpad to be silent, you can disable the trackpad clicking sounds in the **Trackpad** preference pane.

Launch the Trackpad preference pane and select the **Point & Click** tab. Check the checkbox next to **Silent clicking**. Note that this option will not completely turn off the sound your trackpad makes when clicking or Force Clicking. Your trackpad will merely become much quieter when this option is enabled.

Disable Force Click

If you don't like or don't want to use Force Click, macOS gives you the option to disable it. Launch the Trackpad preference pane and uncheck the checkbox next to **Force Click and**

haptic feedback under the Point & Click tab. When this checkbox is checked, you will feel tacile feedback in certain Apple applications. For example, you will feel tacile feedback when aligning objects in the Preview app.

Note that the checkbox next to **Look up & data detectors** will uncheck itself and will revert to **Tap with three fingers** as the only available option. You will need to check the Look up & data detectors checkbox to re-enable this feature.

Mouse Gestures

 Apple's Magic Mouse and Magic Mouse 2 support six gestures with three of the gestures disabled by default. Due to its limited surface space, the Magic Mouse only supports one or two finger gestures. Besides enabling and disabling gestures, the Mouse preference pane also allows you to customize two of the gestures. Apple provides handy videos demonstrating each of the gestures in the Mouse preference pane. I suggest you turn on all of the mouse gestures and spend some time learning them. In no time at all, you'll learn all of the gestures and will wonder how you could have used a computer without them.

Set Up a New Bluetooth Mouse

To set up a new Bluetooth mouse, first ensure your new mouse is turned on. Launch the **Mouse** preference pane and click **Set Up Bluetooth Mouse...** at the lower right. Your Mac will search for your Bluetooth mouse.

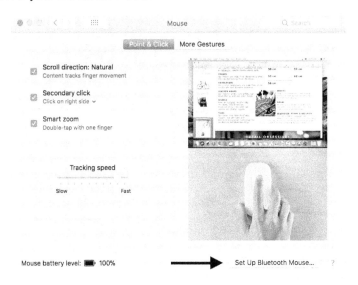

If Bluetooth is off, macOS will display a **Turn On Bluetooth** button at the lower right of the discovery window, which you will need to click to enable Bluetooth on your Mac. Once your mouse is discovered, click **Done**.

You can see your Magic Mouse's battery level at the lower left of the Mouse preference pane.

Configure Mouse Gestures

The standard macOS mouse gestures are enabled, disabled and configured in the **Mouse** preference pane. At the top of the mouse preference pane are two tabs for each category of gestures – **Point & Click** and **More Gestures**. The current tab is highlighted in blue.

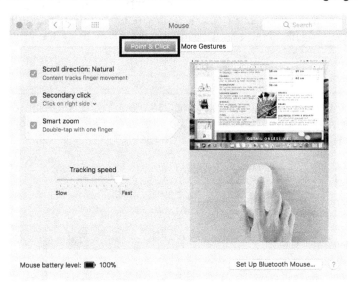

The left side of the pane lists the available mouse gestures with checkboxes next to each. To enable a gesture, check its associated checkbox. Unchecking a checkbox disables the gesture. On the right side of the pane, videos demonstrate how to perform the highlighted gesture and what action the gesture does. Hover over any of the gestures with your pointer and the video will automatically change to demonstrate the gesture and the action it performs.

Scroll Direction: Natural

Natural scrolling was much derided when it first appeared in OS X Lion. This is because the gesture is opposite how most of us learned how to scroll using scrollbars. With a scrollbar you scroll up to move your content down and scroll down to move your content up. Natural scrolling works exactly opposite – your content moves in the same direction as you are scrolling, which, by the way, is exactly how scrolling works on an iPhone or iPad. So in reality, you probably have been scrolling naturally without even realizing it.

With natural scrolling, you swipe in the direction you want to move your content. If you want to move your content up, you swipe up with one finger. Similarly, if you want to move your content down, you swipe down with one finger. While I'll admit I was initially turned off, once I got my head around the fact that natural scrolling works exactly the same on my iPhone and iPad and I had been doing it for years, it made perfect sense.

Scrollbars only appear along the right edge of a window when you are scrolling. This, of course, is customizable. I'll show you several scrollbar customizations in a later chapter.

A neat scrolling trick is to flick your fingers at the beginning or end of your scroll. This will engage a feature called inertia scrolling, which causes your content to continue to scroll a little further until it slowly stops.

Rubberband scrolling lets you scroll a little further past the end of a file or webpage and then bounces back to the end of the content. The rubberband animation lets you know you've reached the end. This is the same animation used by iOS on the iPhone and iPad.

Secondary Click

A secondary click is used to reveal context sensitive menus and is similar to a right button mouse click in the Windows PC world. On the Magic Mouse, secondary click has two options – **Click on right side** or **Click on left side**.

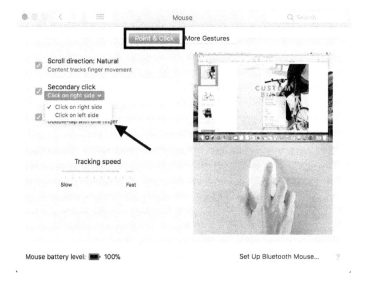

You can also accomplish a secondary click by holding down the ⌘ (command) key while clicking.

Smart Zoom

Smart Zoom is a feature macOS borrows from iOS on the iPhone and iPad. When you want to zoom in on a webpage double tap your Magic Mouse with one finger and Safari will zoom in. Double tap again to zoom out.

Swipe Between Pages

Swiping between pages is very much like thumbing through pages in a book. This gesture is used to move forward and backward through webpages in Safari by swiping right and left, respectively.

This gesture can often be used in other applications and can also be used to scroll horizontally in documents. There are three options – **Scroll left or right with one finger**, **Swipe left or right with two fingers**, or an option to **Swipe with one or two fingers**.

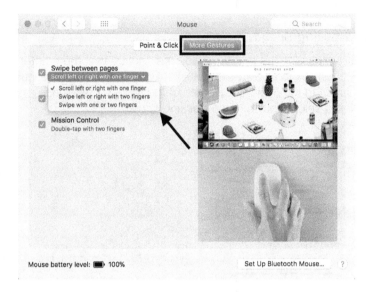

Note that if you configure swiping between pages to use two fingers, the swipe between Full Screen apps checkbox will uncheck itself and this feature will be disabled. If you want to use both gestures, using one finger to swipe between pages is the only option that will allow you to turn on swiping between Full Screen apps.

Swipe Between Full Screen Apps

If you use Full Screen apps or Desktop Spaces, both of which I introduce in Chapter 4, this gesture lets you swipe between them. Swiping left moves the current Desktop Space left to reveal its neighboring Space located to its right. Similarly, swiping right moves the current desktop right, revealing its neighboring Space located to its left. A rubberband animation signifies that you have reached the last space or Full Screen app.

Note that if you want to use the gestures for swipe between pages and swipe between Full Screen apps, you must configure swipe between pages to use one finger. This is the only option that will allow you to use both gestures.

Mission Control

 Mission Control is a handy feature that allows you to create, delete, manage, navigate, and rearrange Desktop Spaces. I will cover Desktop Spaces in detail in Chapter 4. Mission Control also provides a view of every window running in every Desktop Space as well as applications in Full Screen or Split View mode. Using Mission Control, you can quickly jump to another Desktop Space, Full Screen app, Split View app, or another window. Mission Control also allows you to move windows from one Space to another by dragging.

The Mission Control mouse gesture is a double-tap with two fingers and does the same thing as pressing the **F3** key or entering **^up** (control+up arrow). To close Mission Control, double-tap again, press **F3**, or enter **^up** (control+up arrow).

Adjust the Mouse Tracking Speed

If you are using your mouse for the first time, you may notice that the pointer moves pretty slowly across the screen. If you want the pointer to move more or less quickly, you can adjust the tracking speed in the Point & Click tab of the Mouse preference pane. Move the Tracking speed slider to select your desired tracking speed.

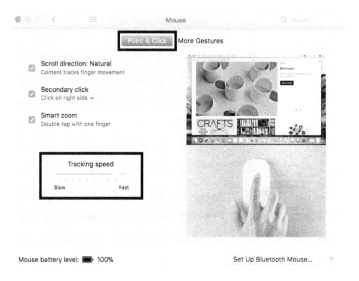

Adjust the Double-Click Speed

To change the double-click speed, launch the **Accessibility** preference pane and select **Mouse & Trackpad** at the left. Use the slider in the right-hand pane to adjust the **Double-click speed**.

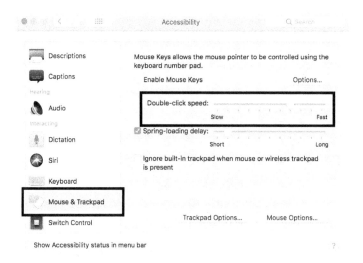

Create Custom Gestures

Now that you are familiar with the out-of-the-box macOS gestures, let's learn how to create your own custom gestures. Creating custom gestures helps you squeeze every drop of productivity from your trackpad or mouse. Creating your own gestures for common tasks will increase your productivity, efficiency, and truly personalize your macOS user experience. A few utilities exist that allow you to create custom gestures, but my favorite app is **BetterTouchTool** by Andreas Hegenberg.

BetterTouchTool lets you assign actions gestures using one, two, three, four, or five fingers combined with a tap, double-tap, tip-tap, swipe, or in combination with one or more modifier keys: ⇧ **fn** ^ ⌥ ⌘ (shift, function, control, option, and command). For those with a Force Touch trackpad, BetterTouchTool offers an additional 24 Force Touch gestures. You can assign any keyboard shortcut or one of over 125 predefined actions to a gesture. BetterTouchTool also includes window snapping functionality. Since we'll cover window snapping in detail in a separate chapter, I won't discuss the basic window snapping capability of BetterTouchTool.

BetterTouchTool is available for a donation as low as $3 at the time of this writing, although the developer is considering switching to a paid model in January 2018. You can download BetterTouch Tool from: https://www.boastr.net.

Set the Security & Privacy Settings

The first time you launch BetterTouchTool, you will be asked to authorize it in the **Security & Privacy** preference pane of System Preferences.

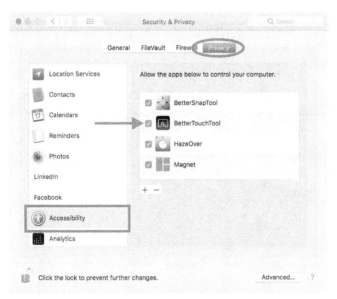

Click on the **Privacy** tab and select **Accessibility** from the left panel. Unlock the pane by clicking on the lock at the lower left and enter your credentials. Check the checkbox next to **BetterTouchTool** to authorize it.

Getting Started

After downloading and installing BetterTouchTool, you'll notice a new Menu Extra in the Menu Bar. Click the BetterTouchTool Menu Extra to reveal the drop-down menu and select **Preferences** to open the BetterTouchTool preferences.

When you open the preference pane, **Gestures** and **Simple** should be highlighted at the top of the window. The black tab bar allows you to select from **BTT Remote**, **Magic Mouse**, **Trackpads**, **Keyboard**, **Drawings**, **Normal Mice**, **Siri Remote**, and **Touch Bar**. BTT Remote is an iPhone and iPad app that allows you to remote control your Mac.

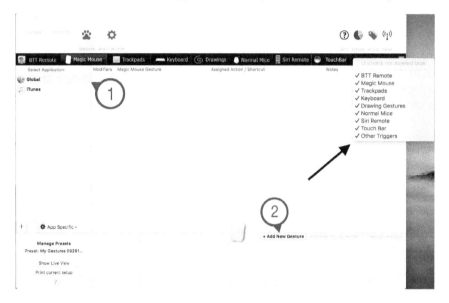

The **Magic Mouse** tab lets you configure custom gestures for Apple's Magic Mouse. **Trackpads** is where you will configure custom gestures for a Magic Trackpad or your Mac's built-in trackpad.

Keyboard allows you to create custom keyboard shortcuts. **Drawings** lets you create drawing gestures. **Normal Mice** allows you to assign specific actions to Windows PC mouse buttons. With **Siri Remote** you can create gestures and configure the buttons on a Siri-capable AppleTV remote.

If you secondary click on the tab bar, you can remove options you do not want to display. Click on the item to remove it.

Basic Settings

Click on **Advanced** at the top left of the preference window and then click the **Advanced Settings** button. Click **General Settings** tab if it is not already highlighted. Ensure the following items are checked: **Show Menubar Icon**, **Launch BetterTouchTool on startup** and **Enable automatic update checking**. The Menu Bar icon is a convenient way to quickly access the BetterTouchTool preferences, documentation, or to send feedback to the developer. Launching BetterTouchTool on startup ensures it runs each time you restart your Mac.

By default, the BetterTouchTool icon does not appear in the Dock. If you want it in the Dock, check the checkbox next to **Show Dock Icon while running** and restart your Mac to take effect.

You can configure one or a combination of the following modifier keys to temporarily disable BetterTouchTool: ⇧ **fn** ^ ⌥ ⌘ (shift, function, control, option, and command). Check the desired modifier keys if you wish to enable this functionality.

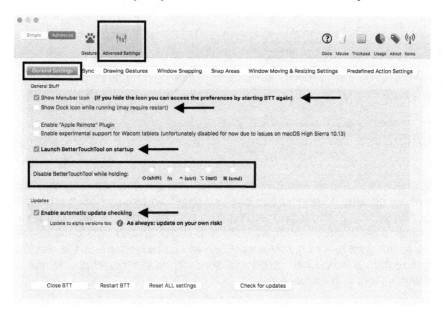

The checkbox next to **Enable automatic update checking**, is checked by default. This allows BetterTouchTool to automatically check for updates and ensures that you always have the latest version. You can decide whether you want to update alpha versions, which warns you that you are updating at your own risk. I suggest sticking with the default, which is to not update alpha versions to ensure you always run a more stable release.

Create Custom Trackpad Gestures

To create a custom trackpad gesture, first click **Gestures** in the BetterTouchTool toolbar at the top of the preference window. Next, click **Trackpads** on the black tab bar to display the trackpad gesture palette where you will create, modify, and delete your custom gestures.

The main window displays existing gestures. In the example below, you can see I have created a number of custom trackpad gestures. My first gesture is a three-finger TipTapLeft, which I use to quickly empty the trash. A three-finger tip tap is performed by placing three fingers on the trackpad and tapping with the left, middle, or right finger while keeping the other two fingers stationary. I have three-finger tip tip center gesture configured to open a Finder window.

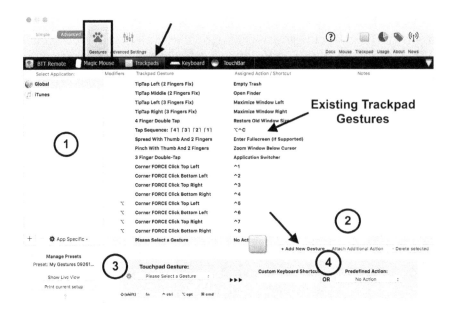

The next set of gestures shown use four fingers, which I use to snap a window to the left or right side of my desktop. The first two are four-finger tip taps, which are performed by placing all four fingers on the trackpad and tapping with the right- or left-most finger while keeping the other three fingers stationary. My four-finger tip tap right gesture snaps the active window to the right half of my desktop while the tip tap left snaps the window to the left half. I can restore a window to its original size with a four-finger double tap, tapping the trackpad with all four fingers twice.

BetterTouchTool will let you create custom tap sequences and an example is the Tap Sequence [4] [3] [2] [1] shown in the picture, which I use to center the active window on my desktop. This gesture is performed by individually tapping the trackpad with each of my four fingers, starting with my pinky finger, then my ring finger, middle finger, and finally my index finger.

Other handy gestures I have created include taking a window to full screen mode by spreading my thumb and two fingers and zooming a window below the cursor by pinching my thumb and two fingers together. I configured a three-finger double tap gesture to display the application switcher. I use the eight Force Click corner gestures to quickly jump between multiple Desktop Spaces. Four Force Click Corner gestures do not use a modifier key while the other four use the ⌥ (option) key as a modifier.

To create a new trackpad gesture first determine if your gesture will be **Global** or specific to an application. Global gestures work regardless of which application is currently active. Application specific gestures work only in the application for which they were created. You can also see that I have created application specific gestures for iTunes, which is listed in the column (**1**) on the left.

If your new gesture is global, click on **Global** at the top of the column at (**1**). If your gesture will be application specific, click the **+** button at the bottom left of (**1**), which will open your Applications folder to select the desired application.

Next, click **+ Add New Gesture** from (**2**) and select your trackpad gesture from the drop-down menu under **Touchpad Gesture** at (**3**). BetterTouchTool supports 1-, 2-, 3-, 4-, and 5-finger gestures, custom gestures you create, and Force Touch gestures in combination with single or double taps, tip-taps, swipes up, down, left, or right, click swipes up, down, left or right, triangle swipes, and trackpad location with 1-, 2-, and 3-finger gestures. Add one or more modifier keys to your gesture, if desired. Modifier keys allow you to use the same gesture for different actions.

Next, assign a keyboard shortcut to your gesture by typing it in the field below **Custom Keyboard Shortcut** at (**4**). Or select from over 125 pre-defined actions from the drop-down menu under **Pre-Defined Action.** You can add notes to your gesture by entering them in the **Notes** field. Close the BetterTouchTool preference pane when finished.

That's how simple it is to create custom trackpad gestures in BetterTouchTool. The only limit to the number of custom gestures is your imagination and the amount of time you have to create them. Have fun creating your own gestures!

To modify an existing gesture, highlight it and make the desired changes in (**3**) and (**4**).

To delete an existing gesture, highlight it and click **- Delete selected** in (**2**).

Create Custom Magic Mouse Gestures

Creating a custom gesture for your Magic Mouse is very similar to creating a trackpad gesture. First click **Gestures** in the BetterTouchTool toolbar. Next, click **Magic Mouse**, if not already highlighted, to display the Magic Mouse gesture palette where you will create, modify, and delete your custom gestures.

The main window displays any existing gestures. In the image below you can see I have created three global mouse gestures. My first custom gesture is a three-finger swipe up, which will open Mission Control. A three-finger swipe down opens App Exposé. Next, a TipTap Right will open Launchpad. A tip-tap is performed by placing two fingers on the mouse and tapping with either the left or right finger while keeping the other finger stationary.

To create a new mouse gesture first determine if your new gesture will be **Global** or specific to an application. Global gestures work regardless of which application is currently active. Application specific gestures work only in the application for which they were created.

If your new gesture is global, click on **Global** at the top of the column at (**1**). If your gesture will be application specific, click the **+** button at the bottom left of (**1**) to open your Applications folder and select the desired application.

Next, click **+ Add New Gesture** from (**2**) and select your mouse gesture from the drop-down menu under **Magic Mouse Gesture** at (**3**). BetterTouchTool supports 1-, 2-, 3-, and 4-finger gestures in combination with single or double taps, tip-taps, and swipes up, down, left, or right. Add one or more modifier keys to your gesture, if desired. Modifier keys allow you to use the same gesture for different actions.

Next, assign a keyboard shortcut to your gesture by typing it in the field below **Custom Keyboard Shortcut** at (**4**). Or select from over 125 pre-defined actions from the drop-down menu under **Pre-Defined Action** at (**4**). You can add notes to your gesture, if you wish, by entering them in the **Notes** field. Close the BetterTouchTool preference pane when finished.

That's how simple it is to create a custom mouse gesture in BetterTouchTool. The only limit to the number of gestures is your imagination and the amount of time you have to create them. Have fun creating your own gestures!

To modify an existing gesture, highlight it and make the desired changes in (**3**) and (**4**).

To delete an existing gesture, first highlight it and click **- Delete selected** in (**2**).

Create a Multiple Action Gesture

BetterTouchTool doesn't limit your gestures to a single action. In the example below, I have created two application specific gestures for Microsoft Word. The first is a Four Finger Tap combined with the ^ ⌥ ⌘ (control, option, and command) modifier keys. This gesture will save and close my currently active Word document, hide the Microsoft Word application, and open a new Finder window.

The second is a Four Finger Double Tap combined with the ^ ⌥ ⌘ (control, option, and command) modifier keys. This gesture will save my currently active Microsoft Word document and then quit Word.

To create a multiple action gesture, first create your trackpad or mouse gesture as described in the last two sections. To attach a second action, highlight the gesture and click **Attach Additional Action**. Next, enter a **Custom Keyboard Shortcut** or select a **Predefined Action** from the drop-down menu. Lather, rinse, and repeat if you want to add more actions. Close the BetterToolTouch preferences and give your new multiple action gesture a try!

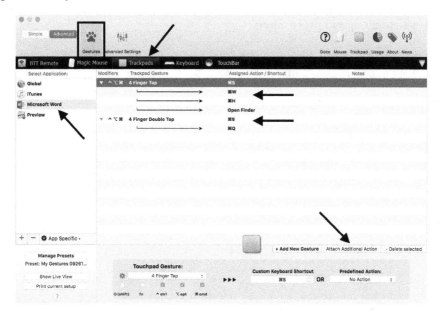

Multiple action gestures are denoted by the small triangle to their left. Click the triangle to expand the gesture and see the other actions.

Import and Export Gestures

If you want to share gestures with friends or want to create a backup of your custom gestures, you can export your BetterTouchTool gestures to a file.

First, click **Gestures**, then **Magic Mouse** or **Trackpads**, as appropriate. Click **Manage Presets** at the lower left of the preferences to reveal a dialog box. Select the gestures from the list of presets and then click **Export**. A save dialog will open. Name your file, choose the save location, and press **Save**.

To import a gesture file, click **Manage Presets** and then click **Import**. Browse to the gesture file, select it, and click **Open**.

3

Desktop

Providing the majority of your user experience, the **Desktop** is the main component of macOS through which you interface with your Mac. All folder, file, and windows appear on the Desktop. Although you will work within an application, all apps are delivered to you via the Desktop.

The Desktop has three major components – the **Menu Bar**, the **Dock**, and the macOS **Desktop** itself – as shown in the picture above. Additional items highlighted are the **Apple Menu**, **Application Menu**, **Status Menu**, **Spotlight**, **Siri**, and **Notification Center** in the Menu Bar and the **Finder** and **Trash** icons and the Dock **Divider** in the Dock.

The translucent bar located across the top of the Desktop is called the **Menu Bar** and it consists of two halves. The left half is comprised of two elements, the **Apple Menu** and the **Application Menu** while the right half contains the **Status Menu**, and icons to access **Siri**, **Spotlight**, and the **Notification Center**.

The **Apple Menu**, denoted by the , is a drop-down menu where you can access system-wide commands to update macOS, purchase and install applications from the Mac App Store, view hardware information, configure System Preferences, open recent applications and documents, force quit misbehaving apps, put your Mac to sleep, restart, shutdown, and log out.

To the right of the menu is the **Application Menu**, a set of application specific drop-down menus for the currently active application. The name of the currently active application is shown to the right of the menu in bold text. In the picture on the previous page, the active application is Microsoft **Word**. The Application Menu is named for the currently active application and in this example it is called the **Word Menu**. The Application Menu will change as you open other applications and make them active. The drop-down menus for **File**, **Edit**, **View**, **Window**, and **Help** contain commands and tools common to almost all applications. Word has additional menus called **Insert**, **Format**, **Tools**, and **Table**.

There are four elements on the right side of the Menu Bar, the **Status Menu**, and icons for to activate **Spotlight**, **Siri**, and **Notification Center**, from left to right, respectively. Note that if you upgraded from a previous version of macOS and customized your Status Menu (as I did), it may look different than what is shown.

The **Status Menu** displays both the status of and provides quick access to various macOS features via small icons called **Menu Extras**. In the picture on the previous page, the Menu Extras are, from left to right, 1Password, Amphetamine, Bitdefender, Unclutter, Deliveries, BetterTouchTool, Magnet, Time Machine, Bluetooth, Wi-Fi, Battery Monitor, AirPlay and Date & Time. We'll cover these apps later. Next to the Menu Extras are icons for **Spotlight**, **Siri**, and **Notification Center**.

Clicking the **Spotlight** icon launches Spotlight, where you can search files, folders, applications, events, reminders, music, movie showtimes, nearby locations, iTunes, the App Store, messages, essentially anything on your Mac or on the Internet. Spotlight is a universal search engine that can search the Internet without having to launch Safari.

Siri is Apple's intelligent virtual assistant application, familiar to anyone who owns an iPhone. If you use Siri on your iPhone, you'll find the macOS version to be quite similar. Siri on macOS features the same natural language interface that adapts to your personal language usage and search preferences.

In the upper right hand corner of the Menu Bar is the icon for **Notification Center**, a one-stop shop that consolidates notifications from any Apple or third party app that supports notifications including Mail, Messages, Reminders, iTunes, Calender, Stocks, Evernote, Facebook, Twitter, LinkedIn and many others. You can also configure Notification Center to provide notifications from websites that support Apple's push notification service.

In this chapter, I'll show you how to personalize your desktop. You'll learn techniques to manage the desktop clutter that inevitably comes with using any computer. Once you've personalized your desktop, I'll show you techniques to manage windows and how to increase your desktop space. Then, I'll teach you how to customize the Menu Bar. The Dock is so customizable, I wrote a chapter specifically focusing on its customization. Because Stacks, which are a component of the Dock, are also extremely customizable, they deserved their own chapter too. After the chapters on the Dock and Stacks, you'll learn about Spotlight and how to customize it and search more efficiently and accurately. Next up is Siri. We'll wrap up the desktop topics by exploring Notification Center's features and personalization options. First, let's start with your first desktop customization, changing the desktop wallpaper.

Change the Desktop Wallpaper

For the default desktop wallpaper in macOS High Sierra, Apple Apple chose a spectacular picture of lush aspens, lit like fire at the peak of their fall color, reflecting off the surface of North Lake, a beautiful little lake on the North Fork of Bishop Creek near Bishop, California.

While the image of North Lake is stunning, you don't have to live with the wallpaper Apple chose for you. Apple included a number of other images from which you can select, including backgrounds from previous releases of macOS. Or if you wish, you can change your wallpaper to any picture or set of pictures you want.

There are often numerous ways to do the same thing in macOS. It is up to you to decide which method works best for you. To change your desktop wallpaper, secondary click anywhere on the Desktop to display the Desktop contextual menu. Select **Change Desktop Background...** to open the **Desktop & Screen Saver** preference pane.

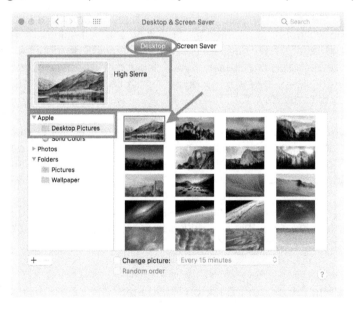

Another option is to open the **Desktop & Screen Saver** preference pane from the System Preferences application. Once the **Desktop & Screen Saver** preference pane opens, ensure the **Desktop** tab is selected. The current desktop wallpaper is shown in the upper left portion of the pane. The left hand pane allows you to select from images provided by Apple, an image or set of images in the Photos application, or images located in a folder on your Mac. Thumbnails of the images are shown in the right pane. If the thumbnail previews are too small for you, use the pinch zoom gesture to make them bigger.

Apple provides a number of standard wallpaper images under **Apple > Desktop Pictures**. If you like one of the standard images, click to select it. Apple also offers a set of solid color wallpaper images under **Apple > Solid Colors**.

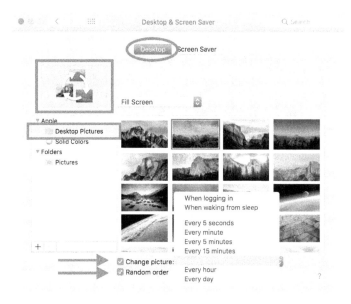

You don't have to settle for one image, you can select any or all of them and macOS will change your desktop wallpaper at an interval chosen by you. Check the checkbox next to **Change picture** and select how frequently you want macOS to change your desktop wallpaper. You have a choice of refreshing your desktop wallpaper image when logging in, when waking from sleep, every 5 seconds, 1 minute, 5 minutes, 15, minutes, 30 minutes, every hour, or every day.

When you check **Change picture**, the picture in the upper left of the **Desktop & Screen Saver** preference pane will change to show a set of circular arrows. By default, macOS will cycle through the wallpaper sequentially from the first picture to the last. Check the checkbox next to **Random order** and macOS will select images randomly.

Now that we know how to change the default desktop wallpaper using the set of images provided by Apple, let's leverage this knowledge to really personalize your desktop using your own images from the Photos application.

Use a Picture from Photos as your Desktop Wallpaper

You can use an image of your choice as your desktop wallpaper, sharing it directly from the **Photos** application. Launch the Photos application, find your desired picture, and click on it. A blue border will appear around the photo. Click the **Share** button located in the upper right of the Photos toolbar and select on **Set Desktop Picture** from the drop-down menu. You can also secondary click on your chosen image to reveal a contextual menu. Select **Share > Set Desktop Picture**. Alternatively, you can select **File > Share > Set Desktop Picture**. The picture on the next page depicts all three available options.

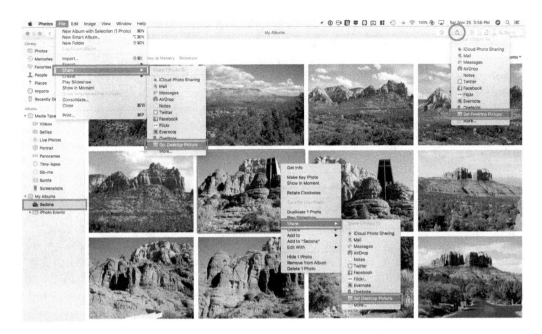

If the size of your photo doesn't match the screen size of your Mac, open the **Desktop & Screen Saver** preference pane in the System Preferences application. Ensure the **Desktop** tab is selected. Use the drop-down menu to the right of the photo you selected. Choose the display option that works best – **Fill Screen**, **Fit to Screen**, **Stretch to Fill Screen**, **Center**, or **Tile**.

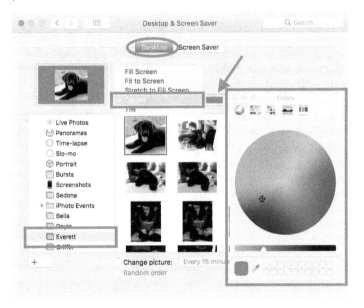

Note that the size of your photo may not match the screen size of your Mac. A photo in portrait mode doesn't fit well since your Mac's screen is in landscape orientation. In that case, you can change how the photo will display using the drop-down menu to the right of the photo you selected. You have five choices: **Fill Screen**, **Fit to Screen**, **Stretch to Fill Screen**, **Center**, or **Tile**. A note of caution when using Stretch to Fill Screen. This selection will change the aspect ratio of the photo and distort the image.

For photos in portrait mode, **Fit to Screen** and **Center** typically work best because the entire photo will be displayed. For photos in landscape mode, **Fill Screen**, **Fit to Screen** or **Center** generally work best. For the **Fit to Screen** and **Center** options, you may notice a colored rectangle to the right of the drop-down menu. Clicking on the colored rectangle reveals a color wheel that lets you choose the color of the bars that appear on the left and right of your photo when the image doesn't fill the entire desktop. This option will not appear if your image fills the entire desktop.

Configure Multiple Pictures from Photos as your Desktop Wallpaper

You can choose multiple pictures in Photos for your Desktop Wallpaper and have macOS rotate through them. Open the **Desktop & Screen Saver** preference pane in System Preferences. Click on the gray triangle next to **Photos** in the left column to open a list of moments, collections, years, places, shared photos, and albums. Click on one of the items in the list and select the photos you want as your wallpaper. Choose to display the photos sequentially or in random order. And don't forget to select how often you want macOS to change your picture.

If your photos are not in the same moment, collection, year, place, or album, create a new album in Photos and add your pictures to it. You can create a new album in Photos by selecting **File > New Album...** or by entering ⌘N (command+N). Once you have finished, open the **Desktop & Screen Saver** preference pane. In the left column, expand Photos using the triangle, scroll to your new album, select it, and choose the display options. Be sure to configure how frequently your pictures change and whether macOS should display them sequentially or randomly.

If the size of your photo doesn't match the screen size of your Mac, use the drop-down menu to the right of the photos you selected and select the option that works best – **Fill Screen**, **Fit to Screen**, **Stretch to Fill Screen**, **Center**, or **Tile**. For photos in portrait mode, **Fit to Screen** or **Center** typically work best because the entire photo will be displayed. For photos in landscape mode, **Fill Screen**, **Fit to Screen** or **Center** generally work best. For both the **Fit to Screen** or **Center** options, you'll notice a colored rectangle to the right of the drop-down menu. Clicking on the color reveals a color wheel that lets you choose the color of the bars that will appear on the left and right of your photo when it doesn't fill the entire desktop. Note that this option will not appear if your image fills the entire desktop. Be sure to configure how frequently the pictures change and whether you want your pictures displayed sequentially or randomly.

Determine Resolution & Aspect Ratio

Another option for your desktop wallpaper is to utilize a folder containing images. I like to collect desktop wallpaper from the Internet, usually landscape scenes. I have hundreds of pictures in a folder called **Wallpaper** located in the **Pictures** folder of my **Home** directory. If you want to download wallpaper from the Internet, the first thing you need to do is to determine the resolution of your display.

When searching Google images (http://images.google.com) or any popular desktop wallpaper site, you don't want just any image, you want images that match the native resolution of your display. An image with a resolution smaller than the native resolution will become pixelated, distorting the image when expanded to fit your higher resolution display.

To find the resolution of your monitor, select > **About This Mac**. Click on the **Displays** tab to see your displays. The resolution of your monitor is listed under the name of the display. For example, the resolution of my 13-inch Retina MacBook Pro's built-in monitor is 2560 x 1600. The numbers represent the width and height of the screen in pixels with the first number representing the width and the second, the height. The larger the numbers, the higher the resolution. I also have an older 27-inch external display, shown on the right in the picture below, with a lower resolution of 1920 x 1080 pixels.

Another important number is the aspect ratio, which is the proportional relationship between a display's width and its height. For my MacBook Pro Retina's built-in display, the aspect ratio is calculated by dividing 2560 (its width in pixels) by 1600 (its height in pixels). The result is 1.6, which equates to an aspect ratio of 16:10. An image with an incorrect aspect ratio will not fit properly on the desktop. When looking for wallpaper to fit my 13-inch Retina MacBook Pro, I look for images with a 16:10 aspect ratio and a minimum resolution of 2560 x 1600 pixels.

Use Images in a Folder as Desktop Wallpaper

To add a folder of images, open the **Desktop & Screen Saver** preference pane in the System Preferences application. Click the **+** (plus) sign at the lower left of the preference pane to open a **Finder** window so you can navigate to and select the folder containing your images.

You can also drag a folder from a Finder window into the left column of the Desktop & Screen Saver preference pane. To make the folder active, click on it and then choose display, frequency, and randomization options. If the thumbnail previews are too small for you, make them bigger using the pinch zoom gesture.

To remove a folder you no longer want to use, highlight it and click the − (minus) button.

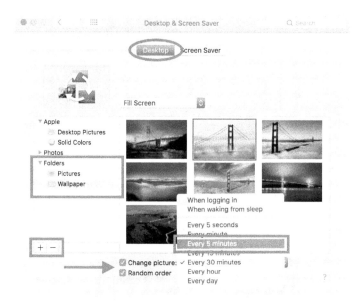

One of the advantages of using a single folder as the source for your desktop wallpaper is that macOS will automatically use any new images you add to this folder without any further configuration on your part.

Access Hidden Wallpaper Collections

Similar to previous versions of macOS, Apple bundled 43 beautiful high resolution images in macOS High Sierra that you can use as desktop wallpaper. There are 17 gorgeous images from **National Geographic** along with 9 **Aerial** images, 9 images of the **Cosmos**, and 8 **Nature Patterns**. Apple had intended for you to use these images as screensavers and it only takes a couple of steps to add them to your wallpaper collection.

To use these hidden screensaver images as wallpaper, open **Finder** and enter ⇧⌘G (shift+command+G) to open the **Go to the folder** dialog box. Enter the following path and click **Go**.

`/Library/Screen Savers/Default Collections/`

Finder will display four folders, numbered from 1 to 4 and labeled **National Geographic**, **Aerial**, **Cosmos**, and **Nature Patterns**, respectively, each containing high resolution images you can use as desktop wallpaper.

To use any of these collections as your wallpaper, open the **Desktop & Screen Saver** preference pane in the System Preferences application. Click on the **Desktop** tab at the top of the pane. Drag each of the folders or just the ones you want to the bottom of the left-hand column under **Folders**. You can now select your desktop wallpaper from any of these folders.

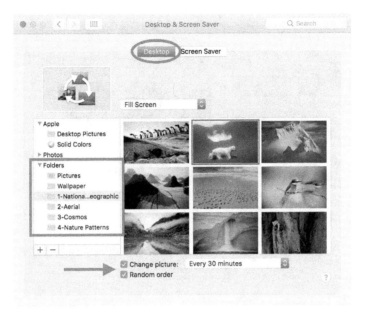

If you already have a folder configured as the source for your desktop wallpaper, another option is to copy the individual picture files into your wallpaper folder. Just open each of the collections by double-clicking its folder. Select the images you like, press the hold the ⌥ (option) key while dragging them into your images folder. The selected images will be copied to your images folder.

Configure the Screensaver

Screensavers are a throwback to the days of cathode ray tube (CRT) monitors. If an image was displayed for too long on a CRT monitor, it would eventually burn a ghost image onto the screen, a phenomenon called phosphor burn in. Screensavers were designed to prevent phosphor burn in by filling the screen with moving images or patterns when the screen was not in use. Modern computers use Liquid Crystal Display (LCD) or Light Emitting Diode (LED) technology which is not susceptible to phosphor burn-in. Today screensavers are primarily used for entertainment purposes.

If you would like to configure a screensaver, open the **Desktop & Screen Saver** preference pane and click on the **Screen Saver** tab at the top of the pane. macOS High Sierra offers 19 different screensaver options, which are shown in the list of screensavers on the left side of the **Desktop & Screen Saver** preference pane.

Any screensaver chosen in the left-hand side of the pane is previewed in the right pane. Apple includes four default collections: **National Geographic**, **Aerial**, **Cosmos**, and **Nature Patterns**, accessible under the drop-down list next to **Source** on the right side of the preference pane.

You also have the option of choosing **Recent Photos Events** or a library from the Photos app or a folder containing images. Select **Photo Library...** or **Choose Folder...**, respectively. Checking the checkbox next to **Shuffle slide order** displays the images randomly.

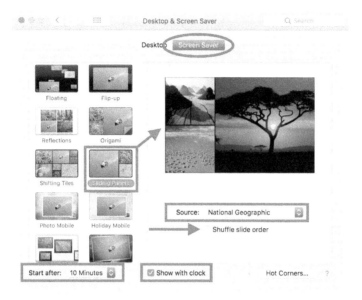

Select an inactivity time from the drop-down menu next to **Start After**. You can start your screen saver after 1, 2, 5, 10, 20, 30, or 60 minutes of inactivity. You also can select **Never**, which effectively disables the screen saver. If you want the screen saver to display the time, check the checkbox next to **Show with clock**.

Display a Message as the Screen Saver

macOS lets you display a message on your computer as your screensaver. To configure your own message, open the **Desktop & Screen Saver** preference pane. Click on the **Screen Saver** tab at the top of the preference pane.

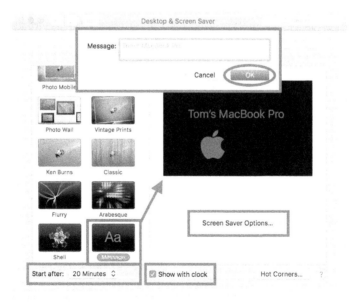

Scroll down to find the **Message** screensaver located towards the bottom of the left-hand pane. By default, macOS will display the name of your computer as the screen saver message. If you would like to display your own message, click the **Screen Saver Options...** button. Enter your message in the drop-down configuration sheet and click **OK** when done.

Don't forget to set the inactivity timer from the drop-down menu under **Start after**. Check the box next to **Show with clock** if you would like to show the time along with your message.

Configure 50 Amazing AppleTV Aerial Screen Savers

If you own an AppleTV you've seen its amazing, high quality screen savers of daytime and nighttime flyover footage of China, Dubai, Greenland, Hawaii, Hong Kong, the Arabian desert of Liwa in Abu Dhabi, London, Los Angeles, New York City, and San Francisco. You can experience these gorgeous screen savers on your Mac if you install the **Aerial** screen saver written by John Coates.

To add the AppleTV Aerial screen savers, download the Aerial screen saver available at: https://github.com/JohnCoates/Aerial. Once the file has downloaded, double-click the Aerial.saver file saved in your **Downloads** folder. Most likely you have the default macOS security settings configured and will see the following pop-up warning that Aerial.saver is from an unidentified developer.

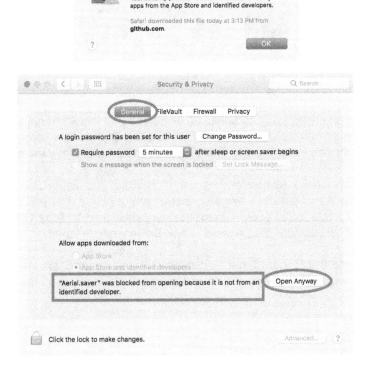

The security warning means that this application has not been registered with Apple. Normally, I wouldn't recommend that you open a file from an unidentified developer since this is a common way malware is distributed. However, I found this application via what I consider to be a reputable source. Click **OK** in the warning box and then launch the **Security & Privacy** preference pane from System Preferences. Click the **General** tab if it is not already highlighted. Under **Allow apps downloaded from:** you will see the following warning. *"Aerial.saver" was blocked from opening because it is not from an identified developer.* Click **Open Anyway**.

Next, select **Install for all users of this computer** from the configuration sheet and click **Install**. Once installed, launch the **Desktop & Screen Saver** preference pane and click on the Screen Saver tab if it is not already highlighted. Scroll to the bottom of the list of screen savers in the left-hand side of the pane. Click on **Aerial** and then select **Screen Saver Options...** to customize the Aerial screen saver.

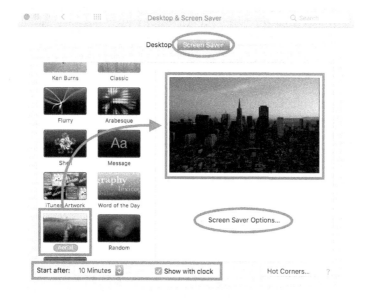

From the configuration sheet, you can select all or a subset of the 50 Aerial screen savers. By default, all of the screen savers are enabled. Scrolling through the screen savers, you will see day and night scenes available. Click on the screen savers to view a preview.

You can disable any of the screen savers by unchecking the checkbox. If you have multiple displays, the Aerial screen saver also allows you to play a different scene on each of your displays, which is really cool. Check the checkbox next to **Play Different Aerial On Each Display** located under the preview. Click **Done** when finished.

Be sure to set the inactivity timer from the drop-down menu under **Start after**. Check the box next to **Show with clock** if you would like to show the time when the screen saver plays.

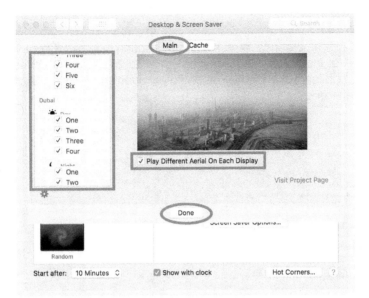

Clicking the **Cache** tab takes you to the cache configuration page, which allows you to change the default location for cached videos. By default, videos are cached as they are played. If you would like to cache all of the videos ahead of time, click the **Download Now** button. Progress bars are updated as each video is downloaded to your Mac. Click **Done** to return the the **Desktop & Screensaver** preference pane.

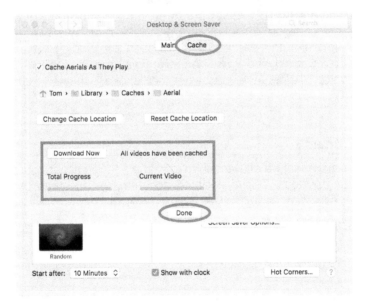

Permanently Disable the Screen Saver

Since screen savers serve no useful purpose with modern computer displays, other than their entertainment value, you may wish to permanently disable the screensaver. To disable the screen saver, select the **Never** option from the **Start After** drop-down menu at the lower left corner on the **Desktop & Screen Saver** preference pane.

Put the Display to Sleep

If you don't want to use a screensaver at all, another option is to simply put your display to sleep after a period of inactivity. The benefit to this feature is that it saves electricity or battery power. To configure the display sleep timer, open the **Energy Saver** preference pane in System Preferences.

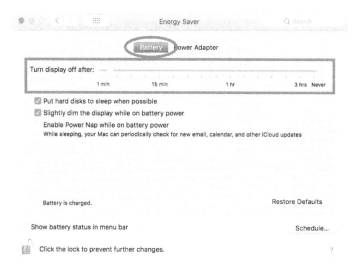

Note that the display sleep timer is configured separately for when your Mac is on battery or AC power. Select **Battery** or **Power Adapter** from the top of the **Energy Saver** preference pane. Next, configure the inactivity timer under **Display sleep** by dragging the slider to the left or right until the desired time has been selected. Be sure to configure inactivity timers for both **Battery** and **Power Adapter** if you own a MacBook, MacBook Air, or MacBook Pro laptop. When the inactivity timer expires, macOS will turn off your computer's display.

Configure Hot Corners

The macOS **Hot Corners** feature allows you to assign a specific action to any or all of the four corners of your desktop. The associated command is executed by moving your pointer to the corner assigned the action you wish to perform.

The supported commands include starting or disabling the screen saver, opening Mission Control, application windows (App Exposé), showing the Desktop, Dashboard, Notification Center, Launchpad, or putting the display to sleep.

To assign commands to Hot Corners, first open the **Desktop & Screen Saver** preference pane. Next, click the **Hot Corners...** button at the lower right of the preference pane to reveal the drop-down configuration sheet. Assign an action to any or all of the four **Hot Corners** using the drop-down menu associated with each corner. Click **OK** when finished, then close the **Desktop & Screen Saver** preference pane.

To execute the command assigned to a **Hot Corner**, simply move your pointer to the appropriate corner. Moving your pointer back to the corner reverses the command.

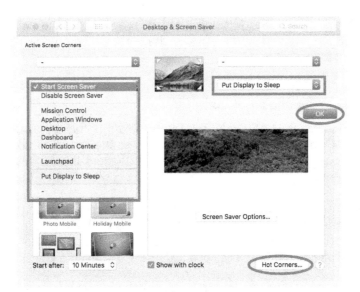

To turn off **Hot Corners**, open the **Desktop & Screen Saver** preference pane and select the **Screen Saver** tab. Next, click the **Hot Corners...** button in the lower right corner of the pane. Select the – from the drop-down menu for each corner that you want to disable.

Hot corners can also be configured in the **Mission Control** preference pane. To set up Hot Corners, first open the **Mission Control** preference pane in the System Preferences.

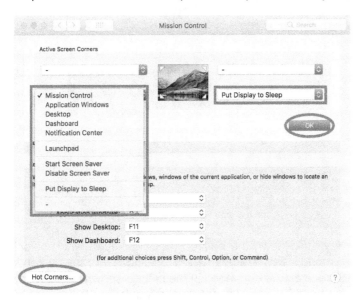

Next, click the **Hot Corners...** button at the lower left of the pane to reveal the configuration sheet. You can assign a command to any or all of the corners. The supported commands are the same as those in the Desktop & Screensaver preference pane.

To turn off Hot Corners, open the **Mission Control** preference pane and click the **Hot Corners...** button in the lower left corner. Select the – from the drop-down menu for each corner that you want to turn off.

Avoid Accidentally Triggering a Hot Corner

The **Hot Corners** feature is very handy, but one problem is that by simply moving the pointer near a **Hot Corner**, you can accidentally trigger the assigned command. Often simply moving the pointer to the menu accidentally triggers the command associated with the upper left corner.

To avoid accidentally triggering a Hot Corner, you can configure Hot Corners to utilize a modifier key. For example, you can configure Hot Corners so that the ⌥ (option) key must be held down to execute the command when the pointer is moved to a Hot Corner. Using a modifier key will eliminate the possibility of accidentally triggering a Hot Corner.

To configure Hot Corners to require a modifier key, open the **Desktop & Screen Saver** preference pane. Click on the **Screen Saver** tab at the top of the pane. Next click the **Hot Corners...** button at the lower right to display the Hot Corners configuration drop down menu.

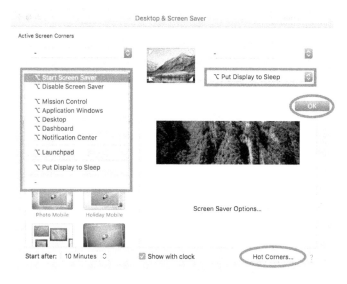

To add a modifier key, hold down the desired modifier key(s) when selecting an action from the drop-down menu. For example, I am holding down the ⌥ (option) key while selecting the **Start Screen Saver** command in the picture shown above. Note that the **Put Display to Sleep** command is already configured to require the ⌥ (option) key. Any of the following modifier keys are supported: ⇧ ⌘ ^ ⌥ (shift, command, control, or option). macOS will even allow you to use any combination of two, three, or even all four of the modifier keys.

You can also configure Hot Corner modifier key in the **Mission Control** preference pane. First open the **Mission Control** preference pane and click the **Hot Corners...** button at the lower left of the pane to reveal the drop-down configuration sheet. To add a modifier key, hold down the desired modifier key(s) when selecting an action from the drop-down menu. Any of the following modifier keys are supported: ⇧ ⌘ ^ ⌥ (shift, command, control, or option). macOS will even allow you to use any combination of two, three, or even all four of the modifier keys.

Once you have configured a modifier key, Hot Corners will only work when you're holding down the modifier key(s) you specified, thereby eliminating the possibility of accidentally triggering a Hot Corner.

Hide Applications to Clean Up Desktop Clutter

Having too many windows open on the desktop can be distracting especially if you are trying to concentrate on a particular window. Of course you could always minimize or close all the windows or quit the applications entirely to clean up the clutter. But that takes time and you may not want to quit all applications because you want to leave them open for later use. In that case, quitting or closing windows are not viable options. You could minimize each window, however that could take a lot of time if you have lots of windows open. And minimized windows clutter the right side of the Dock, making each icon smaller and more difficult to differentiate as the Dock expands across the desktop.

A handy feature is to hide all the other applications except for the one in which you are working. Hiding an application causes all of its windows to instantly disappear without crowding the Dock. Because macOS will remember where the windows were located before you hid them, the windows will return to their original positions when unhidden. If you have lots of applications open and want to hide all but the application in which you are working, enter ⌥⌘H (option+command+H). You can also choose **Hide Others** from the Application Menu.

To hide the currently active application, enter ⌘H (command+H) or select the **Hide** option from the Application Menu, the first menu to the right of the menu.

To unhide any application, simply click on its icon in the Dock and macOS will immediately restore the application's windows to their original locations. You can use **App Exposé** to see the windows of any application, whether hidden or not.

How do you know which applications are hidden and which are not? By default, the macOS Dock does not differentiate between applications that are hidden and those that are not. A tweak I will show you in the chapter on customizing the Dock will allow you to differentiate between hidden and unhidden applications.

Remove Devices from the Desktop

macOS displays icons of external hard drives or optical drives on the desktop when you connect them to your Mac. These icons represent yet more desktop clutter. There is no need to display external devices on the desktop as they are available in the **Devices** list in the Finder Sidebar. macOS allows you to stop external devices from appearing on the desktop. Additionally, turning off the display of external devices is particularly useful when you are using a Volumes Stack, which will display all of your internal and external drives and optical drives as a single stack in the Dock. See the chapter on Stacks to see how to create a Volumes Stack.

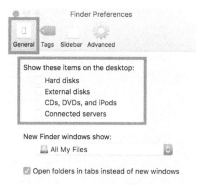

To disable the display of external devices on your desktop open **Finder** and select **Preferences...** from the Finder menu or enter ⌘, (command+comma). By default, macOS will display icons for external hard drives, CDs, DVDs, and connected servers. To disable this feature, uncheck the checkboxes next to each of these items in the Finder preference pane. Changes take effect immediately and any device icons on your desktop will disappear. Don't worry. Your devices have not been removed. They have been hidden and can still be accessed from the Device list in Finder or through a Volumes Stack.

To return to the macOS default, open Finder and enter ⌘, (command+comma) to open the Finder Preferences. Then check the checkboxes next to **External disks** and **CDs, DVDs, and Connected servers**.

Create a Pristine Desktop

Unfortunately for most users, the desktop quickly turns out to be the catch-all location for documents and other stuff they're working on. Screenshots are saved to the desktop by default and many downloaded applications save items there too. Desktop clutter can become overwhelming and detract from your ability to get work done. Not only does the mess make the desktop look unsightly, it steals CPU and memory resources because each icon must be rendered and its contents previewed. If your desktop has more icons than wallpaper, you have inadvertently made your Mac slower by forcing macOS to dedicate resources to render the clutter.

Items saved to the desktop aren't really saved to the desktop. They are actually saved to the **Desktop** folder located in your **Home** directory. The Desktop folder is easily accessible from your Home directory, the Finder Sidebar, or from a Desktop document stack in the Dock. See the chapter on customizing Stacks to learn how to create a Desktop Stack.

If you want a really clean desktop and a faster Mac, this macOS tweak will give you a pristine desktop, completely free of clutter. Essentially this tweak turns off desktop icons, preventing them from being displayed in the first place. This tweak will also prevent you from dragging icons onto the desktop. It will also turn off your ability to secondary click on the desktop to create new folders, Get Info, or change the desktop background. However, all of these features are accessible via other means.

Launch **Terminal** and enter the following commands.

```
defaults write com.apple.finder CreateDesktop -bool FALSE
```

```
killall Finder
```

Any icons that normally would have appeared on your desktop are safely tucked away in the Desktop folder in your Home directory, where they belong. This is a handy tweak if you are about to give an important presentation and you are embarrassed by your lack of desktop cleanliness.

To return to the default and risk a messy desktop and slower Mac, enter the following commands.

```
defaults write com.apple.finder CreateDesktop -bool TRUE
```

```
killall Finder
```

Change the Desktop Icon and Text Size

If you still want to see icons for devices and files on your desktop, macOS gives you the option of changing the icon size. To change the desktop icon size, click anywhere on the Desktop and enter ⌘J (command+J). This will launch the **Desktop** view options panel. Note that the pristine desktop hack must be disabled for ⌘J to work. If it is enabled, open a Finder window and select **Desktop** under **Favorites** in the left hand column and enter ⌘J (command+J).

Use the **Icon size** slider to make the desktop icons appear smaller by dragging the slider to the left. Or, if you want to make the icons appear bigger, drag the slider to the right. Changes take effect immediately. Note that the default size is 64 x 64.

The next slider controls the tightness of the grid separating the desktop icons. For tighter spacing, drag the slider to the left. For more open spacing, drag the slider to the right.

The next section controls the size and location of the text label. macOS places the text label underneath the icon using a 12-point font. macOS lets you choose any text size between 10 and 16 points. The text label can be located at the bottom, which is the default, or to the right of the icon by selecting the appropriate radio button.

By default, **Show item info** is off. Checking this option adds the file size or, in the case of a hard drive, the free space, to a second line of the text label.

By default, the **Show icon preview** checkbox is checked. Unchecking this box disables the macOS preview function. Only default icons indicating the application in which the file was created will be displayed instead of previewing the file contents.

The last option available, **Sort by** allows you to choose a default sort option. By default, the sort is set to **None**. The available sort options include sorting by **Name**, **Kind**, **Date Modified**, **Date Created**, **Date Last Opened**, **Date Added**, **Size**, or **Tags**. The **Snap to Grid** option will organize your desktop icons into a grid. Once you have finished configuring your options, close the Desktop view panel to save.

Find a Lost Pointer

Have you ever lost the pointer? Sometimes it's difficult to find the pointer on the desktop, particularly when it's hidden in the desktop background. How do you find it? Most people either shake the mouse or shake a finger back and forth rapidly hoping they will be able to see the pointer as it moves. Apple added a neat little feature that capitalizes on this behavior by making the pointer grow progressively larger as you move your finger back and forth on the trackpad or shake your mouse. Your pointer will grow from its normal size to gigantic.

To enable shake to locate, launch the **Accessibility** preference pane and select **Display** from the column at the left. Check the checkbox next to **Shake mouse pointer to locate**.

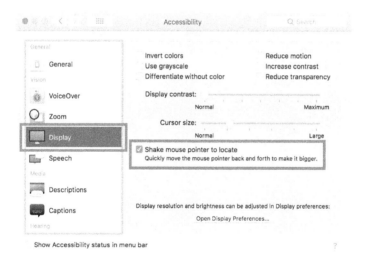

Change the Pointer Size

While you can use the **Shake mouse pointer to locate** feature to find a lost pointer, maybe the default macOS pointer is a little bit too small for you, especially if you're using a larger monitor. For example, the pointer is sized perfectly for my 13-inch Retina MacBook Pro. But when I connect my MacBook to my 27-inch monitor, the pointer is so small I often have trouble finding it. macOS allows you to change the size of the pointer from the default size to a gigantic one.

To change the pointer size, open the **Accessibility** preference pane in the System Preferences application. Select **Display** in the left-hand column if it is not already highlighted. Slide the **Cursor Size** slider until your pointer is at a comfortable size.

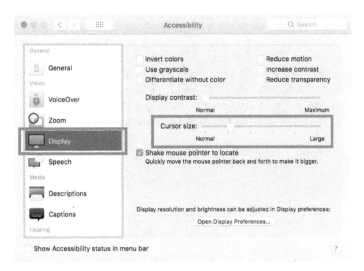

Even a small change makes a big difference when using a large monitor. Note that changing the pointer size also changes the cursor size in word processing applications and the crosshairs used to take screenshots.

Adjust Retina Display Resolution

Mac laptops and desktop computers with Retina displays have the ability to adjust the display resolution to provide larger, more easily readable text or more usable screen real estate. For example, my 13-inch Retina Macbook Pro has a native resolution of 2560 x 1600 pixels at 227 pixels per inch (ppi). Although it's native resolution is 2560 x 1600 pixels, the default resolution is set to appear like 1280 x 800 pixels.

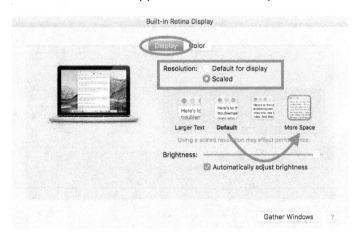

To change the display resolution, launch the **Displays** preference pane from the System Preferences application. Click on **Display**, if not already highlighted, and select the **Scaled** radio button. As you hover your pointer over the available options, from **Larger**

Text to **More Space**, the example display on the left side of the pane will preview the resolution and display what the resolution looks like. The **Default** resolution is selected by default in macOS, which will make your Retina display look like 1280 x 800 pixels.

Depending on your display, you will have either four or five choices. For most, the default setting or the next one to the right of **Default** is usually the best option. If you prefer more screen real estate, click on **More Space**, which will make your Retina display look like 1680 x 1050. The **More Space** setting provides more usable screen real estate but at the expense of readability as windows and fonts will appear smaller. The **Larger Text** setting makes everything appear bigger and easier to read, but with the loss of screen real estate. The following two images compare the **Default** and **More Space** settings, respectively.

A 13-inch Retina MacBook Pro will offer four scaled resolutions – 1024 x 640, the default of 1280 x 800, 1440 x 900, and 1680 x 1050 pixels, from **Larger Text** to **More Space**. A 15-inch Retina Macbook Pro has a native resolution of 2880 x 1800 pixels at 220 ppi and supports scaled resolutions of 1024 x 640, 1280 x 800, 1680 x 1050, and 1920 x 1200 pixels.

If you have multiple displays, changing the resolution of the built-in display will have no impact on external displays. You will need to separately configure your external displays in the Displays preference pane, choosing a separate resolution for each. Or you can let macOS choose a resolution that works best for both displays, which is the **Default for display** setting.

To configure the resolution of an external display, launch the Displays preference pane and select **Display** if it is not already highlighted. A version of the Display preference pane will appear on each of your displays. If you would prefer to see them all on one display, click the **Gather Windows** button in the lower right corner.

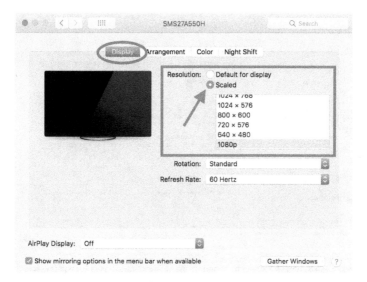

By default, external displays will always run at native resolution unless you have specified a scaled resolution. To set a scaled resolution for an external display, select the **Scaled** radio button and choose a resolution from the list. If you hold down the ⌥ (option) key while clicking the **Select** button, you will get more resolution choices as shown in the image above.

Get More Display Resolutions

 If you want more display resolution options than the standard four or five options provided by Apple, a shareware application called **SwitchResX** can force your Retina display to run at even higher resolutions. Written by Stéphane Madrau, SwitchResX will allow you to select any of the resolutions your display and video card can support.

SwitchResX provides extensive control over display resolution, color depth, mirroring, rotation, and many other display attributes.

SwitchResX comes with a free and fully functional 10-day trial period so you can check it out before deciding to buy. At the time of this writing, SwitchResX is available for $16 at: http://www.madrau.com/srx_download/download.html.

Reduce Transparency

One of the most striking features of macOS is the transparent effect of windows, toolbars, title bars, the Menu Bar, and the Dock. If you own a newer Mac, particularly one with a retina display, this eye candy looks amazing. If your Mac is older, you may notice a considerable drop in responsiveness and speed when opening windows. The one single change you can make to macOS to increase performance on an older Mac is to reduce transparency.

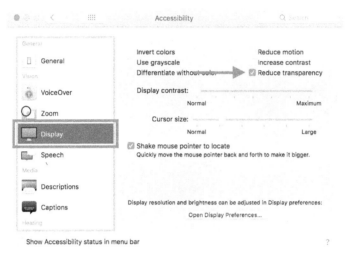

If you don't like transparency or if you feel it is slowing down your older Mac, you can reduce it in the Accessibility preference pane in the System Preferences application. Select **Display** from the left-hand column if it is not already highlighted. Check the box next to **Reduce transparency**. To enable, simply uncheck the checkbox. This change takes effect immediately.

Increase Contrast

OS X El Capitan (version 10.11) replaced Yosemite's Helvetica Neue system font with the slightly more readable San Francisco font. This same font is used in macOS High Sierra. Characters in the San Francisco font are a little taller and less wide than Helvetica Nueu. However, paired with High Sierra's transparency feature, you may find San Francisco challenging to read if you have an older, non-retina Mac. The thinness of the font combined with the lack of contrast can make menu items appear blurry.

You can significantly improve the readability of the system font by reducing transparency and increasing contrast. This setting will increase the contrast of on-screen items such as borders around buttons and darken the text and other interface elements without changing the contrast of the screen itself.

To increase contrast, open the **Accessibility** preference pane in the System Preferences application. Select **Display** from the left-hand column. Check the checkbox next to **Increase contrast**. Note that checking **Increase contrast** also checks the box next to **Reduce transparency**. To revert back to the macOS default, uncheck both boxes, starting with **Increase contrast**. Changes take effect immediately.

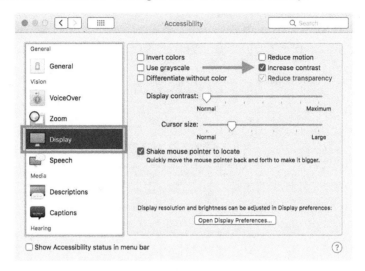

Compare the image of the Accessibility preference pane above with the one shown on the previous page. Note the darker border and text in the window's menu bar. With increase contrast enabled, the text appears sharper and darker and interface elements stand out more clearly from their gray backgrounds.

If you want the Accessibility Menu Extra to appear in the Menu Bar, check the box next to **Show Accessibility status in menu bar**.

Change the Font Smoothing Strength

If you have an older, non-retina Mac, you may find that the macOS system font, San Francisco, appears a little blurry and is harder to read compared to older versions of macOS, which used Lucida Grande. Turning off LCD font smoothing in the **General** preference pane in System Preferences is not a good option as doing so makes the system font appear jagged and thinner. However, manually tweaking font smoothing can make subtle improvements in the appearance of San Francisco on your non-retina Mac.

To change the strength of font smoothing, launch the **Terminal** application and enter the following commands. Note that the command is a single line. Do not press **return** until you have entered the complete command. Log out and log in for this change to take effect.

```
defaults -currentHost write -globalDomain AppleFontSmoothing -int 2
```

When you use this command to change the font smoothing value, a – will appear next to **Use LCD font smoothing when available** in the **General** preference pane in the System Preferences app as shown below.

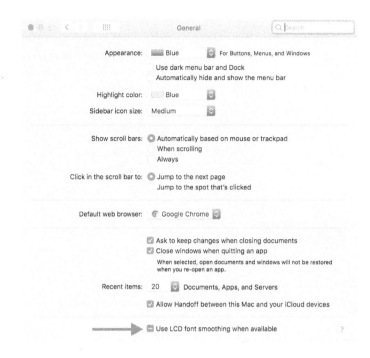

To revert back to the macOS default font smoothing strength, enter the following commands. Note that the command is a single line. Do not press **return** until you have entered the complete command. Log out and log in for this change to take effect.

```
defaults -currentHost write -globalDomain AppleFontSmoothing -int 3
```

Changing the integer to 0 has the same effect as disabling LCD font smoothing in the General preference pane. Another valid entry is the integer 1, however, the difference between 1 and 2 is so subtle that it is almost impossible to discern.

Show the Desktop

Have you ever wanted to look at a beautiful desktop image only to find your desktop is cluttered with windows? macOS offers a number of methods to quickly clear the clutter to view your desktop wallpaper and put the clutter back when done.

If you configured the **Show Desktop** trackpad gesture, the quickest method to show the desktop is by spreading your thumb and three fingers on your trackpad. All open windows will be pushed off screen. Reverse the gesture to return the windows to their original locations. Pressing **fn F11** also clears the desktop. Note that you will have to hold down the **fn** (function) key while pressing **F11** as this key is normally used to lower the volume. Press **fn F11** to return the window clutter.

A couple of other options are to hold down the ⌘ (command) key while pressing **F3,** which is normally used to launch Mission Control. Enter ⌘**F3** again to return the windows to their original locations on the desktop.

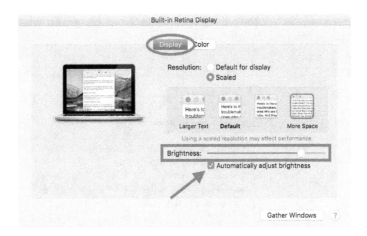

Adjust the Display Brightness

There are a couple of ways to adjust the display brightness of your Mac. First, you can use the **F1** and **F2** keys to manually adjust the brightness. Pressing **F1** will make your display darker while **F2** will make it brighter. Another option is to adjust the display brightness in the **Displays** preference pane by moving the slider to the right to make the display brighter and to the left to make it darker.

Disable Automatic Brightness Adjustment

If your Mac has an ambient light sensor, it will adjust its display brightness automatically based on ambient light conditions. This feature is enabled by default in macOS High Sierra. If you would like to disable it so that brightness can only be manually adjusted, launch the **Displays** preference pane and uncheck the checkbox next to **Automatically adjust brightness**.

Precisely Adjust the Display Brightness

Sometimes it seems you never can get the display brightness adjusted to your liking. One segment more is too much. One less is too little. Wouldn't it be awesome if you could adjust the display brightness in smaller increments? macOS has a solution!

Holding down the ⇧⌥ (shift+option) keys while pressing the **F1** or **F2** allows you to precisely adjust the brightness in quarter-segment increments. This trick also works when adjusting the volume and the brightness of the keyboard backlight.

Remove the Sleep, Restart, & Shutdown Buttons from the Login Screen

At the bottom of the login screen are three buttons – **Sleep**, **Restart**, and **Shut Down**. macOS lets you remove these buttons if you do not want them. Removing these buttons leaves you with only one option on the login screen – to log in.

To remove these buttons from the login screen, open the **Users & Groups** preference pane in the System Preferences application. Next, unlock the preference pane by clicking on the padlock in the lower left corner, if locked. Enter your password when challenged. Select **Login Options** at the bottom left.

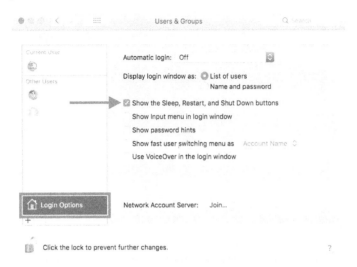

Uncheck the checkbox next to **Show the Sleep, Restart, and Shut Down buttons**. To put the buttons back on your Mac's login screen, check this checkbox.

Sleep Better with Night Shift

The blue light emitted from your Mac's display mimics daylight, which can disrupt your body's sleep cycle. If you work on your Mac at night, your display's blue light tricks your brain into thinking it is daytime, causing your brain to not produce melatonin, which makes it harder for you to fall asleep. **Night Shift** is a macOS feature that adjusts the color temperature of your display based on the time of day. Similar to the iOS Night Shift feature, macOS will adjust your display's color temperature to provide warmer light during nighttime hours to help you sleep better.

To configure Night Shift, open the **Displays** preference pane in System Preferences. Select the **Night Shift** tab. Choose **Custom** or **Sunset to Sunrise** from the drop-down menu next to **Schedule**. If you select **Custom**, **From** and **to** fields will appear for you to set the start and end times for when Night Shift will be enabled. Choosing **Sunset to Sunrise** enables Night Shift based on the when the sun sets and rises in your location. This is a handy feature if you travel with your Mac. A slider lets you select how warm you want Night Shift with the default being **Max Warm**. If you want to enable Night Shift immediately, check the checkbox next to **Turn On Until Sunrise**.

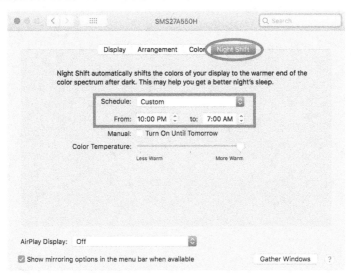

To disable Night Shift, launch the **Displays** preference pane, select the **Night Shift** tab, and choose **Off** from the drop-down menu next to **Schedule**.

4

Mission Control

Mission Control is the macOS feature that provides a view of everything on your Mac – windows, Full Screen apps, Split View apps, Desktop Spaces, and the Dashboard. It allows you to quickly jump to another Desktop, Full Screen app, apps running in Split View mode, an app running in another Space, or to the Dashboard. Mission Control also allows you to move windows to other Desktops and create, rearrange, and delete Desktops.

To open **Mission Control** use the trackpad gesture (swipe up with either 3 or 4 fingers), launch it from **Launchpad**, launch it from **Spotlight**, press the **F3** key, or enter **^up** (control+up arrow).

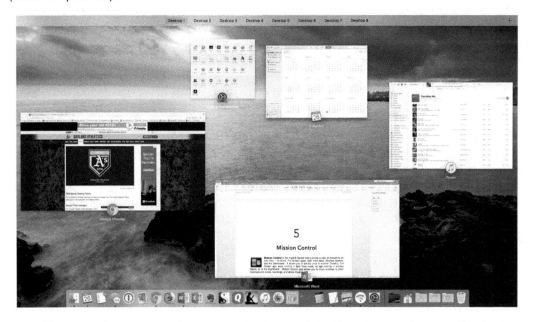

The ribbon at the top of Mission Control simply lists the active Desktops. Moving your pointer into the ribbon expands the Desktops and Full Screen and Split View apps into thumbnails as shown in the image on the next page.

In the example above, Mission Control lists 8 Desktop Spaces, numbered Desktop 1 to 8 from left to right, and iTunes, located between Desktops 2 and 3, which I have expanded to a Full Screen application. Each Desktop Space is a virtual desktop, created using the **Spaces** feature, and each one can have one or more windows assigned to it. The Spaces feature is a nifty way of increasing desktop real estate to accommodate more windows. Spaces are covered in the next section.

You can rearrange the order of the Desktops by clicking, dragging, and dropping them. Any Desktop, Full Screen application, Split View app, or the Dashboard can be rearranged. macOS will renumber the desktops accordingly as you rearrange them. Desktops will always be numbered from left to right starting from Desktop 1 at the left.

Navigating between the Desktops, Full Screen apps, Split View apps, and the Dashboard in Mission Control is done by swiping either three or four fingers to the left or right on the trackpad. If you are using a Magic Mouse, swipe left or right with either one or two fingers. You can also hold down the ^ (control) key and press the left or right arrow to navigate. Clicking on any thumbnail in the Mission Control ribbon makes the Desktop active, bringing it, and the applications which are assigned to it, to the front.

The Dock appears at the bottom of Mission Control, letting you launch applications into the active Desktop, which is highlighted by a blue border at the top of Mission Control. If you try to launch an application while a Full Screen app is selected in Mission Control, the app will open in Desktop 1.

Add More Desktop Space

Desktop clutter can be a real productivity killer. If you have ever opened lots of applications and windows, you know how hard it is to sift through all of the windows looking for a particular one. If you only had more Desktop space, your Desktop would not be so cluttered and life would be so much easier. macOS granted your wish. You can add more desktop space with a macOS feature called **Spaces**.

Spaces is a feature of **Mission Control** that allows you to create virtual desktops. These virtual desktops add more desktop real estate. Using Spaces, you can create additional Desktops, each containing a unique application or set of applications. Multiple Desktops remove clutter by allowing you to assign windows to separate Desktops instead of piling all the windows onto your main desktop. For example, let's say you were writing a book on customizing macOS using Microsoft Word, you can run Word on Desktop 1, and create separate Desktop Spaces for iTunes, Mail, and Safari – effectively quadrupling your desktop real estate! Spaces is so flexible that windows from the same application can even be split between different Desktops.

Mission Control is the command center for Spaces, allowing you to create new Desktops, see and manage your Desktops, and see which windows are assigned to each. To create a new Desktop Space, first open Mission Control by using the trackpad gesture, launching it from Launchpad or Spotlight, pressing the **F3** key, or by entering **^up** (control+up arrow).

If you have never created a Desktop Space, the ribbon at the top of Mission Control will show a single desktop, called **Desktop 1**. Creating a new Desktop Space is as simple as moving your pointer to the **+** sign at the far right edge of the Mission Control ribbon. When your pointer reaches the **+** sign, it will expand to reveal a partial Desktop containing a gray **+**. Clicking this partial desktop or the **+** creates a new virtual desktop.

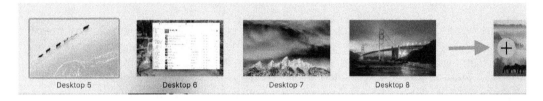

macOS will allow you to create up to 16 Desktop Spaces, numbered sequentially from left to right starting with **Desktop 1**.

The picture above shows 4 Desktops in Mission Control, numbered 1 through 4. Microsoft Word and Chrome are running in Split View mode between Desktops 1 and 2. iTunes is running in Full Screen mode between Desktops 3 and 4. The Dashboard is disabled, and is therefore, not shown. Did you notice anything about the spaces in the picture? Each one can have its own desktop wallpaper.

Remove a Desktop Space

Removing a Desktop is done in **Mission Control**. Hover your pointer over the Desktop you want to remove at the top of Mission Control. An **X** will appear in the upper left corner of the Desktop thumbnail. Click the **X** and macOS will remove the space. Any windows located in the deleted Desktop will be reassigned to the desktop in the foreground. Any Desktop Space with the exception of the Dashboard, Full Screen applications, and Split View apps can be removed in Mission Control.

You can use Mission Control to take an app out of Full Screen or Split View mode. Hover your pointer over a Full Screen or Split View app in Mission Control and two arrows will appear in the upper left corner. Click on the arrows and the app will exit Full Screen or Split View mode and move to the next available Desktop to the left. Note that the Dashboard cannot be removed, but you can disable it in System Preferences.

Another method to remove a desktop is to move your pointer to the Mission Control ribbon and hold down the ⌥ (option) key. An **X** will appear in the upper left hand corner of every Desktop. Remove Desktop Spaces by clicking on the **X** while keeping the ⌥ (option) key depressed. Full Screen and Split View apps will display two arrows, allowing you to exit Full Screen or Split View mode. Release the ⌥ (option) key when finished.

Take an App to Full Screen Mode in Mission Control

You can take any window to Full Screen mode by clicking the green button in the window's Title Bar. Or you can take an app to Full Screen in Mission Control. Activate Mission Control and navigate to the Desktop with the app you want to take Full Screen. Drag the window onto the Mission Control ribbon between two Desktops or after the last Desktop in the ribbon. A new Desktop Space will appear with a **+** sign as shown below. Drop the app onto this new Space to take it to Full Screen mode.

Exit Full Screen Mode

You have a couple of options to exit Full Screen mode. You can hover your pointer over a Full Screen app in the Mission Control ribbon and two arrows will appear in the upper left corner as shown below. Click on the arrows and the app will exit Full Screen mode and its window will move to the next available Desktop.

A second method is make the app active and move your pointer to the top of your screen to reveal the Menu Bar and Title Bar controls. Click on the green button on the Title Bar to exit Full Screen mode and restore the window to its original size. If you click on the red button in the Title Bar, the window will close.

Use Split View to View 2 Apps Side by Side

Two applications can be placed side by side on the same Desktop using a Mission Control feature called **Split View**. Split View is a great feature when you need to compare two documents or need to move information from one document to the other. There are two different methods to put two apps into Split View.

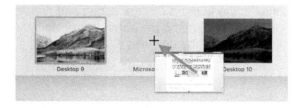

First, ensure that both application windows are in the same Desktop. Next, click and hold the green button in the first application's Title Bar. Release your hold and the window will snap to the left side of your desktop. If you want the window on the right half of the screen, drag it to the right side of the desktop before releasing your hold on the green button. Finally, click on the thumbnail of the second application that you want to occupy the other half of your desktop. It will immediately snap into place.

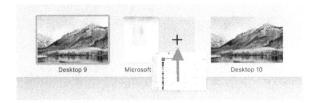

Desktop 9   Microsoft   Desktop 10

The second method is to use Mission Control. The advantage of using Mission Control is that the application windows do not have to start out on the same Desktop. They can be in different desktops or you can create an entirely new Desktop Space for your Split View.

If neither application window is running in Full Screen or Split View mode, open Mission Control and navigate to the desktop with the first application window by swiping left or right with three or four fingers. Drag the first window to an existing desktop or create a new desktop by dragging the window between two desktops or to the the end of the Mission Control ribbon. Next, navigate to the Desktop with the second application window and drag and drop it onto the Desktop where you placed the first window. The occupied half of this Desktop will blur and the other half will have a + sign in it. Drop the app on the + sign.

If the first application is already running in Full Screen mode, simply drag and drop the second application window onto the + sign in the thumbnail containing the first app.

Resize Windows in Split View

Once your two apps are running side by side in Split View, you can adjust how much screen space each occupies. To resize an application window running in Split View mode, place your pointer on the vertical black divider separating the two apps. A double headed black arrow will appear. Click and drag this arrow to resize the windows.

Exit Split View

Similar to exiting Full Screen mode, there are several ways you can exit Split View mode and restore the application windows to their original sizes. You can hover your pointer over the Split View thumbnail in the Mission Control ribbon and two arrows will appear in the upper left corner. Click on the arrows and the apps will exit Split View mode and move to the active desktop in the foreground (the one with the blue border).

Desktop 9   Microsoft Word & iTunes   Desktop 10

Perhaps you don't want to restore both apps to their original sizes. You can restore the application window you no longer want in Split View mode to its original size while keeping the other window in Full Screen mode. Move your pointer to the top of your screen to reveal the Menu Bar and Title Bar controls. Click on the green button on the Title Bar of the app you no longer want in Split View. The other app window will restore to Full Screen mode. Another option is to make the app you no longer want in Split View mode active and press the **esc** (escape) key. The other app window will restore to Full Screen mode.

Turn Off Automatic Space Rearrangement

After working with Desktop Spaces for a while you may notice something odd. Your Desktops seem to automatically rearrange themselves. No, your Mac is not haunted by gremlins and you're not losing your mind. macOS rearranges desktops based on their most recent use. Therefore, Desktop 4 can work its way up to become Desktop 1 if the applications on Desktop 4 are used more recently than the applications on the other desktops. If you find this behavior confusing, macOS allows you to disable it.

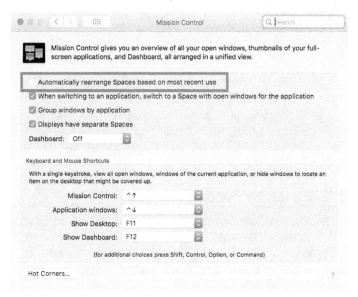

To disable automatic Desktop Space rearrangement, open the **Mission Control** preference pane in the System Preferences application. Uncheck the box next to **Automatically rearrange Spaces based on most recent use**.

Configure Separate Spaces on other Displays

macOS allows you to have a separate, independent set of Desktop Spaces for each display in your system. In a dual-monitor set up, you can have up to 32 desktops! An added benefit to this feature is that when enabled, each display has its own Menu Bar. Since the Menu Bar is available on all displays, you do not have to move your pointer back to the main display to access the Menu Bar. This provides a more independent treatment of each display rather than other displays being merely extensions of the main display.

If you wish to enable this feature, launch the Mission Control preference pane. Check the box next to **Displays have separate spaces**. You will need to log out and log back in for the change to take effect.

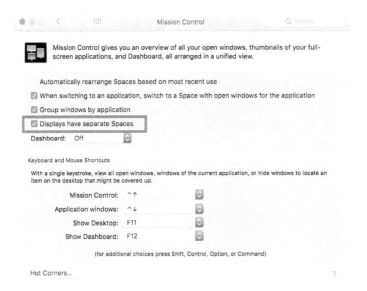

Note that if you disable **Displays have separate spaces**, you will no longer enjoy the benefit of each display having its own Menu Bar. The Menu Bar will only appear on the main display. To learn how to move the Menu Bar to another display, see the next chapter.

Create Keyboard Shortcuts for Spaces

A handy method to quickly navigate between desktops is to set up keyboard shortcuts. Creating a keyboard shortcut for each Desktop Space allows you to jump between Desktops without swiping or using Mission Control. Keyboard shortcuts are by far the quickest way to jump between Desktop Spaces because you can move directly from Desktop 1 to Desktop 4 with a single shortcut.

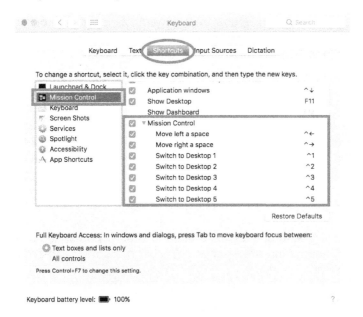

To set up keyboard shortcuts, open the **Keyboard** preference pane. Next, select the **Shortcuts** tab if not already selected. Click on **Mission Control** in the left-hand column.

Scroll to the bottom of the right-hand column to see all of the **Switch to Desktop #** shortcuts. Two shortcuts are enabled by default, **^left** (control+left arrow) and **^right** (control+right arrow), which will move left or right, respectively. However, the **Switch to Desktop #** shortcuts are disabled. Check the checkboxes next to each of your desktops to enable the shortcuts. Once enabled, simply type the number of the desktop space you want to go to while holding down the **^** (control) key. macOS will immediately jump to that space.

Note that if you add new desktops, you will have to go back to the Keyboard preference pane to turn on the shortcuts for any newly created Desktops.

Move a Window to Another Desktop

A window can be moved from one desktop space to another in Mission Control by dragging the window from the active Desktop and dropping it onto your desired destination. Hover your pointer over an application window and it will become highlighted by a blue border. Next, drag and drop the window to your desired destination in the Mission Control ribbon.

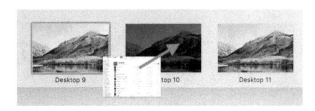

Windows from the same application can be split across multiple Desktops. This is quite handy when working with two or more documents from the same application. The only restriction is that you cannot assign an application window to the Dashboard or to a Full Screen application. If you drag and drop another application onto an application in Full Screen Mode, both apps will enter Split View mode.

Move All Windows of an Application to Another Desktop

Mission Control allows you to move individual windows to another Desktop. But what if you have multiple windows open in a particular application and want to move all of them to another Desktop? macOS has a solution for you.

If you want to move all windows of an application to another Desktop space, first open the **Mission Control** preference pane in the System Preferences application. Ensure the checkbox next to **Group windows by application** is checked

.

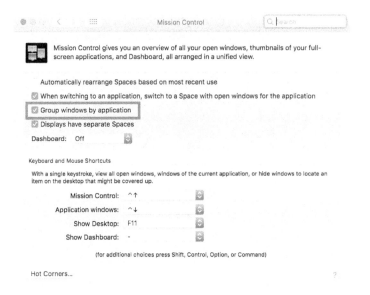

To move all of the windows of an application in Mission Control, click, drag, and drop the application's icon (shown below the application's windows) to the desired destination. All of the windows will move as a group.

Move a Window & Create a New Desktop Space

You can move an application window and create a new destination Desktop for it at the same time. Launch Mission Control and hover your pointer over
the application window you intend to move. The window will become highlighted by a blue border. Drag the window to the upper right corner of Mission Control and onto the **Add Desktop Button** to simultaneously create a new desktop and assign the application window to it.

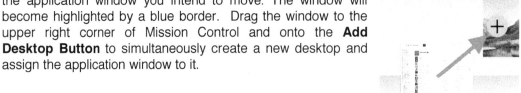

Navigate Between Desktop Spaces

Let's quit Mission Control so I can show you how to navigate between desktops without launching Mission Control. Navigating between desktops outside Mission Control is the same as navigating between them inside Mission Control. Swipe left or right with either three or four fingers on the trackpad. If you are using a Magic Mouse, swiping left or right with either one or two fingers will navigate between your desktops. You can also hold down the ^ (control) key and press the left or right arrow to move left or right through your desktops, respectively. Also, switching to another application automatically switches your active desktop to the Space in which the application resides.

Drag a Window To Another Desktop

There are several methods to move an application window to another Desktop. You could use any of the methods described earlier to move a window in **Mission Control**. Another method is to simply drag the window over to the left or right edge of the desktop until the pointer reaches the edge of the screen and can no longer move any further. macOS will move the window to the neighboring desktop after a short delay.

Note that if you have multiple displays set up as an extended desktop, moving a window to the right or left edge of your desktop will move the application window to the other display. Depending on how you arranged your displays in the **Display** preference pane determines whether your second display is to the left or right of your main display.

Remove the Drag Delay When Moving Windows between Desktops

If you move a window between Desktops by dragging it to the left or right edge, you will notice a slight delay before macOS moves the window to the neighboring desktop. You can completely remove this delay by entering the following commands in Terminal.

```
defaults write com.apple.dock workspaces-edge-delay -float 0
```

```
killall Dock
```

Now you can move a window to the neighboring Desktop without a delay. However, I've found that without a delay, a window will fly across all the Desktops before I have a chance to drop it. So the delay we just eliminated was actually somewhat useful, albeit longer than necessary. The following commands will configure a ½ second delay, just long enough to prevent a window from flying out of control but shorter and more responsive than the default.

```
defaults write com.apple.dock workspaces-edge-delay -float 0.5
```

```
killall Dock
```

Feel free to play with the decimal number after **-float** to adjust the delay to your personal preference.

To revert to the default macOS behavior, enter the following commands in **Terminal**.

```
defaults delete com.apple.dock workspaces-edge-delay

killall Dock
```

Create an Extended Desktop

If you have multiple displays, you can choose to set them up as an **extended desktop** or mirrored displays. Mirroring is covered in the next section. An extended desktop creates one large continuous desktop across your displays, allowing you to drag a window from one display to another.

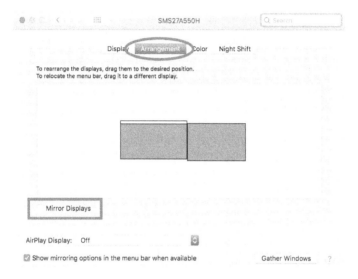

To create an extended desktop across your displays, launch the Displays preference pane and select the **Arrangement** tab. Uncheck the checkbox next to **Mirror Displays**. Choose which display will be on the left and on the right by dragging the displays shown in the center of the preference pane to the positions you desire.

Mirror Displays

Another option for a multiple monitor setup is to mirror the displays. Mirroring displays your Mac's video output on both monitors simultaneously. This feature comes in handy when you need to project your display on screen during a meeting. You will be able to see what the audience is seeing without having to turn around and look at the projected image.

To mirror your displays, open the **Displays** preference pane in the System Preferences application. Select the **Arrangement** tab if not already highlighted. Check the checkbox next to **Mirror Displays**. macOS will attempt to match the closest resolution between the two displays when mirroring. This change takes effect immediately.

Note how the representation of the displays at the center of the preference pane changes when mirroring is enabled.

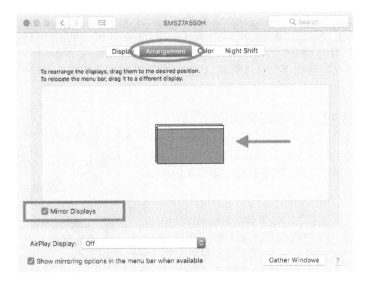

If you ever need to quickly mirror your Mac's display, you can toggle mirroring on and off with the keyboard shortcut ⌘F1 (command+F1).

Assign an Application to a Desktop

If you really value organization, macOS allows you to permanently assign an app to a specific desktop. By assigning applications to desktops, you will insure apps will always open on the desktop of your choice. You can use this feature to create a themed Desktop. For example, you can have one desktop for all of your social media applications, another for your productivity apps, another for browsers, etc. How you organize your apps is up to you.

To assign an application to a specific desktop, first navigate to the desktop to which you want to assign the application. If you need to create a new desktop space, first launch Mission Control and click the **Add Desktop Button**. Find the application in the **Dock**. If the application is not in the Dock, launch the application using **Launchpad** to make it appear in the Dock. Secondary click on the application icon in the Dock to reveal the **Options** menu. By default, the **None** option is checked, which allows the application to be run on any desktop. To assign the app to the current desktop, select **This Desktop** from the menu.

If your Mac has multiple displays, you can assign an app to a Desktop on a specific display. With two displays, the **Options** menu will offer options for each display.

Assigning an application to a desktop does not prevent you from moving that application to another desktop later. Also, the application does not have to be added to the Dock for it to launch to its assigned desktop. Once an application has been assigned to a Desktop, it will always appear on its assigned Desktop regardless of how it was launched.

Assign an Application to Every Desktop

macOS offers an option to assign an application to every desktop. This is a handy feature if you have an application you use frequently and desire quick access to it.

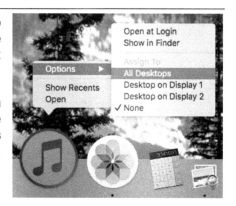

Find the application in the Dock. If the app is not in the Dock, launch it first. Secondary click on the application icon in the Dock to reveal the **Options** submenu. To assign the app to every desktop, select **All Desktops**.

Toggle Mission Control On & Off

There are many ways to launch **Mission Control**. You can launch it using a trackpad gesture, open it from Launchpad, Spotlight or Siri, press the **F3** key, or enter **^up** (control+up arrow).

macOS offers one more alternative that allows you to toggle Mission Control on and off. Press and hold the **F3** key to toggle Mission Control on. The moment you release the **F3** key, Mission Control will toggle off.

Quick Look

When application windows are grouped in **Mission Control**, it is difficult to differentiate between them because they are grouped one on top of the other. This is especially true if you have a lot of windows open on the same desktop and are using a computer with a small screen like an 11-inch MacBook Air. The solution is **Quick Look**.

To see the contents of any window in Mission Control, hover over it with the pointer and when a blue border appears around the window, press the **spacebar**. Mission Control will zoom the highlighted window. To toggle the zoom off, press the spacebar again and the window will shrink back to its original size.

Quick Lock is especially useful when you have windows groups by application enabled, since this feature will allow you to see the contents of windows underneath the top window.

Ungroup Windows in Mission Control

If you prefer that Mission Control not group windows from the same application, you can disable this feature in the Mission Control preference pane. Doing so makes it easier to discern the contents of windows without having to use Quick Look.

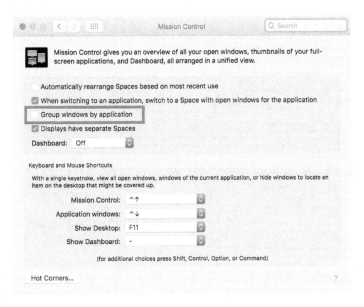

To disable the grouping of windows from the same application, launch the Mission Control preference pane. Uncheck the checkbox next to **Group windows by application**. With this option unchecked, windows from the same application are displayed separately, making it easier to distinguish their contents without resorting to Quick Look.

Change the Mission Control Keyboard Shortcut

The default keyboard shortcut to launch **Mission Control** is ^**up** (control+up arrow). macOS allows you to change this shortcut to utilize any F key from **F1** to **F12**, the left or right ⇧ ^ ⌥ ⌘ (shift, control, option, or command) keys, or the **fn** (function) key.

To change the keyboard shortcut, launch the Mission Control preference pane. Use the drop-down menus next to **Mission Control** under the **Keyboard and Mouse Shortcuts** section located in the lower half of the pane. Select your desired keyboard shortcut to. You can also use the following keys as modifiers: ⇧ ⌘ ^ ⌥ (shift, command, control, or option), alone or in any combination. Hold down the desired modifier key(s) when selecting your desired shortcut from the drop-down menu.

This section of the preference pane also lets you change the keyboard shortcuts for **Application windows** (App Exposé), **Show Desktop**, and **Show Dashboard**.

App Exposé removes desktop clutter to reveal all the windows of a chosen application. To launch App Exposé, select an application with multiple windows open and enter ^**down** (control+down arrow). You can then select the desired window by pointing and clicking to make it active. App Exposé can also be executed with a trackpad gesture by swiping three or four fingers down, depending on how you configured the gesture in the Trackpad preference pane.

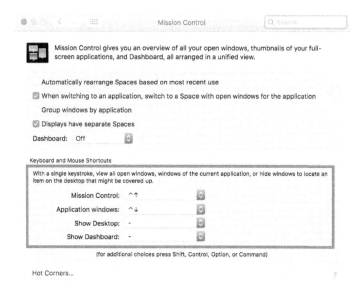

The **Show Desktop** command clears the desktop of all open windows by pushing them off the edge of the screen. The **Dashboard** command launches the Dashboard, if you have it enabled. Choose your desired keyboard shortcuts for Show Desktop and the Dashboard from the drop-down menu next to each command.

To turn off any of the shortcuts, select the – option from the drop-down list.

Open Mission Control by Dragging a Window to the Top of the Screen

This handy trick lets you simultaneously open Mission Control and drag a window to another Desktop. Simply drag a window to the very top of your desktop and continue dragging it as if you were trying to push the window off the top of your screen. Mission Control will launch with its ribbon open, allowing you to move the window to another Desktop or take it to Full Screen or Split View.

5

Menu Bar

macOS offers a number of customizations for the **Menu Bar**. Recall from Chapter 3, that there are two halves to the Menu Bar. The left half contains the **Apple** and **Application** menus while the right half, which is shown below, contains the **Status Menu**. Note that if you upgraded from a previous version of macOS and customized your Status Menu (as I did), it will look different than what is shown below.

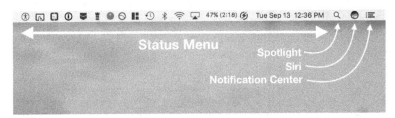

The **Status Menu** displays the status of and provides quick access to various macOS features and applications via small icons called **Menu Extras**. Menu Extras are also called menulets, menu items, or status items. **Menu Extras** are used to configure various macOS features and third party applications.

At the far right of the Menu Extras are icons for **Spotlight**, **Siri**, and **Notification Center**. We will cover Spotlight, Siri, and Notification Center in later chapters.

Enable Dark Mode

The **Menu Bar** is translucent gray by default, using white as its base color. This allows the colors of the desktop wallpaper to show through. **Dark Mode** changes the base color of the Menu Bar, drop-down menus, Spotlight, Siri, and the Dock to black while still maintaining some translucency and the macOS layered 3D appearance. With Dark Mode enabled, the text changes to a higher contrast white against a dark background. The image below compares the translucent gray Menu Bar to the Menu Bar in Dark Mode.

To enable Dark Mode, open the **General** preference pane in System Preferences and check the checkbox next to **Use dark menu bar and Dock.**

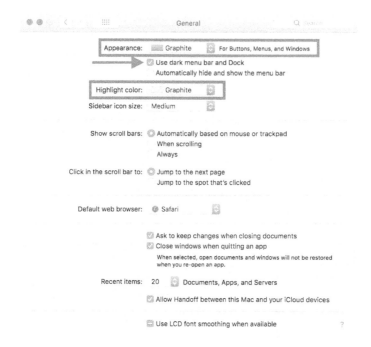

To keep with the general motif of Dark Mode, you might want to change the **Appearance** of buttons, menus, and windows as well as the **Highlight Color** from the default **Blue** to **Graphite**.

Note that Dark Mode also changes the base color of the Dock. The images below compare the Dock in its default mode and with Dark Mode enabled, respectively.

To return to the system default, uncheck **Use dark menu bar and Dock** in the **General** preference pane.

Add a Menu Bar to Each Display

In a multiple display setup, you have a couple of options to configure the behavior of your displays. The first option is to treat each display independently, each with its own **Menu Bar**. Since the Menu Bar is available on all displays, you do not have to move the pointer back to the main display to access Menu Bar features. An added benefit of enabling this feature is that you can have a separate, independent set of Desktops for each monitor in your system. In a dual-monitor set up, you can have up to 32 Desktops!

To add a Menu Bar to each display, open the **Mission Control** preference pane. Check the checkbox next to **Displays have separate Spaces**. You will need to logout and log in for the change to take effect. When you launch Mission Control you will now see an independent ribbon on each display showing the Desktops available on each display.

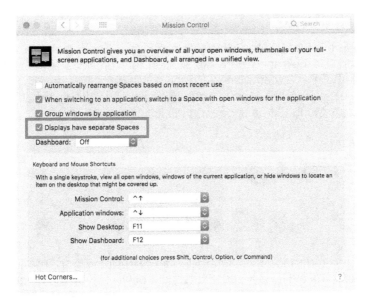

Relocate the Menu Bar to Another Display

Your second option is to treat your second monitor as an extension of your main display. First, ensure that the checkbox next to **Displays have separate Spaces** in the **Mission Control** preference pane is unchecked. If you need to uncheck the box, you will need to logout and log in for this change to take effect.

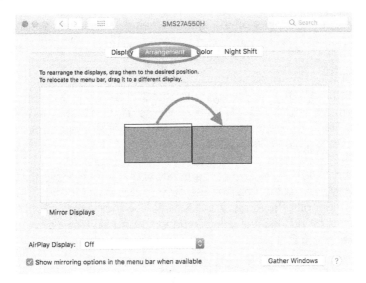

Next, you need to configure on which display the Menu Bar will appear. To relocate the Menu Bar to another display, open the **Displays** preference pane in the System Preferences application. Select the **Arrangement** tab if not already highlighted. Drag the Menu Bar, which is represented by a white bar at the top of one of the displays, to the desired display.

Rearrange the Menu Extras

The **Menu Extras** in the **Status Menu** are displayed generally in the order in which they started. If you launch a new third party application that provides a Menu Extra, it will appear at the far left of the Status Menu. Not all applications have an associated Menu Extra. By default, native macOS Menu Extras will display on the right half of the Status Menu, while third party Menu Extras appear on the left.

Third Party Menu Extras:

Native macOS Menu Extras:

macOS allows you to rearrange the Menu Extras without having to install a third party Menu Bar manager. To move a Menu Extra, hold down the ⌘ (command) key while dragging it to a new location on the Status Bar. The selected Menu Extra will turn gray while you are dragging it. Move it left or right to your desired location. Other Menu Extras will politely move out of the way to make room. Note that you can only reorder the Menu Extras within the Status Bar. You cannot relocate a Menu Extra to the left side of the Menu Bar as it is reserved for the Apple and Application Menus. If you try to move a Menu Extra to the Application Menu, it will bounce back to the far left of the Status Bar. With the exception of Notification Center, you can rearrange any of the Menu Extras, including Spotlight and Siri.

Take care not to drag a Menu Extra off the Menu Bar as you could accidentally remove it.

Remove a Menu Extra

If you have no need for a particular **Menu Extra**, macOS allows you to remove it from the **Status Bar**. To remove a Menu Extra, hold down the ⌘ (command) key while dragging the it off the Menu Bar. Release and poof, the Menu Extra disappears. Note that you cannot remove the Spotlight and Notification Center Menu Extras.

As for third party application Menu Extras, generally you cannot remove them using the ⌘ (command) key. However, some applications provide the ability to hide their Menu Extra in their preferences. For other third party apps, removing their associated Menu Extra can only be accomplished by quitting the app. Depending on the third party application, you may be stuck with its Menu Extra.

Add Native macOS Menu Extras

You can add native macOS **Menu Extras** to the Menu Bar by checking the checkbox in the associated preference pane in System Preferences. Another option is to open the Menu Extras folder and select the Menu Extra you want to add.

Launch **Finder** and press ⇧⌘G (shift+command+G) to display the **Go to the folder** dialog box. Enter the following into the field and click **Go**. Native macOS Menu Extras supplied by Apple are located in this folder:

`/System/Library/CoreServices/Menu Extras`

Find the Menu Extra you wish to add and double-click to add it to the Menu Bar. Note that third party application Menu Extras are added when the application is installed, launched, or by checking an option in the application specific preferences.

Hide the Menu Bar

macOS High Sierra allows you to automatically hide the Menu Bar when it is not in use. Hiding the Menu Bar off screen provides more desktop real estate and less distractions. When combined with the Dock auto hide feature I'll show you in the next chapter, you'll be simply amazed at the amount of clean, uncluttered desktop real estate these two features provide.

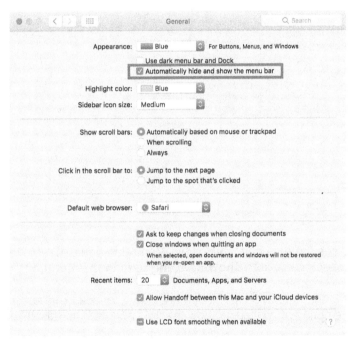

Menu Bar auto hiding is disabled by default. To enable Menu Bar auto hiding, open the **General** preference pane. Check the checkbox next to **Automatically hide and show the menu bar**.

With this feature enabled all you need to do to unhide the Menu Bar is to move your pointer to the top of the screen and leave it there for a moment. The Menu Bar will automatically appear and then disappear when no longer needed.

To return to the macOS default and disable Menu Bar auto hiding, open the **General** preference pane and uncheck the checkbox next to **Automatically hide and show the menu bar**.

Customize the Date and Time

By default, the **Date & Time Menu Extra** displays the the day of the week and current time. Its drop-down menu lets you switch between an analog or digital clock. When the clock is configured as analog, a tiny clock is displayed in the Menu Bar. Clicking it reveals the drop-down menu which displays the day of the week, date, and time in hours, minutes, and seconds. When the clock is configured as digital, the drop-down shows the day of the week and the date.

The Menu Extra also provides direct access to the **Date & Time** preference pane in System Preferences where the configuration options are located. Selecting **Open Date and Time Preferences...** takes you directly to the **Clock** pane of the **Date & Time** preference pane.

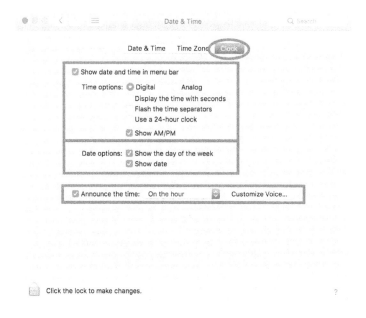

If you don't want to see the date and time in your Menu Bar, you can remove them entirely by unchecking the checkbox next to **Show date and time in the menu bar**.

If you decide to keep the date and time, it does not have to look like the macOS standard clock. You have the option of configuring how the time and date are displayed.

The time can be shown in either analog or digital format. If you select digital, you have 3 additional configuration options. The time can be displayed with or without seconds. The colons separating hours, minutes, and seconds can be set to flash on and off. And you have the option of displaying a 12-hour or 24-hour clock. If you select the 12-hour option, you can choose whether to show AM and PM.

Check the checkboxes next to the options you wish to configure. If you select the analog clock you are prevented from configuring any additional options as they are all grayed out.

For the date, you have the option of showing the day of the week in addition to displaying the date.

You can also configure macOS to announce the time on the quarter, half, or hour by checking the checkbox next to **Announce the time**. Choose how often you want the time announced from the drop-down menu and then click **Customize Voice...** to access the voice configuration sheet to select the voice you wish to use.

Connect to Wi-Fi

The **AirPort Menu Extra** allows you to turn Wi-Fi on and off, connect to a Wi-Fi network, create Wi-Fi networks, or open the Network preference pane. From the AirPort Menu Extra you can connect to any of the Wi-Fi networks listed, which are shown with their relative signal strengths. The more dark lines radiating outward, the stronger the Wi-Fi signal. If your smartphone supports a Wi-Fi hotspot, you'll see it listed here.

A small padlock next to the network name indicates a password is needed to join this Wi-Fi network. Public Wi-Fi networks which are open for anyone to connect to are denoted by the lack of this padlock. Note that public Wi-Fi networks transmit data without any encryption. Therefore, the data you transmit and receive can be seen by others running packet analyzer software. Never do online banking on an unencrypted public Wi-Fi network. Check out the Security & Privacy chapter for information on Virtual Private Network apps.

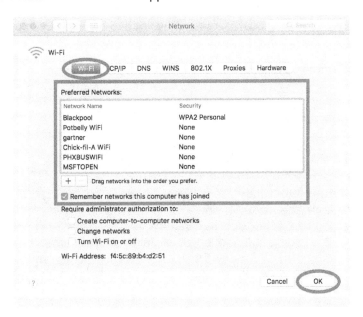

The bottom section of the drop-down menu allows you to join other Wi-Fi networks that are not listed. You can use the **Join Other Network...** option to connect to a network which is hidden (i.e., not broadcasting its network name). A dialog box will appear where you can enter the network name and choose the security option. Once you have selected the security, the dialog box asks you to enter the network password. Checking the **Remember this network** checkbox tells macOS to remember this Wi-Fi network, allowing you to connect again without entering the password. Clicking the **Show Networks** button displays the available Wi-Fi networks to which you can connect.   Click   **Join** when finished.

You can open the **Network** preference pane in the System Preferences application by choosing **Open Network Preferences...** from the AirPort Menu Extra drop-down menu. This preference pane allows you to turn Wi-Fi on and off and connect to Wi-Fi. Clicking the **Advanced** button allows you to see, reorder, and remove the Wi-Fi networks your Mac has previously joined. Drag the Network Name to rearrange your preferred networks. It is best to have the networks you join most frequently at the top of the list. To remove a Wi-Fi network, highlight it and click the – button.

By default, macOS will remember the Wi-Fi networks your Mac has joined and will add them to the Preferred Networks list.   Unchecking the checkbox next to **Remember networks this computer has joined** will disable this feature.

Hold Down the Option Key with the AirPort Menu Extra

Holding down the ⌥ (option) key while clicking on the **AirPort Menu Extra** provides additional Wi-Fi information that can be used to troubleshoot Wi-Fi connectivity issues.

Three diagnostic options are available which help when you are trying to troubleshoot Wi-Fi connectivity problems. **Enable Wi-Fi Logging** enables background logging, saving the log to a .log file. Be sure to disable logging when finished or when restarting as macOS will continue to log until you disable it. **Create Diagnostics Report On Desktop...** will do just that, create a diagnostics report in your Desktop folder for use by Apple technicians to troubleshoot Wi-Fi problems. **Open Wireless Diagnostics...** launches an application that will detect common Wi-Fi problems.

Change How Battery Power is Displayed

If you're working on a MacBook, MacBook Air, or MacBook Pro, you will want to keep the **Battery Menu Extra** in your Menu Bar to keep an eye on how much power is left in your battery. The information displayed by the Battery Menu Extra depends on whether your laptop is plugged into AC power or is running on 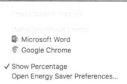 battery. When plugged into AC power, the Battery Menu Extra will tell you whether the battery is charged or is charging and how long it will take to fully charge. When running on battery power, the Battery Menu Extra will tell you how much time remains before your battery runs out of power and which apps are using significant energy, allowing you to close them to save power.

macOS shows a representation of a battery in the Menu Bar. When your battery is almost out of power, the battery will turn red. If you want a more precise reading a battery power, select **Show Percentage** from the Battery Menu Extra drop-down menu.

If you're not interested in seeing how much power your battery has left, you can remove the Battery Menu Extra. Select **Open Energy Saver Preferences...** from the drop-down menu to open the **Energy Saver** preference pane in System Preferences. Uncheck the checkbox next to **Show battery status in menu bar**.

Pair Bluetooth Devices

Bluetooth is a short range wireless technology that lets you pair headsets, smartphones, printers, cameras, tablets, keyboards, a mouse, and a trackpad to your Mac. The **Bluetooth Menu Extra**, lets you turn Bluetooth on and off, pair your Mac with a Bluetooth device, send or browse files on a paired device, and open the **Bluetooth** preference pane.

The Bluetooth Menu Extra lists devices paired with your Mac. If the name of the device is bold, it indicates the device is currently connected. Hovering over any of the connected devices with your pointer allows you to disconnect the device, see its battery level, or open its associated preference pane in System Preferences.

Selecting **Open Bluetooth Preferences...** opens the **Bluetooth** preference pane in System Preferences. From here you can turn Bluetooth off and on, pair Bluetooth devices, and connect and disconnect paired devices. When the checkbox next to **Show Bluetooth in menu bar** is checked, the Bluetooth Menu Extra will appear in the Menu Bar.

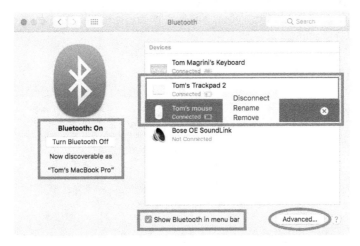

Holding down the ^ (control) key while clicking any device listed will display a submenu allowing you to disconnect, rename, or remove the device. The submenu also displays the address of the Bluetooth device.

Clicking the **Advanced...** button at the lower right of the preference pane displays a drop-down sheet with options to run the **Bluetooth Setup Assistant** if a keyboard, mouse, or trackpad is not detected. You can also configure Bluetooth devices to wake your Mac from sleep.

Hold Down the Option Key with the Bluetooth Menu Extra

Holding down the ⌥ (option) key while clicking on the **Bluetooth Menu Extra** provides additional information and options incudling the version of Bluetooth and Bluetooth MAC address, an option to send files to another Bluetooth device, or to browse files on another Bluetooth enabled device.

Moving your pointer to any of the paired devices will display a secondary menu allowing you to connect or disconnect it, remove it, see its signal strength (RSSI), address, battery level, or open its associated preference pane in System Preferences.

Switch Users with the Fast User Switching Menu Extra

The **Fast User Switching Menu Extra** lets you "fast switch" between users on your Mac. It also provides access to two other features – the **Login Window...** and the **Users & Groups** preference pane. If you have multiple users configured in the User & Groups preference pane, the users are listed in the drop-down menu with the current user grayed out. The Fast User Switching feature allows you to quickly switch users.

Selecting **Login Window...** will lock your Mac without logging you out. Selecting **Users & Groups Preferences...** will take you to the **Users & Groups** preference pane where you can add or remove users, change your password and profile picture, enable parental controls, and choose login items.

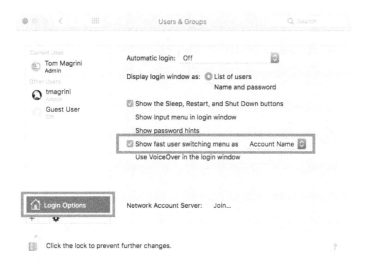

The Fast User Switching Menu Extra can be enabled and disabled from the User & Groups preference pane. Select **Users & Groups Preferences...** or launch System Preferences and choose the **Users & Groups** preference pane. Next, unlock the preference pane by clicking on the padlock in the lower left corner, if locked. Enter your password when challenged. Select **Login Options** at the bottom left.

To enable the Fast User Switching Menu Extra, check the checkbox next to **Show fast user switching menu as**. macOS offers 3 display choices for this Menu Extra: **Full Name**, **Account Name**, or **Icon**.

To disable the Fast User Switching Menu Extra and remove it from the Menu Bar, uncheck the checkbox next to **Show fast user switching menu as**.

Volume Menu Extra

You can view and switch between audio output devices directly from the Volume Menu Extra. You can switch between Bluetooth and AirPlay connected audio output devices directly from the Volume Menu Extra.

If hold down the ⌥ (option) key when clicking the Volume Menu Extra, you can view and switch between your audio input devices.

To add the Volume Menu Extra to the Menu Bar, open the **Sound** preference pane in System Preferences. Check the checkbox next to **Show volume in menu bar** at the bottom of the Sound preference pane.

Mirror your Display to an AppleTV

If you own an Apple TV, the **AirPlay Menu Extra** lets you send video from your Mac to your AppleTV. **AirPlay** only works on Macs manufactured in 2011 or later. If your Mac does not support AirPlay, you will not see the AirPlay Menu Extra.

Open the **Displays** preference pane in System Preferences. Checking the checkbox next to **Show mirroring options in the menu bar when available** in the lower left corner of the pane will display the Airplay Menu Extra. You can select an **Airplay Display** using the drop-down menu.

Backup your Data or Restore Files

Time Machine is the macOS backup utility that automatically backs up your entire Mac to an external drive or AirPort Time Capsule. Not only does Time Machine back up everything, it also remembers how your Mac looked on any given day in the past. The **Time Machine Menu Extra** tells you when and to where Time Machine last backed up your Mac. By selecting **Back Up Now** you can immediately initiate a backup. To restore any lost files, select **Enter Time Machine**, find the files in the Time Machine Finder, select them, and click the **Restore** button.

Selecting **Open Time Machine Preferences...** will open the **Time Machine** preference pane in System Preferences. This preference pane lets you turn **Time Machine** on and off, see the day and time of the last back up, and add or remove back up destinations.

At the bottom of the Time Machine preference pane is a checkbox next to **Show Time Machine in menu bar**. Checking this box will place the Time Machine Menu Extra on your Menu Bar.

Location Services

Location Services is a handy feature of macOS that allows you to get the local weather, restaurant recommendations, use location-based reminders, and a host of other features that require knowledge of your current location. Many apps rely on your location in order to provide relevant information. Maps, Siri, Facebook, Weather, Calendar, and Reminders are a few examples.

When an application accesses your location the icon show below will appear in your Menu Bar. The Location Services Menu Extra's drop-down menu lists applications currently accessing your location.

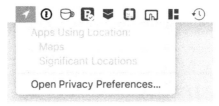

To control which apps can access your location, open the Location Services Menu Extra and select **Open Privacy Preferences...** or open the **Security & Privacy** preference pane from System Preferences and select the **Privacy** tab.

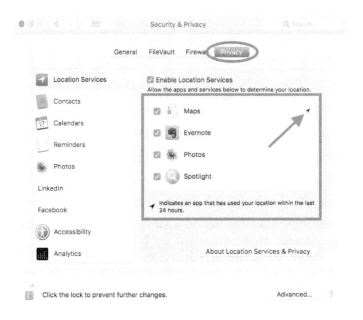

The Location Services icon will identify any app that has accessed your location over the past 24 hours. Check the checkboxes next to the apps you will allow access to your location. Uncheck those which you do not want to access your location.

Note that you do not want to completely disable **Location Services** by unchecking the box next to **Enable Location Services**. Not only does this stop any application from accessing your location, it also prevents you from locating your Mac with the **Find My iPhone** feature.

Third Party Menu Extras

Now that I have introduced you to the native macOS Menu Extras, let's take a look at some very useful third party Menu Extras.

Track Your Packages

Deliveries is a simple and efficient Menu Extra that will keep track of your packages so you'll always know when they will be delivered. Deliveries' simple interface counts down the days left until your package arrives. Deliveries supports all major carriers as well as Amazon's Prime delivery service. You will know when a package is due to arrive and Deliveries will also show you where your package is on a map. Deliveries will also notify you when your package has been delivered.

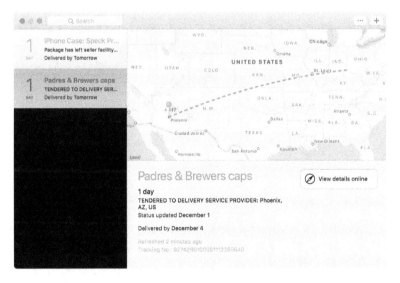

Deliveries is available from the Mac App Store for $4.99 at the time of this writing at: https://itunes.apple.com/us/app/deliveries-a-package-tracker/id290986013?mt=8.

Monitor Battery Status

If you have a MacBook, MacBook Air, or MacBook Pro, I recommend downloading **Battery Monitor**. This app does exactly what its name implies, providing information about your laptop's battery.

Battery Monitor provides more information than the native macOS Battery Menu Extra, displaying the current charge level, time remaining, the cycle count, and battery capacity and current charge in mAh. Battery Monitor is a simple app to manage the health of your laptop's battery.

Battery Monitor is configured from its preference pane, which is accessible by clicking on the drop-down menu icon in the upper left corner of the Battery Monitor information pane. The preference pane allows you to configure behavior and the information Battery provides in its Menu Extra.

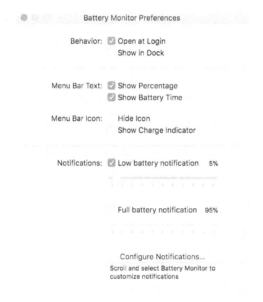

To ensure Battery Monitor is always running, make sure the checkbox next to **Open at Login** is checked. If you would like to see the Battery Monitor icon in the Dock, check the checkbox next to **Show in Dock**.

You can choose what information you want displayed on the Menu Extra and how you want it to appear in the next section. Checkboxes provide the option to **Show Percentage**, **Show Battery Time**, **Hide Icon** (the charge indicator icon in the Menu Bar), and **Show Charge Indicator,** which changes the charge indicator to the native macOS version.

By default, Battery Monitor will notify you of a low battery condition when your battery charge is at 5%. You can change the percentage using the slider underneath **Low battery notification**.

Checking the checkbox next to **Full battery notification**, enables a notification when your Mac laptop's battery reaches full charge. By default, this notification is disabled and set to 95%. Check the checkbox to enable and use the slider to change the percentage for the full charge notification.

Clicking the **Configure Notifications...** button will open the **Notifications** preference pane in System Preferences. See the chapter on Notifications for details on how to customize macOS notifications.

Battery Monitor was available for free in the Mac App Store at the time of this writing at: https://itunes.apple.com/us/app/battery-monitor-health-status/id836505650?mt=12.

Unclutter Your Desktop

 Despite the unsightly clutter, it is often very convenient to store files on the desktop. Say if you are writing a book on how to customize macOS and take a large number of screenshots, which are saved to the desktop by default. Having these files instantly available is not only convenient, it helps with productivity. Too bad it is so unsightly. If you configured the Pristine Desktop tweak to keep your desktop clear of clutter, it would be great if there was an app that could provide the convenience of storing files on the desktop without the clutter.

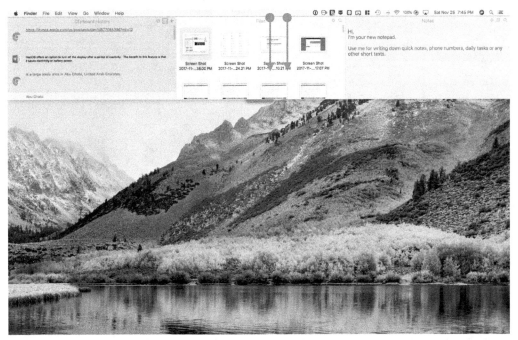

This is where an app, appropriately named **Unclutter**, comes to the rescue. Written by Eugene Krupnov, Unclutter creates a handy place on your desktop to store files, notes, and the clipboard history. Configuring the Pristine Desktop tweak and configuring Unclutter to use the Desktop folder gives you a completely clean desktop while making all files in the Desktop folder instantly available from your Desktop.

To use Unclutter, move your pointer to the very top of your screen and scroll down with two fingers on your trackpad or mouse. The Unclutter window will drop from below the Menu Bar. The default configuration of Unclutter is shown below. Your clipboard history is shown at the left, files in the center, and notes on the right. Click anywhere outside Unclutter, on the desktop or in a window, and the Unclutter window will disappear.

Files can be easily dragged into Unclutter's "drop-zone" located at the very top of your screen above the Menu Bar. Dragging a file into the drop-zone causes the Unclutter window to slide down from under the Menu Bar. Simply drop your file in the files area.

The clipboard history can store the last 10, 25, or 50 items that were cut or copied. You can scroll through them, selecting the one you need, and pasting it again. While I initially purchased Unclutter for quick access to files that would normally be on my desktop, I find the clipboard history to be one of its most useful features.

Let's customize Unclutter. Unclutter places a Menu Extra in the Menu Bar. Click on the Unclutter menu extra and select **Preferences...** or enter ⌘, (command+comma) while the Unclutter window is displayed.

First, let's configure Unclutter's **General** preferences. Click the **General** tab. By default, Unclutter does not run when you start your Mac. I suggest checking the checkbox next to **Launch Unclutter at startup** to ensure Unclutter is always available when you restart.

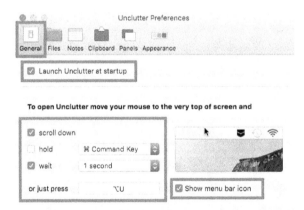

The Unclutter window appears when you move your pointer to the very top of your screen and scroll down with two fingers. You have a number of options to activate Unclutter in addition to the two-finger scroll gesture. By checking the checkbox next to **hold**, you can configure Unclutter to use the ⇧, ^, ⌥, or ⌘ (shift, control, option, and command) keys. Simply hold down your chosen key and scroll to the top of your desktop to activate Unclutter. Check the checkbox next to **wait** to configure Unclutter to activate when you move your pointer to the very top of your screen and wait. You can configure the wait time to a half second, 1 second, or 2 seconds. To configure a keyboard shortcut to reveal the Unclutter window, enter your desired shortcut in the box next to **or just press**. I've configured Unclutter to display its window when I enter ⌥U (option+U). To disable the two-finger scroll, uncheck the checkbox next to **scroll down**.

Unclutter puts a menu extra in the Menu Bar. If you do not want Unclutter's menu extra on your Menu Bar, uncheck the checkbox next to **Show menu bar icon**.

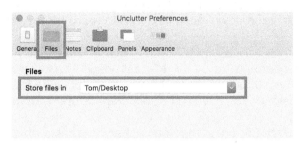

By default, Unclutter saves files to its own location. I find it very convenient to change the default location to the **Desktop** folder in my Home directory. This allows me to use the Pristine Desktop tweak for a completely clean desktop, yet still have quick access to files saved in my Desktop folder. Additionally, Unclutter warns you that to enable Spotlight search for the files it has saved requires you to move files to a different location.

To change the default save location for files in Unclutter, click on the Unclutter menu extra and select **Preferences...** or enter ⌘, (command+comma) while the Unclutter window is displayed. Click the **Files** tab. Select **Open...** from the drop-down menu next to **Store files in**. Navigate to your desired location (I use my Desktop folder) and click **Open**.

Similarly, clicking on **Notes** in the Unclutter preference pane allows you to change the location in which notes are saved.

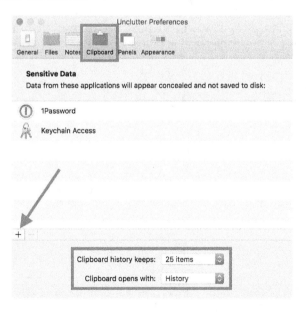

Sometimes you do not want certain data saved to Unclutter's clipboard history. For example, if you use Keychain or another password manager like 1Password, you probably don't want your passwords saved to the clipboard history. To exempt data from certain applications, first click on the **Clipboard** tab in the Unclutter preference pane. Next, click the **+** at the lower left and browse to the application you wish to exempt. Click on it and then click the **Open** button. Unclutter will not show data from any application in its **Sensitive Data** list.

From the **Clipboard** tab, you can configure the number of items Unclutter will save in the clipboard history. Use the drop-down menu next to **Clipboard history keeps** to select 10, 25, or 50 items.

By default, **Clipboard opens with:** is set to **Last view**. Last view displays the last clipboard item viewed. I have found it more convenient to configure this to **History**, which displays the clipboard history. You have a choice of **Item content**, **History, or Last view**.

The **Panels** tab in the Unclutter preference pane lets you disable any panels you do not want to use. By default, the checkboxes next to **Clipboard**, **Files**, and **Notes** are checked. If you do not wish to use a feature, uncheck the checkbox next to it.

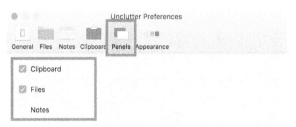

The last customizable item is under the **Appearance** tab. Unclutter matches its theme to how you have configured the Menu Bar when set to **Auto**. If you are using the default Menu Bar, Unclutter will use its **Light** theme. If you have configured the dark Menu Bar, Unclutter will automatically select its **Dark** theme. If you prefer one theme over the other, you can select it using the drop-down menu next to **Theme:**. Unclutter will use your desired theme regardless of the configuration of the Menu Bar.

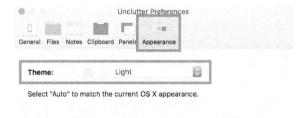

Select "Auto" to match the current OS X appearance.

Unclutter is available from the Mac App Store for $9.99 at the time of this writing at: https://itunes.apple.com/us/app/unclutter/id577085396?mt=12.

Focus with HazeOver

Having lots of open windows can be distracting especially if you are trying to focus on one particular window. All those windows can kill your concentration, making you less productive as each window is another squirrel that demands your attention. Of course, you can always minimize or close windows and hide or quit applications, but all that window and application management is very distracting, drawing your attention from the work at hand.

A better solution is to use **HazeOver**, a distraction dimmer that highlights the active window while automatically dimming all background windows. Written by Maxim Ananov, HazeOver will ensure you stay focused on the the task at hand by letting all the background noise gently fade away.

HazeOver lets you configure the amount background applications are dimmed, from a light, soft dim to a demandingly powerful black that guarantees to eliminate all distractions. The amount of dimming can be configured directly from the HazeOver Menu Extra or from the HazeOver preference pane.

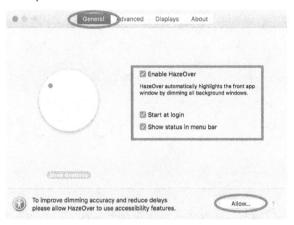

Select the **General** tab if it is not already highlighted. First, check the checkbox next to **Enable HazeOver**. Next, configure the dimming percentage using the large wheel. You can move the wheel with a two-finger up or down scrolling motion. Click **Show Gestures** to view a video demonstrating the gesture. If you want HazeOver to start when you log in to your Mac, check the checkbox next to **Start at login**.

Be sure to click **Allow...** to allow HazeOver to use macOS' accessibility features to improve the dimming accuracy. Click **Open System Preferences** when the security warning appears. The **Security & Privacy** preference pane will open with the **Privacy** tab highlighted. Check the checkbox next to **HazeOver**.

Now back to the HazeOver preference pane. Under the **Advanced** tab, you can change the keyboard shortcut used to toggle HazeOver on and off.

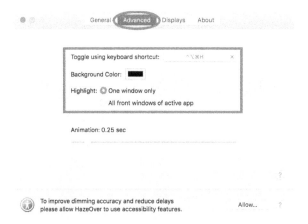

The default shortcut is **^⌥⌘H** (control+option+command+H). You can also select the background color (black is the default) and whether HazeOver will highlight only one or all of the front windows of the active application. The animation speed can also be tweaked in the **Advanced** tab.

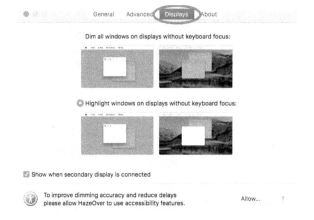

If you have multiple displays, you can configure how windows are dimmed across your displays in the **Displays** tab. You have two choices. The first is to **Dim all windows on displays without keyboard focus**. When selected, this option highlights only the active window on a single display even if the active application has multiple windows open across your displays. Only the active window will be highlighted while all other windows are dimmed. The second option, **Highlight windows on displays without keyboard focus**, will highlight the front windows of the active application on each of your displays.

HazeOver will install a Menu Extra on your Menu Bar, allowing you to quickly access the preferences, turn HazeOver off and on, change the dimming percentage, and quit.

HazeOver is available from the Mac App Store for $4.99 at the time of this writing at: https://itunes.apple.com/us/app/distraction-dimmer-hazeover/id430798174?mt=12.

Keep Your Mac Awake

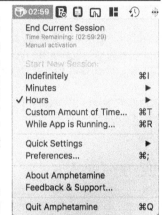

Sometimes you need to keep your Mac awake, overriding its energy saving features. For example, you may need to keep your Mac awake if you subscribe to a cloud back up service. Typically, cloud back up services run more efficiently when you are not using your Mac, and depending on the size of your back up, may need to run for hours. Unfortunately, when you are not actively using your Mac, macOS will force it to sleep after the inactivity timer set in the Energy Savings preference pane expires.

If you want to leave your Mac unattended for a period of time but do not want it to go into sleep mode, you can override its energy saver settings and keep it awake using a free app called **Amphetamine**. You can select one of the preset timers from 5 minutes to 24 hours, create a custom timer, or keep your Mac awake indefinitely. Amphetamine also allows you to schedule activation and deactivation times which is quite handy for nightly back ups.

Other nice features include activating when your Mac connects to a specific Wi-Fi network or when a specific application is running. Its **Drive Alive** feature ensures your hard drive(s) won't go to sleep during a session, which is handy for Time Machine or cloud back ups of external drives.

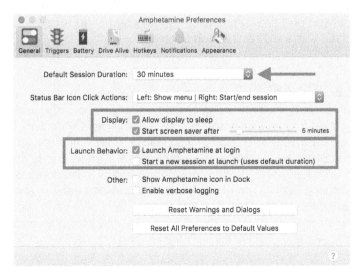

Amphetamine's preference pane is accessed from its Menu Extra, which also allows you to quickly start a new session. From this preference pane, you can set the **Default Session Duration**, which is set to 30 minutes. The options in the drop-down menu mirror the session durations shown in the Menu Extra drop-down, from 5 minutes to 24 hours.

By default, the checkbox next to **Allow display to sleep** is checked. This will allow your display to sleep during a session. You can also enable the screensaver to start by checking the checkbox next to **Start screen saver after** and using the slider to configure the time.

Launch Amphetamine at login is enabled by default. Uncheck it if you prefer to launch Amphetamine each time you want to use it. You also have the option of showing the Amphetamine icon in the Dock, which is disabled by default.

Amphetamine is available from the Mac App Store for free at the time of this writing at: https://itunes.apple.com/gb/app/amphetamine/id937984704?mt=12.

Caffeinate Your Mac

If you prefer to use **Terminal** to keep your Mac awake, you can use the following command to override the macOS inactivity timer.

```
caffeinate
```

If you want to keep your Mac awake for a set period of time, you can set a timer when issuing the caffeinate command. For example, the following command will keep your Mac awake for 12 hours. The time is measured in seconds, therefore 12 hours equates to 43,200 seconds (12 hours x 60 minutes x 60 seconds).

```
caffeinate -t 43200
```

Once you issue the caffeinate command, your Mac will not sleep, dim its display, or play the screensaver until you end the command. You can terminate a caffeinate session by entering ^C (control+C) with the Terminal app open.

Monitor Your Mac's Performance

iStat Menus by bjango is one of the best system activity monitors available for the Mac and an excellent alternative to the macOS Activity Monitor. iStat Menus tracks detailed CPU and GPU data, memory utilization, disk performance and utilization, the temperature at various locations inside your Mac, fan speed, and the current weather and weather forecast, all from the convenience of your Menu Bar. Since iStat Menus also provides battery, and the date and time, it can replace those native macOS Menu Extras. iStat Menus' customizable drop-down panels provide detailed information and graphs. Moving your pointer over an item in the drop-down panel reveals more detailed information and graphs.

What makes iStat Menus such a great alternative to the native macOS Activity Monitor and Menu Extras is the fact that iStat Menus is completely customizable.

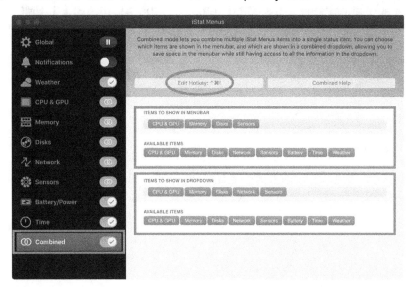

Launch iStat Menus to access its preference pane to enable the menu items that you want shown in the Menu Bar. Move the switch next to each item listed in the black column on the left side of the pane to enable or disable items.

Menu items can be customized. To customize any item, click on it to highlight it. The customization options will be shown on the right side of the pane. Drag items from the **AVAILABLE** bar to the **ACTIVE ITEMS** bar. Items listed in **ACTIVE ITEMS** bar will be displayed on your Menu Bar. To remove an item from the **ACTIVE ITEMS** bar, simply drag it off the bar until you see an **X** appear then release. You can also configure the elements shown on the drop-down panel and configure a hot key to activate the drop-down panel.

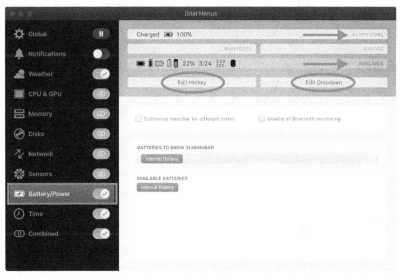

The **Combined** option allows you to combine the **CPU & GPU**, **Memory**, **Disks**, **Network**, **Sensors**, **Battery/Power**, **Weather**, and **Time** items into a single drop-down. You can choose all or a subset of these items. Drag items onto the **AVAILABLE ITEMS** bar from the **ITEMS TO SHOW IN MENUBAR** to add them to your Menu Bar. Move them left or right to rearrange them. Drag items back to the **AVAILABLE ITEMS** section to remove them. The items in the drop-down panel can be customized in a similar fashion.

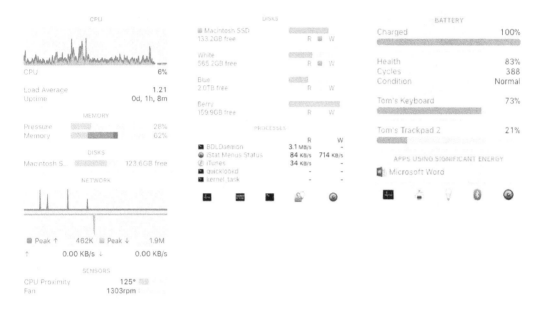

Once you are done customizing iStat Menus, you can close the iStats Menus preference pane by entering **⌘Q** (command+Q). Don't worry, iStats Menus will continue to run in your Menu Bar. You can reorder the items in the Menu Bar by holding the ⌘ (command) key and dragging.

iStat Menus is available from the Mac App Store for $18.99, but was on sale for $9.99 at the time of this writing at: https://bjango.com/mac/istatmenus/.

6

Dock

Whether you are starting your Mac for the first or the thousandth time, the most iconic and recognizable feature of the macOS desktop is the **Dock**. The Dock is one of the most customizable features of macOS. By default, the Dock appears as a strip of application and folder icons at the bottom of the desktop. The Dock serves a twofold purpose, combining the functions of an application launcher and a taskbar to switch between running applications. The Dock is an ingenious feature of macOS that provides a convenient and speedy method to launch applications, open documents and folders, or switch between applications with a single click of your trackpad or mouse.

Since the Dock operates as both an application launcher and switcher, applications that are running are denoted by a tiny black dot beneath their icon. Apps that are not permanently kept in the Dock will appear at the end of the strip of application icons when they are running.

A translucent vertical **divider** separates applications from Stacks, minimized windows, documents, and the trash can. Apps go to the left of the divider. Everything else goes on the right. Clicking the **Yellow** minimize window control in the Title Bar will minimize it to the right side of the Dock. Clicking on a minimized window on the right side of the Dock maximizes it, restoring it to normal size.

Put Apps in Order

The first order of business in customizing the **Dock** is to put the application icons in the order in which you want to see them. This is easily accomplished by moving your pointer to the application icon you wish to move, clicking and holding, and immediately dragging it horizontally, left or right, along the Dock to its new location. If you click and hold too long without moving the icon, a menu will appear and you won't be able to move the icon. In this case, click anywhere on the Desktop and try again. While you are moving the icon other icons will politely move out of the way. Once in its desired location, simply release your hold.

Remove Apps from the Dock

Once you have your application icons in the right order, the next step is to remove apps that you don't want to see in the **Dock**. Note that when you remove an application from the Dock, you are not removing it from your Mac. You only remove its alias from the Dock. The application remains safely tucked away in the **Applications** folder.

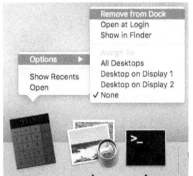

There are always multiple ways of doing things in macOS. It is your personal choice which method you prefer. You can always click and hold the icon you wish to remove until a contextual menu appears. You can also make this menu appear by using a secondary click, holding the control key down while clicking or by using the two-finger tap gesture. If two-finger tap doesn't work, it means you haven't yet customized the trackpad. Select **Options > Remove from Dock**.

An application that is running behaves differently. You can click and hold the icon or use a secondary click to reveal the contextual menu. Select **Options** and a submenu appears. Note the checkmark next to **Keep in Dock**. Select Keep in Dock to remove the checkmark. The menu will disappear along with the checkmark. Since the application is running, its icon will not disappear until you quit.

The fastest and easiest way to remove an app icon from the Dock is to drag it up past the middle of the desktop. About half way up the screen **Remove** will appear above the icon. Release the icon to remove it. If the app icon jumps back to the Dock, it means one of two things. Perhaps you didn't move it far enough away from the Dock. Be sure to move it far enough from the Dock until **Remove** appears above the app's icon. The other possibility is the app is running. If the app is running, it won't disappear from the Dock until you quit.

Oops! Everyone panics the first time they accidentally remove the wrong application icon from the Dock and it disappears. Don't worry. This is an easy fix. Simply add the application back on the Dock. We'll cover how to do that next.

Add Apps to the Dock

Adding an application to the **Dock** is even easier than removing one. Of course, there are multiple ways to do so. The simplest method is to launch the application. Its icon will appear at the end of the strip of apps just to the left of the divider. Drag it to the left to its desired location. The simple act of moving an app icon to the left along the Dock is a signal to macOS that you want to keep the app in the Dock. Another method to add a running application's icon to the Dock is to use the secondary click to reveal the contextual menu. Select **Options > Keep in Dock** and a checkmark will appear next to **Keep in Dock**.

Another method is to open the **Applications** folder in Finder, select the application icon, and drag it to the Dock. Note that you are not moving the app. You are creating an alias on the Dock. Finally, you can add an application to the Dock using a keyboard shortcut. Select the desired application's icon from the **Applications** folder and enter the keyboard shortcut ⇧^⌘T (shift+control+command+T).

Control Application Behavior

The **Options** menu contains several options to control how an application behaves. Checking **Open at Login** opens the app immediately upon logging in to your Mac. This is handy if you have an app or set of apps you open every time you start your Mac. For example, if you always open Safari, Mail, and iTunes, setting these apps to open at login will save you from having to launch each one individually. Use a secondary click to make the **Options** menu appear and select **Open at Login**. A checkmark indicates the application will open when you login or start your Mac. If you no longer want an application to open when you log in, select **Options > Open at Login** to remove the checkmark.

If you want to see the folder where the application is located in Finder, choose **Show in Finder**. This should immediately open the Applications folder with the application highlighted. However, occasionally applications are mistakenly installed in other folders. This is handy if you need to navigate to the application's location to move or uninstall it.

The **Assign To > This Desktop** feature allows you to assign an application to appear on a specific Desktop. This feature is handy if you prefer certain applications to always appear on specific desktops.

It is quite common to have more than one window open for the same application. As your desktop becomes crowded with open windows from multiple applications, it becomes increasingly difficult to find a specific window. This is especially true if you moved a window or two to another Desktop. The **Show All Windows** command executes a feature called **App Exposé**, which removes the desktop clutter to reveal all the windows of the chosen application. You can than select the desired window by pointing and clicking on it, making it active and placing it on top of all other windows.

AppExposé can also be executed with a trackpad gesture. First, click on any open window of the application you are interested in seeing and then swipe down with three or four fingers, depending on how you set up the gesture in the Trackpad preference pane.

Finally, macOS will display the recent items in a list above the **Options** menu. This is a handy feature if you need to reopen a document you recently closed.

The Other Side of the Divider

The Dock's translucent vertical divider separates applications from Stacks, minimized windows, documents, and the trash can. The icon at the end of the Dock that looks like a translucent white trash can is the **Trash**, a temporary holding area for files you want to delete. You can move files to the Trash by dragging them onto its icon. Another option is to utilize a secondary click on a file in Finder to display a contextual menu and select the **Move to Trash** option.

Once items are in the Trash, the icon changes to display a full trash can. If you secondary click on the Trash icon when there are items in it, you have the option to **Empty Trash** or to display its contents in Finder with the **Open** command. The latter feature is handy if you accidentally drag a file into the trash and need to restore it.

To restore a file you accidentally placed in the trash, secondary click on the file and select **Put Back** to return the file to its original location. You can also drag a file out of the Trash back to its folder in Finder.

Select **Empty Trash** to empty the trash can. A warning appears to confirm that you really want to empty the trash.

Delete a File Immediately

You can delete files immediately when they are in the Trash without deleting any of the other files. To delete a file immediately from the Trash, first open the Trash folder by secondary clicking on its icon in the Dock and selecting **Open** from the contextual menu. The **Trash** Finder window will open. Highlight the file you want to delete and secondary click on it to reveal another contextual menu and select **Delete Immediately...**. You also can hold down the ⌥ (option) key while selecting **File > Delete Immediately...** or enter the keyboard shortcut ⌥⌘**delete** (option+command+delete). A dialog box will appear to confirm the deletion and warn you that this action cannot be undone. Click the **Delete** button to delete the file immediately or **Cancel**.

Note that the Delete Immediately option will only appear in the **File** menu when you are holding down the ⌥ (option) key. When the ⌥ (option) key is held down, **Put Back** will change to **Delete Immediately**.

Hide the Dock

Although the Dock is a very useful feature of macOS, it takes up a significant amount of real estate at the bottom of the desktop. This can sometimes be problematic when moving your pointer to the bottom of a window as it will sometimes inadvertently interact with the Dock. macOS gives you the option of hiding the Dock when not in use. And when combined with the Menu Bar auto hide feature I showed you in the last chapter, you'll be simply amazed at the amount of clean, uncluttered desktop real estate these two features provide. See the section "Hide the Menu Bar" in the last chapter to learn how to automatically hide the Menu Bar.

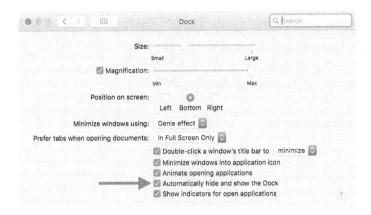

To turn Dock hiding on, open the Dock preference pane from System Preferences. Check the box next to **Automatically hide and show the Dock**. The change will take effect immediately.

The Dock will now slip beneath the bottom of your desktop when not in use. To make the Dock reappear, simply position your pointer at the bottom edge of the desktop or enter ⌥⌘D (option+command+D).

Hiding can also be enabled from the Dock itself. Position your pointer over the Dock divider. When the pointer turns into a two-headed vertical white arrow, use a secondary click to open the Dock contextual menu. Select **Turn Hiding On**. To turn hiding off, secondary click the divider to open the Dock contextual menu and select **Turn Hiding Off**.

You can also use a keyboard shortcut to make the Dock disappear and reappear on demand by entering ⌥⌘D (option+command+D).

Magnify the Dock Icons

Magnification is a handy feature that allows you to conserve desktop real estate by keeping your Dock small and magnifying icons as you move the pointer over them. Magnification is particularly useful if you prefer a small Dock or your Dock is crowded with a large number of icons. As you add more icons to a crowded Dock, it will become smaller, adjusting its size to fit horizontally across the bottom of the Desktop. If you have lots of icons in your Dock or prefer a small Dock, it may be difficult to distinguish application icons from each other. With magnification enabled, the icons in the Dock will magnify as you move the pointer over them.

Magnification is enabled from the **Dock** preference pane in System Preferences. Check the box next to **Magnification**. Use the slider to select your desired level of magnification from "Min," which is no magnification, to "Max," which is 128 pixels. This change will take effect immediately.

You can also enable magnification from the Dock itself. To **Turn Magnification On**, position your pointer over the Dock divider. When the pointer turns into a two-headed vertical white arrow, use a secondary click to open the Dock contextual menu. Select **Turn Magnification On**. To turn magnification off, secondary click the divider to open the Dock contextual menu and select **Turn Magnification Off**.

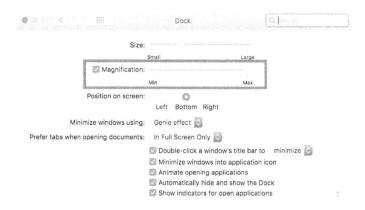

Add More Magnification

If you want more magnification, you can set magnification levels up to a ridiculously large 512 pixels. Open Terminal and enter the following commands. The 256 at the end of the first command doubles the default maximum magnification level of 128.

```
defaults write com.apple.dock largesize -float 256
```

```
killall Dock
```

Why not go all the way and double the magnification level again?

```
defaults write com.apple.dock largesize -float 512
```

```
killall Dock
```

Now that's ridiculously large! You can enter any integer between 1 and 512 toyou're your desired magnification level.

Enter the following commands to revert to the default maximum magnification level.

```
defaults write com.apple.dock largesize -float 128
```

```
killall Dock
```

Toggle Dock Magnification On or Off

Holding down the ⇧^ keys (shift+control) while moving your pointer across the Dock will toggle magnification on or off. If you have Dock magnification disabled, holding the ⇧^ keys while moving your pointer across the Dock will temporarily turn magnification on.

Conversely, if you have Dock magnification enabled, holding the ⇧^ keys while moving your pointer across the Dock will temporarily turn magnification off.

Relocate the Dock

The default position of the Dock is at the bottom of the Desktop. macOS allows you to relocate the Dock to either the left or right edges of the Desktop.

To relocate the Dock, open the **Dock** preference pane in System Preferences. Select the **Left**, **Bottom**, or **Right** radio button next to **Position on screen**.

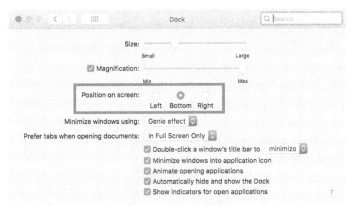

You can also relocate the Dock from the Dock itself. Position your pointer over the Dock divider. When the pointer turns into a two-headed vertical white arrow, use a secondary click to open the Dock contextual menu. Select **Position on Screen** and select **Left**, **Bottom**, or **Right**. Your selection takes effect immediately.

The image on the previous page shows what the Dock looks like when configured at the left, bottom, or right edge of the desktop. You can see that the Dock icons are smaller when the Dock is configured for the left and right edges of the desktop.

Change How Windows Minimize

macOS features two standard animation effects when windows are minimized or maximized. The default is **Genie effect**, in which windows minimize or maximize like a genie entering or exiting a magic lamp. The second option is the **Scale effect**, where a window scales smaller and smaller until it finally reaches the Dock. When maximizing, the window scales larger as it restores itself to its original size.

To change how windows minimize, open the **Dock** preference pane in the System Preferences application. Choose **Genie effect** or **Scale effect** from the drop-down menu next to **Minimize windows using**.

You can also change how windows minimize from the Dock itself. Position your pointer over the Dock divider. When the pointer turns into a two-headed vertical white arrow, use a secondary click to open the Dock contextual menu. Select **Minimize Using** and choose **Genie effect** or **Scale effect**.

Minimize Windows with the Hidden Suck Effect

macOS offers two standard animations when minimizing windows, the Genie and Scale effects, with the default being Genie. macOS offers one more hidden animation, the **Suck effect**, which is not available from the Dock preference pane. As the name suggests, a minimized window appears as if it is being sucked into the Dock by a powerful vacuum cleaner. Maximizing reverses the effect with the window shooting back to its original position as it pushed by a powerful leaf blower.

To enable the suck effect, open Terminal and enter the following commands. Be sure to press the **return** key after each line. The change takes place immediately, so minimize a window and check it out.

```
defaults write com.apple.dock mineffect -string suck
```

```
killall Dock
```

You could have also replaced **suck** with either **genie** or **scale** in the above write command to configure either window animation directly in Terminal.

To revert to the default Genie animation, enter the following commands in Terminal.

```
defaults delete com.apple.dock mineffect
```

```
killall Dock
```

Minimize or Zoom Windows by Double-Clicking

Double-clicking the Title Bar to minimize does the exact same thing as clicking the Yellow minimize window control. Zooming an app by double-clicking causes the window to expand to cover all available desktop space between the Menu Bar and the Dock. If you have chosen to hide both the Menu Bar and Dock when not in use, the window will expand to cover the entire desktop. While this sounds like Full Screen mode, it is not. Mission Control does not recognize zoomed windows as Full Screen apps. You can still take an app to Full Screen mode when zoomed by clicking the green button in its Title Bar.

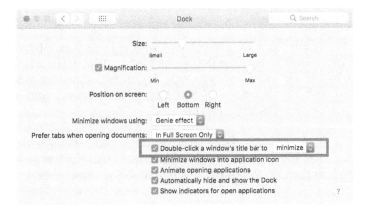

Double-clicking to minimize or zoom is configured in the **Dock** preference pane in System Preferences. Make your selection from the drop-down menu next to **Double-click a window's title bar to**.

Size the Dock

The Dock will automatically resize itself based on the number of icons docked. As you squeeze more icons into the Dock, it stretches across the bottom of the desktop. The Dock's maximum size is limited by the size of the screen. macOS will not allow you to make the Dock so big that it won't fit on the screen, although the left- and right-most icons will likely slide off screen when using magnification.

Once the Dock reaches the maximum size allowed by the screen, you can continue to add icons. However, each icon will become smaller in order to allow all icons to fit. If your

Dock has become overcrowded with app icons, check out the next chapter where I show you a nifty method to group apps into stacks and use them as application launchers.

Sizing the Dock is accomplished through the **Dock** preference pane in the System Preferences application. At the top of the pane is the **Size** slider, which controls the size of the Dock. Making the Dock smaller means it will take up less desktop real estate. Sometimes it seems that sliding the size towards large has no effect. This is because macOS scales the Dock to the maximum size horizontally (or vertically if positioned along the left or right edge of the desktop) that will fit given the number of icons in the Dock.

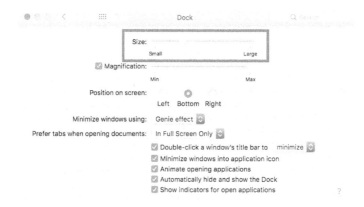

A second option is to change the size of the Dock from the Dock itself. Move your mouse pointer over the divider. It will turn into a double headed vertical white arrow. Click, hold and drag the white arrow up to make the Dock bigger and down to make it smaller. Remember, the maximum size is limited by the size of the screen. And while you can make the Dock very small, macOS limits you here too.

When you resize the Dock, you are essentially changing the size of each of the icons displayed in the Dock. Therefore you can utilize Terminal to more precisely size the icons. Try out the following commands. They will make your Dock small. Don't worry you can resize it.

```
defaults write com.apple.dock tilesize -int 32
```

```
killall Dock
```

macOS will allow you to replace the 32 in the first command to any integer from 1 to 256. The smaller the number, the smaller the Dock. Try using the integer 1.

```
defaults write com.apple.dock tilesize -int 1
```

```
killall Dock
```

Don't worry, your Dock is still there. It's that half-inch long blob where your Dock used to be. A Dock this small is really not useable even with magnification. Let's change the Dock to a more reasonable size.

```
defaults write com.apple.dock tilesize -int 64
```

```
killall Dock
```

There, that's better. You can try other integers between 1 and 256. If you were hoping for a gigantic Dock, you're out of luck. Even if you use 256, the size of the Dock is limited to the maximum size that will fit on the screen.

Sometimes getting the Dock sized properly is like adjusting the driver's seat in your car. It's never quite right. If you want to return the Dock to its default size and start over, open Terminal and enter these commands.

```
defaults delete com.apple.dock tilesize
```

```
killall Dock
```

Clean Up a Cluttered Dock

By default, macOS minimizes windows to the right side of the Dock divider. This can become problematic if you minimize a large number of windows. As you minimize each window, the Dock expands across the Desktop. Once the Dock reaches its maximum size, each successive window minimization causes it to become smaller as macOS crowds more minimized window icons into the right side of the divider. Eventually the overcrowding causes the icons in the Dock to become extremely difficult to differentiate, especially the minimized windows.

macOS has a solution, available in the Dock preference pane. Open the Dock preference pane in the System Preferences application. Click the checkbox next to **Minimize windows into application icon**.

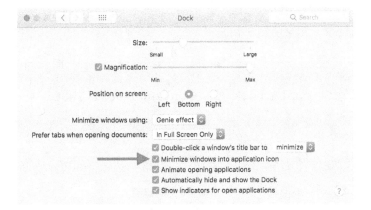

When this option is checked, macOS will minimize windows into their associated application icon. Minimized windows will no longer clutter the right side of the Dock and increase its size. This saves a great deal of Dock real estate.

When you want to see all the windows of an application, simply use **App Exposé** on the associated application icon. **App Exposé** is activated by hovering the pointer over an application icon in the Dock and swiping down with either three or four fingers on the trackpad. Note that **App Exposé** has to be activated in the Trackpad preferences.

Stop Bouncing App Icons

Application icons in the Dock will bounce when one of two events occur: upon launching the app or if the app needs your attention. The latter event typically occurs when a dialog box opens with a warning, needs your input, or the app wants to tell you a task has been completed. Bouncing can be disabled in the **Dock** preference pane in the System Preferences application.

Animate opening apps is enabled by default. Uncheck this box if you do not like this animation. This will stop apps from bouncing when you open them from the Dock. However, some applications will bounce their icon continuously until you respond by clicking the bouncing icon. The incessant bouncing can be irritating if you are busy doing something else and are not at a convenient break point. Stopping icons from bouncing in response to a warning or when the app needs your attention requires configuration using the Terminal application.

To disable application bouncing, launch Terminal and enter the following commands.

```
defaults write com.apple.dock no-bouncing -bool TRUE
```

```
killall Dock
```

To turn bouncing back on for warnings, enter the following commands.

```
defaults delete com.apple.dock no-bouncing
```

```
killall Dock
```

Turn Off Open Application Indicators

macOS puts a tiny black indicator dot underneath the icon of open applications. If you moved the Dock to the left or right edge of the Desktop, the indicator will be on the left or right, respectively. If you don't care to know which applications are open, you can disable this feature in the **Dock** preference pane. Uncheck the box next to **Show indicators for open applications**.

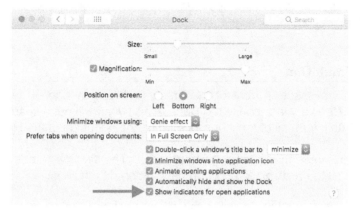

You can also turn off open application indicators using Terminal. To turn off the indicator lights for open applications, launch Terminal and enter the following commands.

```
defaults write com.apple.dock show-process-indicators -bool FALSE
```

```
killall Dock
```

Enter the following commands to turn the indicator lights back on.

```
defaults write com.apple.dock show-process-indicators -bool TRUE
```

```
killall Dock
```

Space Out the Apps

All of the application icons are equally spaced next to each other on the Dock. If you'd like to better organize your apps, you can group similar apps together and put a blank space between groups. Launch Terminal and enter the following commands. The first two lines are a single command. **Do not** hit the **return** key until you have entered both lines.

```
defaults write com.apple.dock persistent-apps -array-add '{tile-data={};tile-type="spacer-tile";}'
```

```
killall Dock
```

A blank space will appear at the end of the app icons permanently kept in the Dock. Note the blank space between the icons for Calculator and Terminal in the image below. Drag the blank space to your desired position. Repeat the Terminal commands if you want to add another space.

Removing the space is rather interesting. Drag it off the Dock to remove. What makes this interesting is it will appear as if you are dragging nothing because the blank space is invisible! If that is too weird for you, secondary click on the blank space to display the **Remove from Dock** option.

Space Out the Trash Can

This command adds a space in front of the Trash on the right side of the divider. By default, the Trash is the very last icon in the Dock. This tweak will put a space to the left of the Trash to separate it from all of the icons located on the right side of the Dock divider.

Open Terminal and enter the following commands. The first two lines are a single command. **Do not** hit the **return** key until you have entered both lines.

```
defaults write com.apple.dock persistent-others -array-add '{tile-
data={};tile-type="spacer-tile";}'
```

```
killall Dock
```

A blank space will appear to the left of the Trash. Drag the space to your desired location. Repeat the commands if you want to add more spaces.

Remove the space by dragging it off the Dock past the middle of your desktop and release. Remember the blank space is invisible so it will appear that you are dragging nothing. If you prefer, you can secondary click on the blank space and select **Remove from Dock**.

Dim Hidden Apps

How do you know which applications are hidden? An indicator light under the icon denotes a running app, but the Dock provides no feedback to tell you which applications are hidden versus which ones are not. The Dock can be customized to dim the icon of a hidden application, allowing you to spot the applications you have hidden at a glance. Note the difference between the icons for Safari, Microsoft Word and Excel versus Mail and Evernote. Mail and Evernote are hidden and their icons appear dimmed.

To enable this feature, open Terminal and enter the following commands.

```
defaults write com.apple.dock showhidden -bool TRUE
```

```
killall Dock
```

If you hid applications before entering the commands above, you'll notice no change to the icons. Click on the hidden apps and then hide them again. They will now dim.

Use the following commands to change the Dock back to its default behavior.

```
defaults write com.apple.dock showhidden -bool FALSE
```

```
killall Dock
```

Turn the Dock into a Taskbar

The Dock serves a twofold purpose, combining the functions of an application launcher and a taskbar to switch between open apps. macOS lets you change the behavior of the Dock so that it operates only as a taskbar, showing only the applications that are currently open.

Enter the following commands into Terminal to switch the Dock to taskbar mode.

```
defaults write com.apple.dock static-only -bool TRUE
```

```
killall Dock
```

Once the Dock is operating in taskbar mode, you may want to turn off the indicator lights for the running applications. Since the Dock now shows only running apps, the indicator lights are superfluous. You can disable indicator lights from the **Dock** preference pane by unchecking the box next to **Show indicators for open applications**.

Running the Dock in taskbar mode is particularly useful if you don't want to use the Dock to launch applications or you have categorized your applications into App Stacks as described in the next chapter. Often users want to put all of the applications they routinely use into the Dock. The problem is the Dock's maximum size is limited and once reached, each application icon becomes smaller and more difficult to differentiate from the others.

macOS offers several alternative methods to launch applications. First, Launchpad offers a quick and easy method to access and launch any of your applications. Another method is to categorize applications into folders for easy access and to combat sprawl and clutter. Applications can be organized into App Stacks and launched directly from the Dock in taskbar mode. If you are an ex-Windows user, you may want to create aliases on the desktop for your applications. Alternatively, if there is a particular set of applications you use constantly, you can set them to launch when you start or log into your Mac. Another option is to enter **⌘space** (command+space) to activate **Spotlight** and use it as an application launcher. Or you can hold down the **⌘space** (command+space) keys to activate **Siri** and use it to launch your applications.

To change the Dock back to its default behavior, enter the following commands.

```
defaults write com.apple.dock static-only -bool FALSE
```

```
killall Dock
```

Surprise! macOS remembered what your Dock looked like and restored it back to its original state.

Activate App Exposé with a Two-Finger Scroll Gesture

App Exposé can only be accessed using a trackpad, so you are out of luck if you use a Magic Mouse unless you activate this tweak. This tweak allows you to open App Exposé using a scroll up gesture on an application icon in the Dock. Scroll up with one or two fingers on an Apple Magic Mouse or with two fingers on a trackpad. Scroll in the opposite direction with the same number of fingers to close App Exposé.

Open Terminal and enter the following commands to activate this feature.

```
defaults write com.apple.dock scroll-to-open -bool TRUE
```

```
killall Dock
```

Once active, you'll be able to open App Exposé by moving the pointer to an application icon in the Dock and scrolling up. Scroll down to close App Exposé. An additional benefit of this feature is that it also allows you to open and close a stack by scrolling up or down, respectively.

Enter the following commands in Terminal to deactivate this feature.

```
defaults delete com.apple.dock scroll-to-open
```

```
killall Dock
```

Single Application Mode

Hiding applications is a handy technique to keep your desktop free of clutter and distractions to help you stay focused. A Dock shortcut allows you to accomplish two commands simultaneously – launching an application while hiding all other apps.

Hold down the ⌥⌘ (option+command) keys while clicking on an application icon in the Dock. The app will open and all other open windows from other running applications will instantly be hidden. You can also use this shortcut even if the application is already open.

If you like this behavior, you can make it permanent by configuring the Dock to operate in single application mode. Anytime you open a new application from the Dock or switch applications, all other apps will be hidden. Note that this tweak does not affect applications launched from Launchpad, Spotlight, or from the Applications folder.

Enter the following commands in Terminal to turn on single application mode.

```
defaults write com.apple.dock single-app -bool TRUE
```

```
killall Dock
```

To turn off single application mode and return the Dock to its default behavior, enter the following commands.

```
defaults delete com.apple.dock single-app
```

```
killall Dock
```

Change the Hide/Show Animation Speed

If you like keeping your Dock hidden, you'll notice that macOS animates the Dock's disappearance and reappearance to and from underneath the desktop. macOS allows you to completely eliminate this animation, making the Dock hide and unhide instantly.

Enter the following commands in Terminal to eliminate the Dock animation.

```
defaults write com.apple.dock autohide-time-modifier -float 0
```

```
killall Dock
```

macOS also allows you to increase the length of the animation. Setting the animation to a larger number slows the animation down. A smaller number speeds it up. The following commands will set the animation to 2.5 seconds so you can see the Dock animation in slow motion. You can even use decimals like 0.15 and 0.5 to tune the length of the animation to your exact specification.

```
defaults write com.apple.dock autohide-time-modifier -float 2.5
```

```
killall Dock
```

To restore the Dock to its default animation, enter the following commands.

```
defaults delete com.apple.dock autohide-time-modifier
```

```
killall Dock
```

Find an App's Location

Another handy Dock shortcut is to hold the ⌘ (command) key while clicking on an app icon. This shortcut opens the application's location in Finder with the application highlighted.

Spring Loaded Dock Icons

Applications icons in the Dock are spring loaded like folders in Finder. If you drag and drop a file, pause, and hover over an application icon, **App Exposé** will launch, allowing you to drop the file onto the app to launch it.

Add a Preference Pane to the Dock

If you find yourself frequently using a specific preference pane in the System Preferences application, you may find it convenient to add it to the Dock. A preference pane can be added to the right side of the Dock.

To add a preference pane to the Dock, open Finder. Enter ⇧⌘G (shift+command+G) to open the **Go to the folder** dialog box. Enter the following into the field and click **Go**.

`/System/Library/PreferencePanes/`

Locate the preference pane you want to add to the Dock and drag it to the right side of the divider. You are now able to access it directly from the Dock without having to first launch the System Preferences application. In the example below, I added the Time Machine preference pane between the Home and the Applications folders.

To remove a preference pane from the Dock, drag it off like any other item you wish to remove from the Dock.

Add iCloud Drive to the Dock

Like many features of macOS, there are several ways to access your **iCloud Drive**. I find that the most convenient and quickest way to open iCloud Drive is from the Dock, where it is immediately accessible without having to first launch Finder to open iCloud Drive from the Finder Sidebar.

To add the iCloud Drive icon to the Dock, open a **Finder** window. Enter ⇧⌘G (shift+command+G) to open the **Go to the folder** dialog box. Enter the following into the field and click **Go**.

`/System/Library/CoreServices/Finder.app/Contents/Applications/`

Locate **iCloud Drive** in this folder and drag and drop it where you want it on the Dock.

Lock the Dock

You just spent a significant amount of time customizing the Dock to get it to look and perform exactly the way you like it. However, it is very easy to accidentally reorder or remove icons or resize or reposition the Dock. All it takes is one bad click from your trackpad or mouse to ruin your customization. It is easy to prevent this from happening by locking the Dock. If you are satisfied with the way your Dock looks, macOS allows you to individually lock the Dock's contents as well as its size, position, magnification, and autohide settings. You will need to ensure that the Dock preference pane is closed before executing any of the following commands.

Lock the Dock Contents

To prevent unintentional changes to the contents of the Dock, launch Terminal and enter the following commands. Hit the **return** key after each line.

```
defaults write com.apple.dock contents-immutable -bool TRUE
```

```
killall Dock
```

Lock the Dock Size

The following commands will prevent accidental changes to the size of the Dock. After running these commands, you'll notice the **Size** slider in the Dock Preference pane will be grayed out.

```
defaults write com.apple.dock size-immutable -bool TRUE
```

```
killall Dock
```

Lock the Dock Position

To lock the Dock's position on the Desktop, enter the following commands.

```
defaults write com.apple.dock position-immutable -bool TRUE
```

```
killall Dock
```

Lock Dock Magnification

To prevent changes to your Dock's magnification setting, enter the following commands.

```
defaults write com.apple.dock magnify-immutable -bool TRUE
```

```
killall Dock
```

Lock Dock Autohide

To lock the Dock's autohide feature, enter the following commands.

```
defaults write com.apple.dock autohide-immutable -bool TRUE
```

```
killall Dock
```

Although you have locked the Dock autohide feature, you can still use the ⌥⌘D (option+command+D) keyboard shortcut to make the Dock disappear and reappear on demand.

Completely Lock the Dock

To completely lock all Dock features, enter the following commands in Terminal.

```
defaults write com.apple.dock contents-immutable -bool TRUE
defaults write com.apple.dock size-immutable -bool TRUE
defaults write com.apple.dock position-immutable -bool TRUE
defaults write com.apple.dock magnify-immutable -bool TRUE
defaults write com.apple.dock autohide-immutable -bool TRUE
killall Dock
```

Unlock the Dock

What happens if you want to make changes to a locked Dock? Well, unlock it, of course! Each of the locks for contents, size, position, magnification, and hiding can be unlocked individually.

Unlock the Dock Contents

To unlock the Dock contents so you can make changes to its content or order, enter the following commands. Press the **return** key after each line.

```
defaults delete com.apple.dock contents-immutable
```

```
killall Dock
```

Unlock the Dock Size

To unlock the Dock so you can change its size, enter the following commands.

```
defaults delete com.apple.dock size-immutable
```

```
killall Dock
```

Unlock the Dock Position

To unlock the Dock's position on the Desktop, and enter the following commands.

```
defaults delete com.apple.dock position-immutable
```

```
killall Dock
```

Unlock Dock Magnification

To unlock the Dock magnification to make changes, enter the following commands.

```
defaults delete com.apple.dock magnify-immutable
```

```
killall Dock
```

Unlock Dock Autohide

To unlock the Dock's autohide feature, enter the following commands.

```
defaults delete com.apple.dock autohide-immutable
```

```
killall Dock
```

Completely Unlock the Dock

To completely unlock the Dock, enter the following commands in Terminal.

```
defaults delete com.apple.dock contents-immutable
defaults delete com.apple.dock size-immutable
defaults delete com.apple.dock position-immutable
defaults delete com.apple.dock magnify-immutable
defaults delete com.apple.dock autohide-immutable
killall Dock
```

7

Stacks

Stacks are another cool feature of macOS, offering quick access to frequently used folders directly from the Dock. Stacks are located to the right of the divider, the thin translucent vertical line separating applications from the stacks, minimized windows, and the trash can. Applications go to the left of the divider. Everything else goes on the right.

Unless you upgraded from a previous version of macOS where you customized the Dock, macOS gets you started with one stack, which is linked to the **Downloads** folder. The Downloads stack is the exact same Downloads folder you see under Favorites in the Finder Sidebar. Anything downloaded using Safari, Mail, Messages, or AirDrop is saved to this folder.

When you click on the **Downloads** stack, its contents spring from the Dock in a fan. Clicking on any item in a stack opens it. At the very top of the fan is a link to open the Downloads folder in **Finder**. Of course, you can change this behavior and view the contents as a **Fan**, **Grid**, or **List**. An **Automatic** option lets macOS select the most appropriate view depending on the number of items in the stack. Secondary click on the Downloads stack to access the contextual menu to configure how the stack is displayed and how its contents are viewed and sorted.

Sort by
Name
✓ Date Added
Date Modified
Date Created
Kind

Display as
Folder
✓ Stack

View content as
✓ Fan
Grid
List
Automatic

Options ▶

Open "Downloads"

macOS offers four options to view stack contents. **Automatic** is the default, automatically switching between **Fan** and **Grid** depending on the number of items in the stack. Choosing Fan will always display the contents as a stack fan, however, only the first ten or so items will display. macOS will tell you how many more items are available at the top of the fan. Clicking this circular icon with the arrow will open the folder in a Finder window so you can see the remaining items.

As their names imply, **Grid** displays stack contents as a grid and **List** as a list. Both the Grid and List options behave differently than the Fan view. Clicking on a folder in a Fan stack will open the folder in Finder. Clicking on a folder in a Grid or List stack will open the sub-folder directly in the Grid or List view, allowing you to navigate through your folder hierarchy to your intended destination. If you don't want to navigate further in the grid or list, holding down the ⌘ (command) key while clicking a folder will open it in Finder. In addition to changing how you want the contents to display, the stack contextual menu allows you to change the stack icon to a folder.

macOS offers five sorting options. A stack's contents are sorted by **Name**, **Date Added**, **Date Modified**, **Date Created**, or **Kind**. The default is to sort by Name. In a Fan, the closest icon to the Dock is based on the sort type. For example, if a Fan is sorted by name, the closest item to the Dock is the first item in alphabetical order. Similarly, when the Fan is sorted by date added, the item with the most recent date will be closest to the Dock.

Add Stacks

You can customize the right side of the Dock by adding stacks for folders like the Applications folder or other frequently accessed folders or devices. Adding folders you frequently use as stacks is much more efficient than navigating through Finder. The picture shows stacks for my Microsoft Office 2016 Applications and Home, Applications, Desktop, and Downloads folders.

To add a folder stack to the Dock, simply locate the folder you wish to add in Finder and drag it to the Dock. It's that easy. Another method is to locate the folder in the Finder Sidebar and secondary click on it to open a contextual menu. Choose **Add to Dock**. Any item in the Finder Sidebar can be added to the Dock as a stack with the exception of **AirDrop** and **iCloud Drive**. However, folders located in iCloud can be added to the Dock as stacks. macOS allows you to create as many stacks as you want or can fit on the Dock.

To add a disk drive, look under **Devices** in the Finder Sidebar. Secondary click the device and select **Add to Dock**. Note that the icon for a removable storage device will turn into a question mark on top of a disk drive icon when the media is removed.

Once your stacks are in the Dock, you can arrange their order. Rearrange stacks by dragging them left or right. Remember, you cannot drag a stack to the left of the vertical divider. macOS will not allow you to move stacks to the left of the divider as that side is reserved for applications.

You can even drag individual documents into the Dock, although technically, a document is not a stack, it is an **alias**. The only options available with a secondary click are to **Remove from Dock**, **Open at Login**, **Show in Finder**, and to open the document. Despite these limitations, adding a document to the Dock is particularly useful if you frequently access it.

You can drag and drop items in a stack to move them to another folder, stack, onto the Dock, to the Desktop, into the Trash, to an external disk drive, or any other location.

Remove Stacks

Removing a stack is done the same way as you would remove any item from the Dock. Simply drag it off the Dock until **Remove** appears above the icon. Release and the stack will disappear. Stacks can also be removed by secondary clicking on the stack and selecting **Options > Remove from Dock**.

This Happens All the Time

You think you are dragging a file from the Downloads stack, but you accidentally drag the entire Downloads stack off the Dock and poof, it's gone! Don't panic. You can put the Downloads folder back with one command.

Open Finder, navigate to the Downloads folder and drag it back onto the Dock. If the Downloads folder is in the Finder Sidebar, secondary click on it and select **Add to Dock**. To avoid accidentally removing or rearranging items in the Dock, lock it. See "Lock the Dock" in the last chapter to learn how to lock and unlock the Dock.

Highlight Stack Items

macOS offers a feature that will highlight an item in a Stack as you hover over it with the pointer. Highlighting is disabled by default. To enable highlighting, open Terminal and enter the following commands. Don't hit the **return** key until you have completely entered the first two lines.

```
defaults write com.apple.dock mouse-over-
hilite-stack -bool TRUE
```

```
killall Dock
```

To turn off highlighting and go back to the default, enter the following commands.

```
defaults delete com.apple.dock mouse-over-hilite-stack
```

```
killall Dock
```

Temporarily Highlight Stack Items

If you don't want to permanently highlight stack items, macOS lets you use highlighting as needed. If you want to temporarily highlight items, click and hold the Stack icon. Do not remove your finger from the trackpad or mouse as the Stack expands. With your finger still pressing down on the trackpad or mouse, move up the Stack listing. Whichever item your pointer is hovering over will be highlighted. Continue to hold the trackpad or mouse until you hover over the item you want to open and then release. The highlighted item will open immediately.

Another option is to click and hold the stack icon. Release immediately after the stack expands. Now type the first few letters of the desired item's name. macOS will highlight items as you type. Once the desired item is highlighted, press the **return** key to open it immediately.

Add a Recent Items Stack

To save you the trouble of looking for a recently opened application, document, or server, macOS keeps a list of **Recent Items** under the (Apple) Menu. Select **> Recent Items** to display a list of the last ten applications, documents, and servers. Ten is the default and can be changed in the **General** preference pane. Access the pane by clicking **System Preferences > General**. Look for **Recent Items** near the bottom of the pane and select **None**, **5**, **10**, **15**, **20**, **30**, or **50** items.

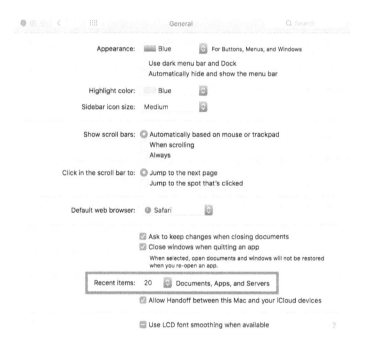

But what if you want to use the Dock instead of the (Apple) menu to access your recent items? Adding a recent items stack to the Dock is one of the most useful macOS tweaks. Open Terminal and enter the following commands. Do not press the **return** key until you have completely entered the first three lines.

```
defaults write com.apple.dock persistent-others -array-add '{
"tile-data" = { "list-type" = 1; }; "tile-type" = "recents-tile";
}'
```

```
killall Dock
```

macOS will place a recent items stack on the Dock to the left of the Trash. By default, the recent items stack will list the most recently accessed applications with the contents viewed as **Automatic**. A secondary click on the stack icon will open a contextual menu of options, allowing you to change the type of recent items in the stack and how the stack is viewed. The recent items stack can show **Recent Applications**, **Recent Documents**, **Recent Servers**, **Recent Volumes**, or **Favorite Items**. Like all stacks, contents can be viewed as a **Fan**, **Grid**, **List**, or **Automatic**.

macOS allows you to create as many stacks as you want. If you want another recent items stack, run the commands again. By default, each new stack will first appear as a **Recent Applications** stack. Use a secondary click to change to **Recent Documents**, **Recent Servers**, **Recent Volumes**, or **Favorite Items**. The contents of a newly created Recent Items Stack are viewed as **Automatic**. Secondary click on the Recent Items Stack to set the **View content as** option. To remove a Recent Items stack, drag it off the Dock or secondary click on it and select **Remove from Dock**.

If you ever need to clear the recent items displayed in a stack or set of stacks, select > **Recent Items** > **Clear Menu**. If you have a large number of recent items, you will have to scroll down to access the **Clear Menu** command at the very bottom. The recent items stack will look like it disappeared, but it is still there. It just has no contents to display as shown in the image below.

Create an App Stack

If your Dock is crowded with applications making it difficult to quickly find the app you are looking for, a solution to the overcrowding is to organize your apps into App Stacks. You can organize your apps by any method imaginable – by application type like productivity, social media, utilities, or browsers or by how often you use them. This feature is particularly useful if you like a neat and tidy Dock or if you switched the Dock to taskbar mode, where it only shows the running applications.

Follow these simple steps to create an App Stack:
1. Create a new folder in your Home Directory called "Stacks."
2. Open the folder.
3. Create and name a new folder for your App Stack using ⇧⌘N or **File > New Folder**.
4. Open a new Finder Window using ⌘N or **File > New Finder Window**. Click on the Applications folder in the Sidebar.

5. Select an application you wish to add to your App Stack from the Applications folder and drag it into your App Stack folder. This will create an **alias** in your App Stack folder.
6. Repeat step 5 for each application you want to add to your App Stack.
7. Drag and drop your App Stack folder onto the right side of the Dock.
8. Repeat starting at step 3 to create another App Stack, if desired.

Dragging a folder from the Stacks folder to the Dock creates the App Stack. By default, the contents of an App Stack are sorted by **Name**, displayed as a **Stack**, and content viewed as **Automatic**. Secondary click on the App Stack to set the **Sort by**, **Display as**, and **View content as** options.

The images below show the contents of my Microsoft Office 2016 App Stack folder and how this App Stack appears in the Dock.

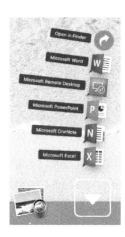

To add a new application to an existing App Stack, open the Applications folder and drag the new app to your App Stack in the Dock. To remove apps from an App Stack, open the App Stack in the Dock and drag the app alias to the Trash. To remove an App Stack, simply drag it off the Dock. Release and the stack disappears.

Create a Document Stack

If you have a certain set of documents you access frequently, the quickest and easiest method to access these items is to create a **Document Stack** on the Dock. A Document Stack can be created for any folder in Finder including your Home folder.

To create a Document Stack, simply locate the desired folder or create a new one in Finder, then drag it to the right side of the Dock. By default, the contents of a Document Stack are sorted by **Name**, displayed as a **Stack**, and content viewed as **Automatic**. Secondary click on the Document Stack to set the **Sort by**, **Display as**, and **View content as** options.

To remove a Document Stack, simply drag it off the Dock until **Remove** appears above the icon, release, and poof, the stack disappears.

Create a Desktop Stack

If you like a clean and clutter-free desktop like I do, you probably configured the macOS tweak "Create a Pristine Desktop" in Chapter 3. However, a lot of items are saved to the desktop by default. If they no longer appear on the desktop, where do they go? In reality, macOS doesn't save these items to your desktop. They are saved to a folder in your **Home** directory called **Desktop**. You can access this folder in Finder, but because so many items get saved to the Desktop folder by default, I suggest you add a Desktop Stack to your Dock for quicker access to those items.

To create a Desktop Stack, open Finder. If the Desktop folder is in the Finder Sidebar, drag it to the right side of the Dock or secondary click on it and select **Add to Dock**. If the Desktop folder is not in the Finder Sidebar, find it in your Home directory. Drag it to the right side of the Dock. You may want to also drag the Desktop Folder to the Finder Sidebar to provide another method to quickly access it. By default, the contents of a Desktop Stack are sorted by **Name**, displayed as a **Stack**, and content viewed as **Automatic**. Secondary click on the Desktop Stack to set the **Sort by**, **Display as**, and **View content as** options.

To remove a Desktop Stack, drag it off the Dock until **Remove** appears above the icon, release, and poof, the stack disappears.

Create a Volumes Stack

If you have multiple internal or external drives, wouldn't it be cool to see them all in one stack? While macOS allows you to drag each one individually from the **Devices** list in the **Finder** Sidebar, you have to use this tweak to see them all in a single stack.

If you like a clean, uncluttered desktop, you probably wish macOS wouldn't show all of your disk drives on the desktop. See Chapter 3 to learn how to disable this feature. Once macOS is no longer displaying your hard drives on your desktop, a **Volumes Stack** makes accessing any of your internal or external hard drives a breeze.

Creating a Volumes Stack is a multi-step process.
1. Open Finder and enter ⇧⌘G (shift+command+G) to open the **Go to the folder** dialog box.
2. Enter **/Volumes** in the dialog box and hit **return** to open the **Volumes** folder.
3. Click **Column** View in the Finder toolbar. The **Volumes** folder will be highlighted and grayed. This is because **Volumes** is a hidden folder.
4. Drag and drop the hidden **Volumes** folder to the right side of the Dock to create a Volumes Stack.

By default, the contents of a Volumes Stack are sorted by **Name**, displayed as a **Stack**, and content viewed as **Automatic**. Secondary click on the Volumes Stack to set the **Sort by**, **Display as**, and **View content as** options.

To remove a Volumes Stack, simply drag it off the Dock until **Remove** appears above it. Release and it disappears. If you changed the **Finder** preferences so external drives no longer display on the desktop, you may wish to turn this feature back on. Otherwise, the only place you will be able to see your external drives is under the **Devices** list in the

Finder Sidebar. See Chapter 3 on customizing the Desktop to learn how to change the Finder preferences to make external drives appear on your desktop.

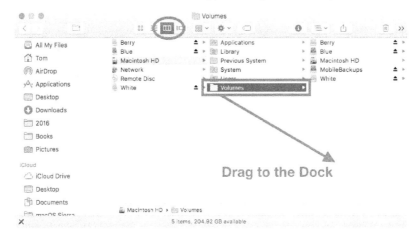

Drag to the Dock

Activate Stacks with a Scroll Gesture

Typically a stack is opened using a single click or click and hold when using temporary highlighting. Another method available is to use a scroll up gesture with a single finger on an Apple Magic Mouse or with two fingers on a trackpad.

To activate this feature, launch Terminal and enter the following commands.

```
defaults write com.apple.dock scroll-to-open -bool TRUE

killall Dock
```

Once active, you'll be able to open a stack by moving the pointer to the stack and scrolling up with a single finger on a mouse or with two fingers on a trackpad. Scroll down to close the stack. An additional benefit of this feature is that it also activates **App Exposé** when you use the scroll gesture on an application icon in the Dock. Give it a try on an application with multiple windows open. All open windows of the application will be shown in App Exposé.

Enter the following commands to deactivate this feature.

```
defaults delete com.apple.dock scroll-to-open

killall Dock
```

Slow Motion Stack Animation

Next time you open a stack, hold down the ⇧ (shift) key while clicking on the stack. The stack will open in slow motion. Try holding the ⇧ (shift) key while closing the stack to see the same animation in reverse.

Quickly Open a Stack in a Finder Window

If you ever need to open a stack in Finder, hold down the ⌥⌘ (option+command) keys while clicking on the stack. The folder linked to the stack will immediately open. This is the same as clicking on the **Open in Finder** control at the top of a fan or the bottom of a grid or list stack. This is a handy feature when you need to update the contents of a Stack. This trick works for any stack except a Recent Items Stack.

Locate a Stack

Another handy Dock shortcut is to hold the ⌘ (command) key while clicking on a stack. This shortcut opens the stack's location in Finder with the item highlighted. This trick works for any stack except a Recent Items Stack and a Volumes Stack.

Spring Loaded Stacks

Try dragging a file onto a Stack, pause while hovering over the Stack and suddenly a Finder window will open allowing you to move the file into the folder. If you hold down the ⌥ (option) key while dragging and hovering, you will copy the file instead of moving it. Holding down ⌥⌘ (option+command) will create an alias.

8

Spotlight

Spotlight is the macOS search application that will locate almost anything on your Mac. In addition to finding stuff on your Mac, Spotlight will make suggestions from the Internet, iTunes, the App Store, find movie showtimes, nearby locations, provide sports scores, weather forecasts, and find online videos. Spotlight retains its same front and center look and feel in macOS High Sierra as in previous versions of macOS.

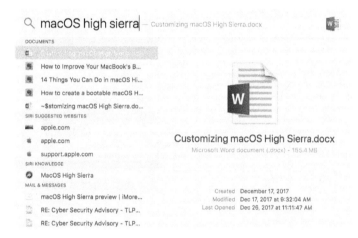

Spotlight has the ability to search 20 different categories of data, which is configurable in the **Spotlight** preference pane. To make suggestions more relevant, Spotlight includes your location in its search request to Apple.

Spotlight is accessed by clicking on its icon, located in its usual spot in the upper right corner of the Menu Bar next to Notification Center. Clicking on the Spotlight icon opens a large search window in the center of your desktop. The default keyboard shortcut remains the same as in earlier versions, **⌘space** (command+space).

As you type in the Spotlight search field, Spotlight will offer results it thinks are likely matches, refining them as you type and organizing them into categories directly below the search field. Results are displayed in categories, with the **Top Hit**, the result Spotlight determined to be the most likely, highlighted at the top of the list. If you press **return**, macOS will immediately open the Top Hit. Spotlight displays search results in the categories listed in the Spotlight preference pane, skipping categories that lack a result.

A large preview pane on the right allows you to preview results selected in the left pane. Any item in the search results can be previewed by highlighting it. Clicking on an item in the Spotlight search results opens it. If an item is already highlighted because you were previewing it, pressing the **return** key will open it. To see the location of an item in the file system, hold down the ⌘ (command) key while clicking on the item. The file path is shown at the bottom of the preview pane.

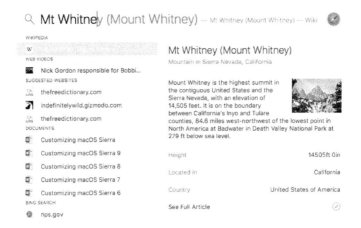

One of the coolest features of Spotlight is its ability to search the Internet without first having to launch Safari. Spotlight will display a preview of the webpage in its preview pane. Highlight the result and hit **return** to open Safari and go to the website.

Avoid Spotlight Information Overload

By default, **Spotlight** will search 20 different categories including files on your internal and external drives, the web, folders, music, movies, images, bookmarks, web browsing history, events, reminders, contacts, (take a deep breath), mail, messages, definitions, applications, system preferences, fonts, documents, presentations, spreadsheets, PDFs, System Preferences, plus an other category for those things not listed above. Spotlight can even do unit conversions so you never have to remember that formula to convert temperatures in Celsius to Fahrenheit.

Depending on your point of view, this could be pretty darn awesome or just a lot of information overload. If you think this is information overload, the Spotlight preference pane allows you to remove categories that do not interest you.

To remove Spotlight search categories, open the Spotlight preference pane in the System Preferences application. Next, click **Search Results** at the top of the pane if it is not already highlighted. Feel free to uncheck as many categories as you like. You can always add them back later.

Exclude Volumes or Folders from Spotlight

Spotlight searches everything on your Mac by default. However, macOS High Sierra allows you to exclude specific volumes or folders from being searched.

To exclude a volume or folder, open the Spotlight preference pane in the System Preferences application. Click **Privacy** at the top of the pane if it is not already selected.

Click the **Add Button**, denoted by the **+** at the bottom left, to open a **Finder** window. Browse to the volume or folder you want to exclude. Click the **Choose** button. Your selection will be added to the exclusion list.

To remove a volume or folder previously excluded, highlight it in the list of excluded folders and click the **−** at the bottom left.

Change the Spotlight Keyboard Shortcut

The default keyboard shortcut for **Spotlight** is **⌘space** (command+space). macOS lets you configure any keyboard shortcut you desire.

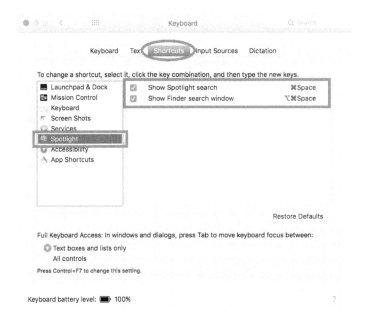

To change the keyboard shortcut for Spotlight, open the Spotlight preference pane in the System Preferences application. Click the **Keyboard Shortcuts...** button found in the lower left hand corner of the preference pane. This button is available on both the **Search Results** and **Privacy** tabs. The **Keyboard shortcuts...** button will launch the **Keyboard** preference pane.

From the **Keyboard** preference pane you can choose any combination of keys as Spotlight's keyboard shortcut. Click on the **Shortcuts** tab if it is not already highlighted. Next, select **Spotlight** in the left-hand column. **Show Spotlight search** is the first choice in the list of shortcuts in the right-hand pane. Click on **Show Spotlight search** to highlight it and click on **⌘space**. You can now enter your own custom shortcut in the field provided. Be sure to select a shortcut that is not already in use. If you select a shortcut already in use, a yellow triangle will appear to warn you of the conflict. A yellow triangle will also appear in the left column next to the category containing the conflict.

You can also change the keyboard shortcut for the Finder search window that is used to search for files in Finder. Click on **Show Finder search window** to highlight it and click on **⌥⌘space**. You can now enter your own custom shortcut in the field provided.

To revert back to the macOS defaults for both Spotlight and Finder Search Window, click the **Restore Defaults** button at the lower right of the Keyboard preference pane.

Improve Spotlight Search Results

Spotlight allows you to narrow your search to specific types of files using the search modifier **kind**. For example, if you are looking for a specific file type, such as a spreadsheet created in Excel, you can enter **kind:excel** followed by the name of the file. Spotlight will limit the search results to only Excel files.

The following list of search modifiers can be used to improve your Spotlight searches. Enter the search term after the modifier. Entering a Spotlight search modifier alone without a search term returns all files of that type.

kind:alias	Returns results that are aliases.
kind:app	Used to locate applications.
kind:audio	Returns search results that are audio files.
kind:avi	Returns results that are AVI files.
kind:bookmark	Used to search Safari bookmarks.
kind:chat	Used to search the Messages logs.
kind:contact	Searches Contacts.
kind:developer	Returns results from the developer category.
kind:document	Used to search for document files.
kind:event	Searches Calendar events.
kind:folder	Finds folders.
kind:font	Used to search for fonts.
kind:gif	Returns images in GIF format.
kind:history	Searches your Safari history.
kind:image	Returns results that are image files.
kind:jpeg	Used to search for images in JPEG format.
kind:mail	Used to search Mail.
kind:message	Returns results from Messages.
kind:movie	Returns results that are movies.
kind:music	Used to search for music.
kind:pdf	Used to locate PDF files.
kind:preferences	Used to search for system preferences.
kind:presentation	Returns files that are presentations.
kind:quicktime	Used to locate QuickTime movies.
kind:reminder	Used to search for Reminders.
kind:spreadsheet	Returns files that are spreadsheets.

`kind:tiff`	Returns images in TIFF format.
`kind:webpage`	Searches your Safari history.

Search by Specific Application

Spotlight has the capability to search for files created by specific applications.   For example, to search for this book, written in Microsoft Word, I would enter **kind:word macOS** into the Spotlight search field.

The following list shows search modifiers that you can use to look for specific files produced by Apple's iWork suite and the Microsoft Office productivity suite.

`kind:pages`	`kind:word`
`kind:numbers`	`kind:excel`
`kind:keynote`	`kind:powerpoint`

Search Using Tag Color

If you use Finder tags, **Spotlight** allows you to search for files based on the color of their tag using the search modifier **tag**.   For example, to find files with a red tag, you would enter **tag:red** into the Spotlight search field.   Valid tag colors are red, orange, yellow, green, blue, purple, gray, and white.

Once you have begun to routinely tag files, you most likely will rename tags to something more descriptive. macOS allows you to search for tags based on their color or their name. Let's say you renamed the green tag to "vacation."   Either of the following searches would return all of your files tagged with the green tag "vacation." For more information on using tags, see the chapter on Finder.

`tag:green`

`tag:vacation`

Search by Document Author

Spotlight allows you to use the search modifier **author** to search for documents written by a specific author.   For example, to search for documents written by myself, I would enter the following into the Spotlight search field.

`author:Magrini`

Search by Date

Spotlight has the capability to search for files based on the date they were created or modified using the search modifier **date**.   The date can be a specific date, a range, today, or yesterday. For example, entering **date:7/4/17** in the Spotlight search field will return files created or modified on July 4, 2017.

Spotlight also allows you to search for ranges. The following search would return all files created or modified during the month of July 2017.

date:7/1/17-7/31/17

You can use greater than and greater than or equal to in order to find files created or modified on or after a certain date. The following search would return all files created or modified after September 1, 2017.

date:>9/1/17

This search returns all files created or modified on and after September 1, 2017.

date:>=9/1/17

You can also look for files created or modified before a specific date. In this example, Spotlight returns all files created or modified before September 1, 2017.

date:<9/1/17

This search returns all files created or modified on and prior to September 1, 2017.

date:<=9/1/17

Spotlight also allows you to search for files created or modified yesterday or today.

date:yesterday

date:today

Spotlight understands yesterday and today. What about tomorrow? Yes, Spotlight does understand what tomorrow means. However, results are limited to Calendar events and Reminders since your Mac can't predict the files you will create or modify in the future.

date:tomorrow

In addition to the **date** search modifier, Spotlight understands **created** and **modified**.

created:<=10/1/17

modified:7/1/17

Use Multiple Search Modifiers

Any of the search modifiers can be used together to narrow your search. For example, the following Spotlight search would find all Microsoft Word documents I created or modified during the month of September 2017.

```
kind:word date:9/1/17-9/30/17 author:Magrini
```

This search looks at Safari's history and returns any webpages about High Sierra that I visited after August 1, 2017.

```
kind:history created:>8/1/17 High Sierra
```

Handy Keyboard Shortcuts

Spotlight features a number of useful keyboard shortcuts. Use any of the following shortcuts after Spotlight displays search results.

⌘B	Opens **Safari** and searches the Internet for the terms listed in the Spotlight search field.
⌘D	Opens the **Dictionary** application and looks up the term in the Spotlight search field.
⌘K	Opens **Safari** and looks up the terms in Wikipedia.
⌘O	Opens the currently highlighted search result, the same as pressing **return**.
⌘R	Opens the containing folder of the currently highlighted result.
⌘T	Launches the **Top Hit**.
⌘down	Jumps down and highlights the first result in the next category of search results.
⌘up	Jumps up and highlights the first result in the category of search results above.

Show the File Path

Pressing the ⌘ (command) key while a Spotlight search result is highlighted will display the item's path at the lower right of the window. Entering **⌘R** (command+R) or **⌘return** (command+return) will open the containing folder in Finder with the item highlighted.

Save a Spotlight Search

macOS allows you to save **Spotlight** searches to reuse later. To save a Spotlight search, highlight the **Show All in Finder** result at the bottom of the search results and then click on the large Finder icon in the right pane. This will open a Finder window displaying all of the results from the Spotlight search. Click the **Save** button at the upper right of the Finder window to save the search.

A drop-down configuration sheet will appear asking you to specify a name for the search and location to save it. macOS saves searches to the **Saved Searches** folder in your **Home** directory. A checkbox, which is checked by default, allows you to add the saved search to the Finder Sidebar. Click the **Save** button to save your search or **Cancel**. If you left the **Add To Sidebar** box checked, your search will appear in the Finder Sidebar.

What you have just created is a **Smart Folder**, a saved instance of a Spotlight search that will dynamically update its content based on your search criteria. Simply click on the Smart Folder under **Favorites** in the Sidebar to run the search again. We'll cover Smart Folders in more detail in the chapter on Finder.

Use Spotlight as an Application Launcher

Spotlight makes a pretty handy application launcher. This is a great feature if you're trying to launch an application that is not in the Dock or if you're running your Dock in taskbar mode where it only displays running applications. The best part is that your fingers never have to leave the keyboard to launch an app.

Start Spotlight by clicking on its icon in the Menu Bar, but that defeats the purpose of your fingers never leaving the keyboard; use ⌘**space** (command+space) instead. Begin typing the name of the application into the search field. Spotlight will zero in on the application after you enter a few letters of its name. The application will appear as the **Top Hit**. You can launch the application by pressing **return**, entering ⌘**T** (command+T), or clicking on the app within the search results. Spotlight will learn which applications you launch most and will often find your target application after you've typed just one letter.

You can use an application's initials to quickly find and launch it. For example, **Photos** can be launched by entering **ph**. QuickTime can be launched using **qt**. Similarly, you can use **ib** for **iBooks**, **it** for **iTunes**, **wo** for **Word**, **ex** for **Excel**, **pa** for **Pages**, **ev** for **Evernote** and so forth.

Search for Comments

Adding **Comments** to your files is a convenient way to organize related content without having to create folders in Finder. The Comments feature allows you to enter descriptive metadata into a file's **Get Info** window. This metadata will facilitate searching.

For example, if you are working on a large project, you may create or collect a number of different files from several applications. While all are related to your project, they may not be saved in the same location in Finder. Of course, you could create a folder in Finder and save or move your files to that folder. Another option is to use Comments and never care where your files are located.

To add Comments to a file, first locate the file in Finder. Next, highlight it, secondary click, and select **Get Info** or press ⌘i (command+i). This will open the Get Info window. Expand the Comments section, if necessary, by clicking on the little triangular shaped caret to the left of **Comments**. Enter your comments in the field provided. Enter multiple words by separating them with commas.

To do a Spotlight search using Comments, use the search modifier **comment:** followed by one of your comments.

```
comment:manuscript
```

To search for files tagged with multiple comments, type **comment:** into the Spotlight search field before each comment.

```
comment:macOS comment:manuscript
```

Comments are a great way to quickly find files while keeping them organized in their respective folders.

Use Spotlight as a Calculator

An neat feature of Spotlight is that it can also be used as a calculator. Simply type the formula in the Spotlight search field and Spotlight will calculate the answer. If you have no need for this functionality, you can disable it in the Spotlight preference pane in System Preferences. Uncheck the checkbox next to **Calculator** in the Search Results tab.

Use Spotlight to Convert Currency

Another nice Spotlight feature is that you can use it as a currency converter. For example, if you want to know what 500 euros is in U.S. dollars, simply enter 500 euros in the Spotlight search field. Spotlight will tell you that 500 euros equals $620.89 on the day I wrote this sentence. If you have no need for this functionality, you can disable it in the Spotlight preference pane in System Preferences. Uncheck the checkbox next to **Conversion** in the Search Results tab. Note that by doing so you will disable all conversions in addition to currency conversion, so you'll have to remember the formula to convert temperatures in Celsius to Fahrenheit.

Rebuild the Spotlight Index

Sometimes you'll swear that Spotlight is not finding a file you know is on your Mac or on an external drive. You're not crazy. Sometimes the Spotlight index becomes corrupt, causing inaccurate searches. When this happens, it is time to rebuild the index.

To rebuild the Spotlight index, launch Terminal and enter the following command. The command erases the existing Spotlight index, forcing Spotlight to reindex the drive. Enter your password into Terminal when prompted.

```
sudo mdutil -E /
```

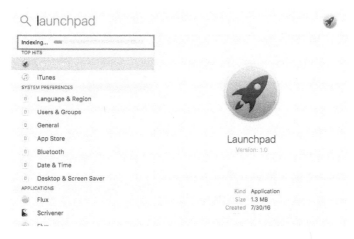

You can verify Spotlight is rebuilding its index by launching and looking for the indexing progress bar. The rebuilding process takes some time and is dependent upon the size and speed of your drive and the number of files it contains. Once the rebuilding process is complete, Spotlight will provide more accurate search results.

9

Siri

 Siri is Apple's intelligent virtual assistant application, which is familiar to anyone who owns an iPhone or iPad. Siri works just like it does in iOS, with the exception being you can't say "Hey Siri" to activate it. Although I'll show you how to do this with a dictation command later. Siri features the same natural language interface as it does in iOS, which adapts to your personal language usage and search preferences.

Like many features in macOS, there are several ways to invoke Siri. You could click the Siri icon in the Dock, which macOS conveniently placed during its installation. You could click on the Siri Menu Extra, located between Spotlight and Notification Center in the Menu Bar.

If you prefer to use a keyboard shortcut, the default shortcut for Siri is **⌘space** (command+space). But wait, isn't **⌘space** (command+space) the keyboard shortcut for Spotlight? Yes it is. To use Siri, you will need to hold down **⌘space** (command+space) until you hear the familiar Siri tone and have finished speaking. Releasing **⌘space** (command+space) tells Siri you are finished speaking and that it should execute your command or search for your answer. When you press **⌘space** (command+space, the Siri window will appear in the upper right corner of your desktop. That's where Siri will provide its response. Dismiss the Siri window by clicking the **X** in the upper left corner.

I find that Siri works best for routine everyday tasks like searching the web, finding the weather forecast, getting sports scores, launching applications, and looking for files on my Mac. For web searches, you can ask Siri to specifically search for images, which you can then drag into folders or documents. Siri can modify a limited set of system preferences like adjusting the volume and brightness, enabling the Notification Center Do Not Disturb feature, or turning Bluetooth or Wi-Fi on and off.

The easiest way to master Siri is to try a bunch of commands, starting with the mundane everyday stuff you do on a Mac like launching applications, opening files, or searching the web. Ask Siri questions and request various information like movie showtimes, the weather, or scores for your favorite team. Siri can give you a list of things you can ask it. Activate Siri from the Menu Bar, Dock, or by using its keyboard shortcut and do not ask it a question. Siri will respond with a list of things you can ask it. Click on any of the items to see more detailed questions.

Relocate the Siri Menu Extra

By default, macOS placed the Siri Menu Extra in the Menu Bar between Spotlight and Notification Center. If you don't find this location to be convenient, you can change the location of the Siri Menu Extra by holding down the ⌘ (command) key while dragging it to your desired location.

Remove the Siri Menu Extra

If you don't want the Siri Menu Extra in your Menu Bar, you can remove from the Siri preference pane in System Preferences.
To remove the Siri Menu Extra, launch the Siri preference pane and uncheck the checkbox next to **Show Siri in menu bar**.

You can also remove the Siri Menu Extra from the Menu Bar by holding down the ⌘ (command) key while dragging it off the Menu Bar.

To revert back to the macOS default, launch the Siri preference pane and check the checkbox next to **Show Siri in menu bar**.

Configure "Hey Siri"

In macOS High Sierra, Apple did not include the ability to invoke Siri with the "Hey Siri" command like you can do in iOS. However, you can configure the same functionality using a dictation command. To configure "Hey Siri," launch the **Accessibility** preference pane. Scroll down the left column and select **Dictation**.

First, check the checkbox next to **Enable the dictation keyword phrase:**, which is the keyword that tells your Mac you are about to dictate a command to it. The default keyword is "Computer."

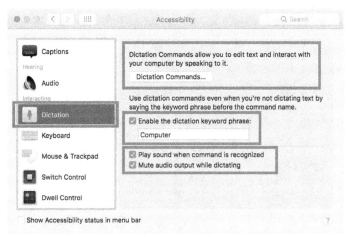

You can check the checkbox next to **Play sound when command is recognized** to provide audio feedback that your Mac has understood your command.

Verify that the checkbox next to **Mute audio output while dictating** is checked. Next, click the **Dictation Commands...** button to reveal the configuration sheet shown in the image below.

Check the checkbox next to **Enable advanced commands** and then click the **+** to add a new user command. Then enter "Hey Siri" in the **When I say:** field. Since you'll want to access Siri at any time, ensure that **Any Application** is listed in the **While using:** field. From the **Perform:** drop-down menu, select **Run Workflow** and then select **Other...** which opens a Finder window. Browse to your Applications folder, click on **Siri**, and then click the **Open** button. Click **Done** in the Accessibility preference pane to finish.

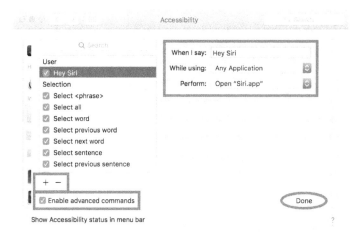

To start dictation, you will need to say "computer" followed by the command "Hey Siri." Siri will open and you can immediately ask it your question or give it a command.

Change Siri's Language

Siri supports over 40 different languages. To change Siri's language, launch the **Siri** preference pane in System preferences. Select your desired language from the drop-down menu next to **Language:**.

Change Siri's Voice

When Siri's language is set to American English, the default voice is an American female.

To change Siri's voice, launch the **Siri** preference pane in System Preferences. Select your desired voice from the drop-down list next to **Siri Voice:**. Your choices include male and female American, Australian, and British voices.

Disable Voice Feedback

If you prefer to read Siri's responses rather than having Siri speak to its responses to you, macOS allows you to disable **Voice Feedback** in the **Siri** preference pane. This feature comes in handy if you prefer that Siri's responses are not overheard by others or if Siri's responses would be disruptive in a quiet office environment.

To disable voice feedback, launch the Siri preference pane and select the **Off** radio button to disable Voice Feedback. Siri will no longer speak to you when responding.

Change the Mic Input

If you Mac has multiple audio input sources, you can select which one will be used to ask Siri questions. The **Internal Microphone** is the default **Mic Input**. To select a different Mic Input, select another input from the drop-down menu next to **Mic Input:** in the **Siri** preference pane.

Change the Siri Keyboard Shortcut

By default, Siri's keyboard shortcut is to hold down **⌘space** (command+space) until you are finished speaking. If you want to change Siri's shortcut, launch the **Siri** preference pane in System Preferences.

There are four **Keyboard Shortcut** choices available: **Hold ⌘space** (command+space), **Hold ⌥space** (option+space), **Press fn space** (function+space), or **⌘space** (command+space). The **Customize...** option lets you choose your own keyboard shortcut. To completely disable the Siri keyboard shortuct, select **Off**.

Type Siri Requests

A new feature in macOS is the ability to type your requests to Siri instead of speaking them. This feature is useful if you don't want your Siri requests to be overheard by others, speaking to Siri in a quiet office environment would be disruptive, or if speaking is difficult. Another time you may want to enable **Type to Siri** is when you are listening to music on your Mac and want to use the Siri feature without Siri interrupting your music.

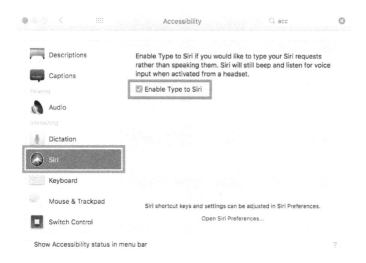

To enable **Type to Siri**, launch the **Accessibility** preference pane from System Preferences. Scroll down and select **Siri** in the left column. Then check the checkbox next to **Enable Type to Siri**. Uncheck the checkbox to disable this feature.

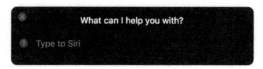

With Type to Siri enabled, you activate Siri by holding down ⌘**space** (command+space) or the keyboard shortcut you configured if you decided to change the default. The normal Siri input dialog box will appear in the upper right corner of your desktop awaiting your input. Type the question you want to ask Siri and press the **enter** key.

Add Siri to the Dock

If you have a new Mac that came with macOS High Sierra pre-installed, the Siri icon should be located in the Dock. If you upgraded your Mac from a previous version of macOS and had customized your Dock and now want to add Siri to your Dock, adding it is simple.

First open the **Applications** folder in Finder and scroll down to the **Siri** application icon. Drag it to where you want it on the Dock.

To remove the Siri icon from the Dock, simply drag it off until **Remove** appears and then release.

Disable Siri

Don't like or don't want Siri on your Mac? macOS allows you to disable it. To disable Siri, launch the **Siri** preference pane and uncheck the checkbox next to **Enable Ask Siri**.

If you change your mind later, check the checkbox to enable Siri.

10

Notification Center

Notification Center is a hidden panel at the right edge of the Desktop that consists of two different views – the **Today** view and the **Notifications** view. The **Today** view features Apple and third-party widgets that provide quick access to information. The **Notification** view collects and displays notifications and alerts from various apps. Similar to the iOS feature of the same name, you can choose which applications will save their alerts to the Notification view.

The gesture to display Notification Center seems a little odd at first because you actually start off the trackpad. Starting at the right edge, swipe left with two fingers to reveal the Notification Center panel. Swipe in the opposite direction or click anywhere outside the Notification Center panel to hide it. Alternately, you can click on the Notification Center Menu Extra in the Menu Bar. Click the Menu Extra again or press the **esc** key and Notification Center will slide off the right edge of your screen.

Customize Today View

macOS lets you customize your **Today** view, choosing the items you wish to display and their order. To edit the Today view, slide out the Notification Center panel and click on the **Today** tab at the top of the panel. Scroll down to the very bottom of the Today view and click the **Edit** button.

The panel will expand to display a second column to the right, presenting a list of any available widgets that you can add to your Today view. To add a new widget, click on the green **+** button to the right of the widget's name.

To remove a widget from your Today view, click the red – button at the upper left corner of the widget.

Widgets can be rearranged within your Today view by using the handle to the right of the widget's name to drag the widget to your desired location.

Clicking the **App Store** button will open Safari and take you to the **Notification Center Widgets** page in the Mac App Store where you can find and install new widgets.

The control in the lower right corner of the panel that looks like a gear launches the Notification Center preference pane in System Preferences.

Click the **Done** button at the bottom of the panel when finished.

Add Widgets to Notification Center

macOS lets you add widgets to your Today View. Open Notification Center and click the **Edit** button at the bottom of the panel. When the panel expands click the **App Store** button at the bottom center of Notification Center. This will take you to the **Notification Center Widgets** section of the Mac App Store where you can search for and install new widgets.

Here are a number of handy third party widgets that I recommend you consider for your Today view. All are available in the App Store at the time of this book's publication.

iStat Mini

iStat Mini by Bjango provides a quick overview of some basic Mac performance statistics. It shows the CPU percentage, memory, and storage your Mac is currently using as well as your battery status. iStat Mini, as its name implies is a scaled down version of its big brother, iStat Menus that I introduced in the Menu Bar chapter. iStat Mini was available for $2.99 in the App Store at the time of this writing.

Wunderlist

Wunderlist is a full featured task list application. It offers native applications for macOS and iOS as well as a full featured web version, allowing you to seamlessly access your task lists regardless of platform. Changes made on one platform are pushed to your other devices, keeping everything synchronized. Each task list can contain a limitless number of sub-tasks.

At the time of this writing, Wunderlist was free to download from the Mac App Store. There is an optional upgrade to the Pro version for $4.99 a month or $49.99 a year. The Wunderlist Pro upgrade provides unlimited access to assignments, subtasks, and attachments.

Deliveries

Deliveries will help you keep track of your packages and will always know when they are supposed to be delivered. Deliveries syncs with iCloud so you can track your packages on all of your Apple devices. Deliveries includes a Menu Extra and is the same application I recommended in the Menu Bar chapter. Deliveries is available for $2.99 in the Mac App Store.

Countdowns

Countdowns is a Notification Center widget that keeps track of the days until or since an important event that you configure. The countdown is displayed in the Notification Center. Countdowns syncs with iCloud so you can keep track of the days to an important event on all of your Apple devices. At the time of this writing, Countdowns is available as a free trial from the Mac App Store and requires a 99-cent in-app purchase to unlock its full functionality.

Battery Monitor

Battery Monitor does just what its name implies, allowing you to access and monitor information about your MacBook's, MacBook Air's, or MacBook Pro's battery from the Notification Center. Battery Monitor also includes a Menu Extra for the Menu Bar and is the same application I recommended in Chapter 5. Battery Monitor displays the current charge level, time remaining, the cycle count, and time remaining in the Notification Center. Its Menu Extra provides additional information including battery capacity and current charge. Battery Monitor is available for free in the Mac App Store.

Select Widgets for Today View

You can also configure the widgets displayed in Notification Center's **Today View**, by opening the **Extensions** preference pane in the System Preferences application.

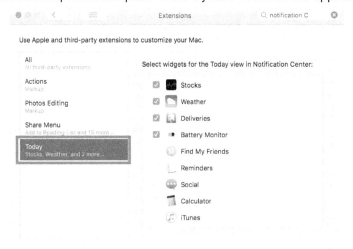

Select **Today** from the left column if not already highlighted. Use the checkboxes in the right side of the pane under **Select widgets for the Today view in Notification Center** to add or remove widgets.

Customize Notifications

The other half of Notification Center should be very familiar to macOS and iOS users. The **Notifications** view is a one-stop shop consolidating all notifications from a variety of Apple applications including Messages, Mail, Calendar, Reminders, iTunes, Safari, FaceTime, Game Center, iMovie, and Maps. Notification Center supports notifications from social media applications like LinkedIn, Facebook, and Twitter, as well as from many third party applications and websites.

Notifications are delivered to the upper right hand corner of your desktop in the form of a **Banner** or **Alert**, depending on the style chosen in the Notifications preference pane in System Preferences. **Banners** appear and disappear automatically after a set period of time. An iTunes notification with the name and artist of the current song it is playing is an example of a Banner. **Alerts** stay on your desktop until you dismiss them. Reminders are an example of an Alert, requiring you to take some action to dismiss the notification. All previous notifications, regardless of style, are stored in Notification Center.

To unhide Notification Center, start with two fingers on the right edge of your trackpad and swipe left. Select **Notifications** if it is not already highlighted. Alternately, you can click on the Notification Center Menu Extra in the Menu Bar. Click the Menu Extra again to close Notification Center or press the **esc** key.

Clicking on a notification launches the application that created it. For example, clicking on a Mail notification takes you to the Mail application. Doing so will mark the notification as read and the notification will be removed. Clicking the **X** at the top right of any application dismisses all notifications associated with that application.

Any application utilizing Apple's push notification service or local notifications can send notifications to Notification Center. macOS allows you to customize which applications are allowed to send notifications to the desktop and Notification Center in the **Notifications** preference pane located in the System Preferences application.

Choose Which Apps Will Notify

By default, all of the applications listed in the **Notifications** preference pane will display alerts in the upper right-hand corner of your desktop and deposit a notification in **Notification Center**. The number of applications configured in Notification Center could easily inundate you with annoying and superfluous alerts. macOS allows you to turn off notifications from any of the apps listed in the Notifications preference pane.

To turn off notifications, open the **Notifications** preference pane in System Preferences. This preference pane is split into a left column and a right pane. The left column lists the applications that are able to send an alert or banner to your desktop and deposit a notification in your Notification Center.

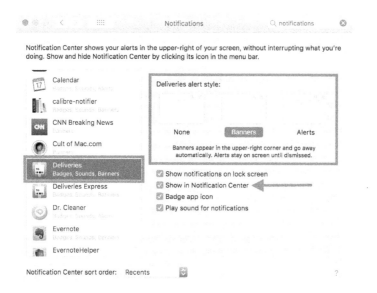

To stop an application from placing a notification in Notification Center, first highlight the application in the left column. Next, uncheck the checkbox next to **Show in Notification Center**. With the checkbox unchecked, the application will not save its alerts to Notification Center. However, the application will continue to send notifications to your desktop if **Banners** or **Alerts** are configured as the alert style. This is a completely valid configuration. Another valid configuration is for an app to not send notifications to the desktop and only save them in Notification Center.

If you want to stop an application from sending notifications to your desktop, select **None** under the **alert style** at the top of the right-hand pane. When **None** is selected as the notification style, the application will stop sending notifications to your desktop.

If you want the application to save notifications in Notification Center but not send them to the desktop, choose the **None** alert style and ensure the checkbox next to **Show in Notification Center** is checked.

Choose the Notification Style

The macOS **Notification Center** can be configured to send banners or alerts to your desktop. There is a difference between a banner and an alert. A **Banner** is a notification that will appear and disappear after a set amount of time. An **Alert** is a notification that will stay on your desktop until you respond or dismiss it. Alert styles and options such as history, badging, and sound are configured on a per application basis in the Notifications preference pane.

To choose a notification style, open the Notifications preference pane in the System Preferences application. Click on an application in the left column. Once an application has been selected, the right-hand pane will change to show the alert style currently configured, which is highlighted in blue, and any available configuration options. Choose **Banners** or **Alerts** to change the alert style that will appear on your desktop. If you choose **None**, the application won't send notifications to your desktop.

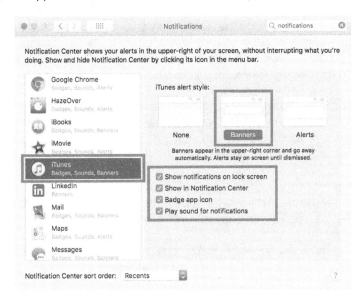

Once you have chosen your alert style, you can configure the various options shown below the alert style. Depending on the application, there may be 2 or 4 options available. Generally, the options are: **Show notifications on lock screen**, **Show in Notification Center**, **Badge app icon**, and **Play sound for notifications**. All of the checkboxes are usually checked by default.

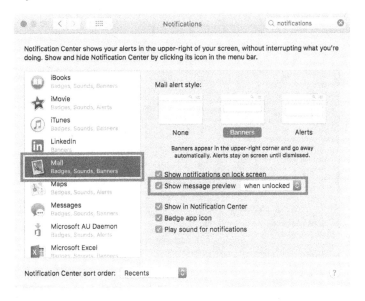

macOS will show alerts when your Mac is locked. This creates a potential privacy issue since anyone can read your notifications when your Mac is locked and you are away from it. If you want to disable this feature, uncheck the checkbox next to **Show notifications on lock screen** for the apps with messages you prefer to keep private.

The **Show message preview** option is only applicable to apps such as **Mail** and **Messages**. You have two options: to show a message preview **when unlocked** or **always**. The **always** option will show message previews regardless of whether your Mac is locked or not, presenting a potential privacy issue. As its name implies, the **when unlocked** option will only show message previews when your Mac is unlocked. Uncheck the checkbox to turn message preview off.

By default, the **Show in Notification Center** option is checked, which means the message will be saved in Notification Center. You have the option of disabling this feature by unchecking the box. If you do so, you will only see messages on your desktop and only if the alert style is set to **Banners** or **Alerts**.

The **Badge app icon** option will show the number of notifications in a red circular badge on the app's icon in the **Dock**. The app must be in the Dock for badges to appear. If you don't want the application icon to get badged, uncheck this checkbox.

Some notifications play a sound when they appear. If you prefer silent notifications, uncheck the checkbox next to **Play sound for notifications**.

Change the Notification Sort Order

Notification Center displays notifications using the sort order configured in the Notifications preference pane. Notifications are sorted with the most recent ones on top.

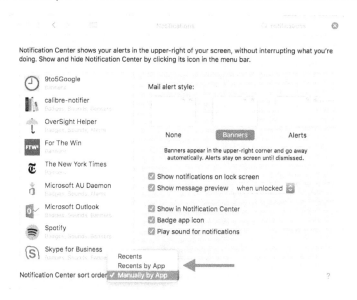

To change the sort order for notifications, open the **Notifications** preference pane in the System Preferences application. Change the sort order using the drop-down menu next to **Notification Center sort order**. You can sort by **Recents** where the most recent notifications, regardless of application, appear at the top of Notification Center. This is the macOS default. Another sort option is to sort **Recents by app**, which organizes notifications by application where the app with the most recent notification is placed at the top of Notification Center.

The final option, **Manually by app**, allows you to reorder the list of applications displayed in the left column of the Notifications preference pane. When selecting this option, you'll notice the list of applications in the left column will rearrange themselves to what Apple suggests is a logical sort order. You don't have to accept Apple's suggestion. Simply drag and drop the applications in the left column into the order in which you want to see your notifications. Once finished, close the preference pane. The notifications will be displayed in your desired order. Any application without a notification is skipped.

Keep Banners Around Longer

Banners delivered to the upper right hand corner of your desktop automatically disappear after 5 seconds. Often this is not enough time to read them. I find myself forced to check Notification Center to read the Banner I just missed. This tweak allows you to set the amount of time in seconds that Banners will stay on your desktop before they disappear.

To increase the Banner time, launch Terminal and enter the following command. This command will increase the Banner time to 30 seconds. You can change the 30 in the command below to any whole number you wish. You will need to log out and log back in for the change to take effect.

```
defaults write com.apple.notificationcenterui bannerTime 30
```

If you want Banners to stick around until you dismiss them, enter the following command in Terminal. You will need to log out and log back in for the change to take effect.

```
defaults write com.apple.notificationcenterui bannerTime 86400
```

To return to the macOS default of 5 seconds, enter the following command in Terminal. Log out and log back in for the change to take effect.

```
defaults delete com.apple.notificationcenterui bannerTime
```

Set Up Social Media Accounts

Notification Center can be configured so you can receive alerts from and post messages to LinkedIn, Facebook, and Twitter. To add your social media accounts open the **Internet Accounts** preference pane in the System Preferences application.

To add a social media account, click on the account type you wish to add. Once configured, you'll receive notifications from and be able to post to your social media accounts directly in Notification Center.

Post to Social Media Directly from Notification Center

You can post to your social media accounts or send a Message directly from Notification Center's Today view. To add social media to the Today view, open the Notification Center panel. Click **Today**, if not already highlighted. Click the **Edit** button at the very bottom of the pane. The Notification Center pane will expand to reveal a column of available widgets. Click the green button with the **+** sign next to **Social** to place buttons for Linkedin, Facebook, Twitter, and Messages in Notification Center's Today view.

Clicking any one of the Social buttons will open a window in Notification Center for you to create your post.

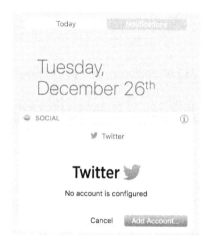

If you haven't configured any of the social media accounts, macOS will provide an **Add Account...** button. Clicking this button will take you to the Internet Accounts preference pane where you can enter your credentials for your social media account.

Swipe to Dismiss a Notification

macOS allows you to dismiss any desktop notification by swiping on the notification from left to right with two fingers on your trackpad. If you are using a Magic Mouse, swipe left to right with one finger. The notification will fade away as it moves towards the right edge of the screen.

Some desktop notifications include controls. For example, the iTunes notification allows you to skip a song. Hover your pointer over the iTunes notification and a **Skip** button will appear to the right. Click **Skip** to skip the current song.

Enable Do Not Disturb

Finding all those desktop notifications a little distracting? The **Do Not Disturb** feature turns Notification Center off for the remainder of the day. To enable the **Do Not Disturb** feature, first open Notification Center. Next, swipe in a downward motion with two fingers with your pointer located anywhere within Notification Center to reveal the Do Not Disturb switch at the top below the **Night Shift** switch.

Click the switch to the **ON** position. When Do Not Disturb is enabled the Notification Center Menu Extra turns gray. Any notifications received while Do Not Disturb is enabled are still available in Notification Center, but Banners and Alerts will not be sent to your desktop. macOS will automatically turn Do Not Disturb off tomorrow. To disable Do Not Disturb, switch the Do Not Disturb switch to **OFF**.

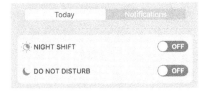

A quick way to enable the Do Not Disturb feature is to hold down the ⌥ (option) key while clicking the Notification Center Menu Extra. Click while holding the ⌥ (option) key again to disable Do Not Disturb.

Enable Night Shift

You can quickly enable **Night Shift** from Notification Center by switching the Night Shift switch to **On**. **Night Shift** is a macOS feature that adjusts the color temperature of your display based on the time of day. Similar to the iOS Night Shift feature, macOS will adjust your display's color temperature to provide warmer light during nighttime hours to help you sleep better.

To enable Night Shift, first open Notification Center. Next, swipe in a downward motion with two fingers with your pointer located anywhere within Notification Center to reveal the Night Shift switch at the top above the **Do Not Disturb** switch.

Schedule Do Not Disturb

macOS allows you to schedule the **Do Not Disturb** feature to turn on and off automatically at a scheduled time each day. To schedule Do Not Disturb, open the **Notification** preference pane. Click on **Do Not Disturb** in the left column. Next, check the checkbox next to **From:** and **to:** and select the times during which you do not want to be disturbed by banners and alerts.

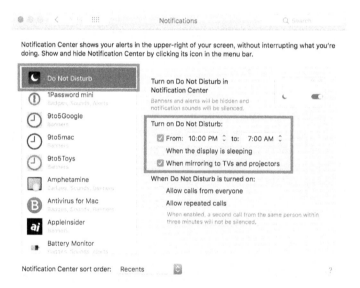

By default, macOS enables Do Not Disturb while your Mac is mirroring its display to TVs and projectors. Enabling Do Not Disturb when you are mirroring your display to a TV or projector is quite handy if you are streaming a video to your AppleTV or giving a presentation to a group of people and don't want notifications interrupting you. However, if you do want to receive banners and alerts when mirroring, you can disable this behavior by unchecking the checkbox next to **When mirroring to TVs and projectors**.

Your Mac will not disturb you if you receive a FaceTime call when Do Not Disturb is enabled. If you would like to accept all FaceTime calls, check the checkbox next to **Allow calls from everyone**. Another option is to accept only repeated calls by checking the **Allow repeated calls** checkbox. If a second call is received from the same person within 3 minutes, you will be notified. Both of these options are disabled by default.

Safari Push Notifications

Websites supporting Apple's push notification service can send notifications of breaking news, sports, a new post, or other relevant info. These notifications will appear on your desktop and in Notification Center. Before a website can send you push notifications, you must choose to opt in. If a website supports push notifications, you'll be asked if you would like to receive notifications when browsing to the website in Safari. Click **Allow** to opt in or **Don't Allow** to opt out. Don't worry, you can always change your mind later. You can configure how you receive these notifications in the Notifications preference pane in System Preferences.

If you no longer find notifications from a particular website useful, you can opt out. Similarly, if you opted out, you can opt back in.

To change your Safari notification choice, launch **Safari** and open the Safari preference pane by selecting **Safari > Preferences...** or by entering **⌘,** (command+comma). Once the Safari preferences launch, select **Websites**.   The websites that have asked for permission to send you push notifications will be listed. Next to each website is a drop-down menu with two choices: **Allow** and **Deny** with the current status displayed.

If you wish to delete a website from the list, highlight it and click the **Remove** button.   If you would prefer that websites not ask you to opt in to their push notification service, uncheck the checkbox next to **Allow websites to ask for permission to send push notifications**.   Checking this checkbox stops websites from asking you if you want to receive notifications from them.

Change the Keyboard Shortcut for Notification Center

macOS allows you to assign keyboard shortcuts to execute any number of actions. If you would like to change the keyboard shortcut to open Notification Center, open the **Keyboard** preference pane from System Preferences. Click on the **Shortcuts** tab.

Select **Mission Control** from the left column. By default, the keyboard shortcut for Notification Center is ⌥⌘**left** (option+command+left arrow). To change the keyboard shortcut, ensure the checkbox next to **Show Notification Center** is checked and select a shortcut in the field provided. Be sure to select a shortcut that is not used by another function. If you select a shortcut that is already assigned, a yellow triangle will appear to the right of the shortcut. The yellow triangle will also appear in the left column.

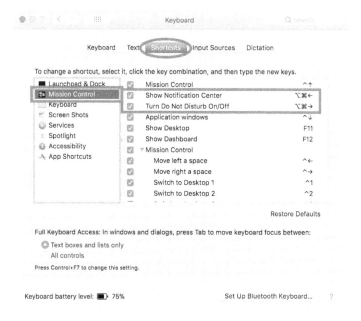

To disable the shortcut, simply uncheck the checkbox next to **Show Notification Center**. If you want to restore all keyboard shortcuts to their macOS defaults, click the **Restore Defaults** button at the lower right of the preference pane.

Change the Keyboard Shortcut for Do Not Disturb

By default, the keyboard shortcut to toggle **Do Not Disturb** on and off is ⌥⌘**right** (option+command+right arrow). If you want to change this shortcut, open the **Keyboard** preference pane and select the **Shortcuts** tab.

Next, select **Mission Control** in the left column. Ensure the checkbox next to **Turn Do Not Disturb On/Off** is checked and select a shortcut key combination. Once configured, the shortcut will act as a toggle to enable and disable Do Not Disturb. Remember that you can check the status of Do Not Disturb by looking at the Notification Center icon in the Menu Bar. If it is grayed out, Do Not Disturb is enabled.

To disable the shortcut, simply uncheck the checkbox next to **Turn Do Not Disturb On/Off**. If you want to restore all keyboard shortcuts to their macOS defaults, click the **Restore Defaults** button at the lower right of the preference pane.

Disable Notification Center

Don't like Notification Center? macOS lets you completely disable it. Launch Terminal and enter the following command. Note that this command is a single line and there is a space after **–w**. Be sure to enter the entire command before pressing the **return** key. This change takes effect immediately. The Notification Center icon remains in the Menu Bar, but clicking on it does nothing. In addition to disabling Notification Center, this tweak will also disable desktop notifications.

```
launchctl unload -w
/System/Library/LaunchAgents/com.apple.notificationcenterui.plist
```

Miss Notification Center? You can bring it back by entering the following command in Terminal. Note that this command is a single line and there is a space after **–w**. Be sure to enter the entire command before pressing the **return** key. You will need to log out and log back in for this change to take effect. Note that Do Not Disturb may be enabled when you log back in. Look for the grayed out Notification Center icon.

```
launchctl load -w
/System/Library/LaunchAgents/com.apple.notificationcenterui.plist
```

11

Dashboard

The **Dashboard** is a macOS feature that runs mini-applications called widgets on a dedicated desktop space or as an overlay with the widgets appearing in the foreground of your acive desktop. The Dashboard is disabled by default in macOS High Sierra. When enabled, the Dashboard can be accessed using the **F12** key or by clicking on the Dashboard icon in the Dock or Launchpad. Note that you will have to hold the **fn** (function) key while pressing **F12**. On older Macs, use the **F4** key.

Enable the Dashboard

The **Dashboard** is disabled by default. To turn it on, open the **Mission Control** preference pane. From the drop-down menu next to **Dashboard**, choose either **As Space** or **As Overlay**.

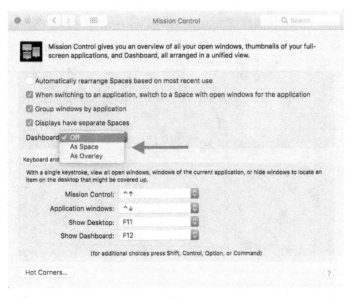

As the name implies, **As Space**, enables the Dashboard as a separate dedicated desktop space. If you have an older Mac, pressing **F4** will reveal the Dashboard. On newer Macs, you can access the Dashboard by pressing **F12**, through Mission Control, or by swiping your Desktop Spaces all the way to the leftmost space. The picture below shows the Dashboard running in its own space to the left of Desktop 1.

| Dashboard | Desktop 1 | Desktop 2 | Desktop 3 | Desktop 4 |

Like any other desktop in macOS you can relocate the Dashboard space. Initially, the Dashboard will always appear to the left of Desktop 1. The Dashboard is accessed like any other space in Mission Control by clicking on it to make it active.

| Desktop 1 | Desktop 2 | Dashboard | Desktop 3 | Desktop 4 |

As Overlay allows you to display the widgets in the foreground of your active desktop. Launching the Dashboard will dim your desktop and the widgets will appear in the foreground. Configuring the Dashboard to run in the foreground provides convenient access to the widgets without changing Desktop Spaces.

Disable the Dashboard

Dashboard is getting a bit long in the tooth and appears to be on its last legs. The fact that Apple disabled it by default appears to be an admission that it is less than useful. I'm surprised Apple didn't kill it outright, especially considering the more functional widget features in Notification Center. Browsing Apple's Dashboard widget page, which is not incorporated into the Mac App Store, is like taking a trip back in time before iPhones and iPads. Most of the widgets haven't been updated in years and few are being actively developed or maintained. Many Mac users feel that the Dashboard has outlived its usefulness and wonder when Apple will eliminate it for good. I'm hoping that High Sierra is the last release where we'll see the Dashboard, but I've been hoping for years now. The Dashboard widget page is located at: http://www.apple.com/downloads/dashboard/.

If you want to disable the Dashboard, open the **Mission Control** preference pane in the System Preferences application and select **Off** in the drop-down menu next to **Dashboard**.

You can also remove the Dashboard by entering the following commands in Terminal.

```
defaults write com.apple.dashboard mcx-disabled -bool TRUE
```

```
killall Dock
```

If you change your mind and want Dashboard back, launch Terminal and enter the following commands.

```
defaults write com.apple.dashboard mcx-disabled -bool FALSE
```

```
killall Dock
```

Add New Widgets

macOS comes with a rather spartan **Dashboard** containing only four widgets: a calculator, calendar, clock, and weather, which shows the weather in Cupertino, of course.

You add widgets by clicking on the large, circled **+** sign located at the lower left corner of the Dashboard. This will open what appears to be a Launchpad for widgets, listing the available widgets installed on your Mac.

If these widgets aren't enough for you, Apple's website has a page dedicated to Dashboard widgets: http://www.apple.com/downloads/dashboard/. This page contains thousands of widgets, organized into categories.

If you configured the Dashboard to run as an overlay, adding widgets is done in a similar fashion. You'll find the large circled **+** sign in the lower left corner of your Desktop.

Remove a Widget from the Dashboard

Dashboard widgets are deleted much the same way as they are added. To delete a widget, click on the large circled **−** sign at the lower left of the Dashboard, if run as a separate space, or at the lower left of the desktop when run as an overlay. An **X** will appear at the upper left corner of each widget. Click the **X** to remove a widget. Widgets are only removed from the Dashboard. They are not deleted and can be added back later.

Rearrange Widgets

Dashboard widgets can be rearranged by dragging them to a new location. This method works in both space and overlay modes.

Open Duplicate Widgets

If you haven't tried to open multiple copies of the same widget, you may never know this feature exists. macOS doesn't limit you to one instance of a Dashboard widget. One obvious use is to open multiple weather or clock widgets so you can see the weather or time in different locations.

To open duplicate widgets, repeatedly add the same widget as many times as needed. This method works in both space and overlay modes.

Change the Dashboard Keyboard Shortcut

The default keyboard shortcut for the **Dashboard** is **F12** (or **F4** on older Macs). You can assign another keyboard shortcut for the Dashboard by opening the **Mission Control** preference pane in the System Preferences application. Select your desired **F** key from the drop-down list next to **Show Dashboard** or choose – to disable the keyboard shortcut for the Dashboard. The following modifier keys are supported: ⇧, ^, ⌥, or ⌘ (shift, control, option, and command). You can use one, two, three, or all four modifier keys together.

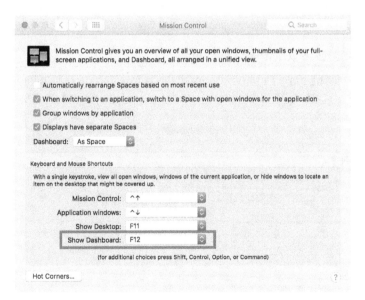

You can also configure a mouse shortcut from the Mission Control preference pane using the drop-down list in the second column next to **Show Dashboard**. You have a choice of the **Secondary Mouse Button** or the **Middle Mouse Button**.

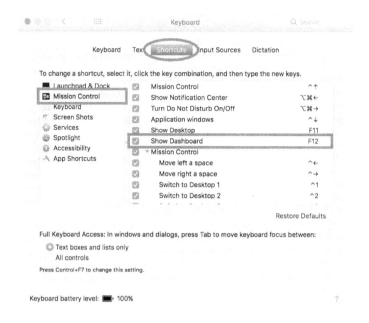

What if you want to use a keyboard shortcut other than the **F** keys? Easy. Configure your keyboard shortcut using the **Keyboard** preference pane. Open the Keyboard preference pane in the System Preferences application. Click on **Shortcuts** if not highlighted already.

Choose **Mission Control** from the left column and check the checkbox next to **Show Dashboard** if it is not checked. Next, click on the shortcut (**F12**, by default) in the right column. Change the shortcut by entering your desired keyboard shortcut.

Move the Dashboard to Another Display

You can move the **Dashboard** to another display in a multiple display system. You have to configure separate spaces on each display and run the Dashboard as a space.

Launch the **Mission Control** preference pane. Select **As Space** from the drop-down list next to **Dashboard**. Next, check the checkbox next to **Displays have separate Spaces**. You will need to log out and log in for this change to take effect.

To move the Dashboard to another display, simply drag it over to the destination display via the right or left edge of the screen.

12

Launchpad

Launchpad is a feature that blurs the line between iOS and macOS. Like the iOS home screen, Launchpad allows you to see every application installed on your Mac on one or more full screen pages. Launchpad serves as an application launcher, providing an alternative method to launch applications. From Launchpad, you can search, launch, organize, and delete apps.

To open Launchpad, click on its icon in the Dock, press the **F4** key or pinch your thumb and three fingers together on the trackpad. When you open Launchpad, your desktop background will blur and any windows will disappear and reveal a grid of application icons similar to the home screen on an iPad or iPhone. The Dock, if hidden, will reappear.

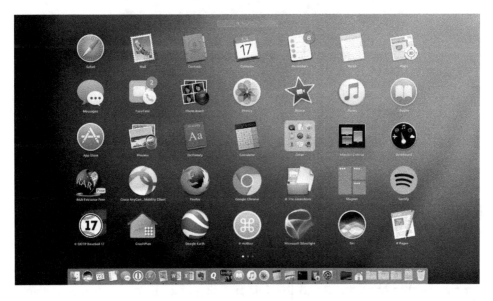

Launchpad provides a search field at the top center allowing you to easily find applications, particularly ones that may be hidden in a folder. Small dots at the bottom center represent pages. You can swipe left or right with one finger on a mouse or two fingers on a trackpad or hold down the ⌘ (command) key while pressing the left or right arrow keys to navigate between pages. You also can click on one of the dots to jump directly to that page. All four arrow keys can be used to move up, down, left, or right within the grid to highlight an application. Pressing the **return** key launches the highlighted application, as does directly clicking on its icon.

Folders can be created the same way they are in iOS, by dragging one icon on top of another. Once a folder is created, it can be renamed and other applications can be dragged into it. Folders are opened by clicking on them. Close an open folder by clicking anywhere outside the folder.

You can close Launchpad by clicking on the desktop wallpaper, pressing the **F4** key again, pressing the **esc** key, or using the Show Desktop gesture by spreading your thumb and three fingers apart on your Mac's trackpad.

Rearrange the App Icons

The application icons in **Launchpad** can be rearranged by dragging them into the order you desire. To move an icon between pages, simply drag it to the edge of the screen and hold it there until the page flips. Drop the icon on the desired destination page.

Delete an App Using Launchpad

Some applications can be deleted from your Mac using **Launchpad**. To delete an app, click and hold on an icon until all of the app icons begin shaking. Some icons will have an **X** in the upper left corner. Clicking the **X** will delete the app.

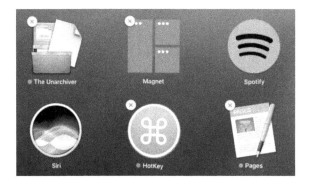

Add Finder to Launchpad

Open **Launchpad**. Now type **Finder** in the search field. No Results. Noticeably absent from Launchpad is one of the most critical apps in macOS, Finder.

To add Finder to Launchpad, first open a **Finder** window. Enter ⇧⌘G (shift+command+G) to open the **Go to the folder** dialog box. Enter the following into the field and click **Go**.

```
/System/Library/CoreServices/
```

Locate **Finder** in this folder and drag and drop it onto the **Launchpad** icon in the Dock. Now, check out Launchpad and there's Finder.

Change the Number of Apps per Page

macOS lays out a 7 column by 5 row grid in Launchpad, displaying 35 icons per page. If you want more application icons to appear on each Launchpad page, you do so by making the grid larger by adding more columns and rows.

For example, if you want Launchpad to display 60 application icons per page, you would need to resize the grid to 10 columns by 6 rows. To resize Launchpad, open Terminal and enter the following commands.

```
defaults write com.apple.dock springboard-columns -int 10
```

```
defaults write com.apple.dock springboard-rows -int 6
```

```
killall Dock
```

I suggest you experiment, trying different combinations of column and row sizes until you find the right combination. Simply replace the number after **-int** in each command with an integer to find your perfect size.

Increasing the size of the grid decreases the size of each icon. With Launchpad displaying more icons per page, it takes less pages to display all of your applications. In the picture below, Launchpad is configured to display 60 icons in a 10 column by 6 row grid. Why aren't there 60 icons on this page? macOS doesn't automatically rearrange the icon layout in Launchpad when you change the rows and columns. You have to do that manually.

Conversely, you can make the Launchpad grid smaller – i.e., fewer columns and rows – so that fewer application icons are displayed on each page.

For example, if you want Launchpad to display 20 application icons per page, you would need to resize the grid to 5 columns by 4 rows. To resize Launchpad, enter the following commands in Terminal.

```
defaults write com.apple.dock springboard-columns -int 5
```

```
defaults write com.apple.dock springboard-rows -int 4
```

```
killall Dock
```

Decreasing the size of the grid increases the size of each icon. With Launchpad displaying less icons per page, it takes more pages to display all of your applications. In the example, it now takes 5 pages to display all of the application icons.

To revert back to the macOS default of 7 columns by 5 rows, enter the following commands.

```
defaults delete com.apple.dock springboard-columns
```

```
defaults delete com.apple.dock springboard-rows
```

```
killall Dock
```

You probably noticed that as you changed the Launchpad grid size, your application icons spread out across multiple pages. Launchpad does not automatically rearrange the icons for you as you experimented with different grid sizes. Unfortunately, you'll have to rearrange the app icons manually.

Remove the Page Scrolling Delay

macOS introduces a delay when scrolling between pages in Launchpad. If you prefer pages appear immediately without the delay, enter the following commands in Terminal.

```
defaults write com.apple.dock springboard-page-duration -int 0
```

```
killall Dock
```

To restore the default scroll animation between Launchpad pages, enter the following commands.

```
defaults delete com.apple.dock springboard-page-duration
```

```
killall Dock
```

Change the Launchpad Keyboard Shortcut

The default macOS keyboard shortcut for Launchpad is the **F4** key on newer Macs. (Older Macs use the **F4** key to launch the Dashboard.)

If you would like to change this keyboard shortcut, open the **Keyboard** preference pane. Next, select **Shortcuts** if not already highlighted. Select **Launchpad & Dock** from the left-hand pane. **Show Launchpad** is the second choice in the list of shortcuts in the right-hand pane. To change the shortcut, enter a shortcut key combination in the field at the right.

To remove the shortcut, simply uncheck the checkbox next to **Show Launchpad** or click the **Restore Defaults** button at the lower right of the preference pane.

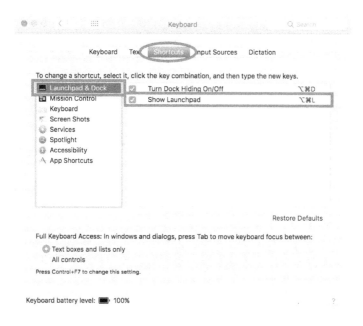

Add Launchpad to the Dock

If you have a new Mac that came with macOS High Sierra pre-installed, the Launchpad icon should be in the Dock. If you upgraded from a previous version of macOS and now want to add the Launchpad icon to the Dock, adding it is simple.

First open the **Applications** folder in Finder and scroll down to the **Launchpad** application icon. Drag it to where you want it on the Dock.

To remove the Launchpad icon from the Dock, simply drag it off until **Remove** appears and then release.

Need to Start From Scratch?

If you need to revert back to the macOS **Launchpad** defaults for any reason, enter the following commands in Terminal. This will reset Launchpad to its out-of-the-box settings. Any tweaks, including folders you may have created, will be reset to their defaults.

```
defaults write com.apple.dock ResetLaunchPad -bool TRUE
```

```
killall Dock
```

13

Finder

 Finder is the macOS file manager, providing a graphical user interface to manage files, disk drives, network drives, and to launch applications. A Finder window has three major components. At the very top of the Finder window is the **Toolbar**, which contains various tools to manipulate the window and its contents. The **Sidebar** is located at the left and is divided into four sections. **Favorites** lists shortcuts to favorite or frequently used items such as your Home, Desktop, Applications, Documents, Movies, Music, and Pictures folders. The Favorites category also allows access to AirDrop. Underneath Favorites is **iCloud**, which lists the contents of your iCloud drive. Below iCloud is **Shared**, a list of shared computers and network shares to which your Mac is connected. Next is the list of **Devices**, which lists the internal and external drives attached to your Mac. The final section is the list of **Tags**, which are useful method of organizing your files. The contents of any folder selected in the Sidebar are displayed in the large pane on the right.

Clicking on the Finder icon in the Dock launches a Finder window showing the **All My Files** view, which displays files organized by file type and chronologically with the most recent at the top of the window. You can return to this view by clicking **All My Files** under **Favorites** in the Sidebar.

iCloud Desktop & Documents

 macOS features the seamless integration of **iCloud**, making online storage part of the operating system instead of an add-on app like Dropbox, Box, or OneDrive. iCloud can be configured to automatically store your **Desktop** and **Documents** folders in Apple's cloud.

iCloud Desktop and Documents makes it easy, seamless, and effortless to synchronize and access your data across multiple devices since your data lives in iCloud. The advantage is that these folders and the files contained within them are accessible across all of your Apple devices (Mac, iPhone, iPad, AppleTV), through a browser, or even from Windows PCs. This is feature is huge for those of us who work on multiple devices throughout the day. And since these folders are where a majority of files are saved, saving them to iCloud frees up storage space on your Mac's solid state drive.

There are some caveats, of course. iCloud requires an Apple ID, which is a no-brainer. Apple gives you 5 GB of storage for free, which may or may not be sufficient depending on the size of your Desktop and Documents folders. All files stored in those folders will count against your iCloud storage allocation. You can, of course, purchase more storage from Apple. The table below lists the monthly cost of iCloud storage in the United States when this book went to press. Apple lets you share the 200 GB and 2 TB plans with your family. You can see how much iCloud storage costs in your country at Apple's iCloud Storage pricing page: https://support.apple.com/en-us/HT201238.

50 GB	99¢
200 GB	$2.99
2 TB	$9.99

There are minimum device requirements to access iCloud and to take advantage of the latest iCloud features. You must be running macOS High Sierra on your Mac. iOS devices need to be running iOS 10. AppleTVs must be at tvOS 7.2.1 or later. And Windows PCs must be running Windows 10 and have iCloud for Windows 6 installed. Minimum browser requirements for Macs are Safari 9.1, Firefox 22, or Chrome 28. On PCs, the minimum browser requirements are Internet Explorer 11, Firefox 45, or Chrome 50. If you are using Apple's iWork suite, you'll need Pages 5.5, Numbers 3.5, or Keynote 6.5 or later. On iOS, Pages, Numbers, and Keynotes should be version 2.5 or later.

Enable iCloud Desktop and Documents

iCloud Drive Desktop and Documents will automatically save your Desktop and Documents folders to your iCloud Drive. There is no need to move or copy documents to iCloud. macOS will keep your documents synchronized. iCloud Drive will safely store all of your documents, allowing you to access them from any of your Apple devices, even Windows PCs.

To enable iCloud Drive Destop and Documents, launch the **iCloud** preference pane in System Preferences. Check the checkbox next to **iCloud Drive**.

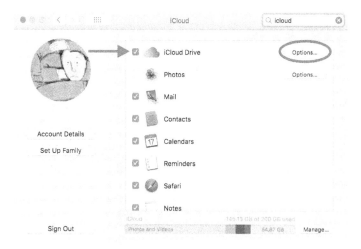

Next, click the **Options** button and check the checkbox next to **Desktop & Documents Folders**. Click **Done** to finish. Your Desktop and Documents folders will now be moved to iCloud. The time this takes depends upon the number and size of your documents and the speed of your Internet connection.

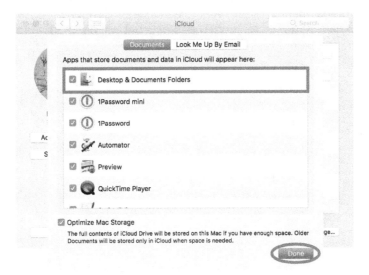

Your Desktop and Documents folders will now be listed under the iCloud section in the Finder Sidebar.

Manage iCloud Storage

To manage the contents of your iCloud storage, click the **Manage...** button in the lower right corner of the iCould preference pane.

A configuration sheet will appear, which lists the applications utilizing iCloud storage in a column at the left. Select an app to manage its documents and data. For example, **Backups** often contains old backups of devices you no longer own. Deleting old, unneeded backups frees iCloud storage space. Click **Done** when finished.

Upgrade your iCloud Storage Plan

You can upgrade your iCloud storage plan directly from the iCloud preference pane. Click **Manage...** in the lower right corner of the preference pane. Next, click the **Change Storage Plan...** button in the upper right of the configuration sheet. A new panel will appear with your storage options. Click **Next** to continue or **Cancel** to cancel the upgrade. Note that the credit card attached to your iTunes account will be charged immediately for cost of your new storage plan.

If you want to downgrade your current plan to one with less storage, click the **Downgrade Options**... button. Note that your new storage plan must be of sufficient size to accommodate the amount of data you are currently storing in iCloud.

Add iCloud Drive to the Dock

 Like many features of macOS, there are several ways to access your **iCloud Drive**. I find that the most convenient and quickest way to open iCloud Drive is from the Dock, where it is immediately accessible without having to first launch Finder.

To add iCloud Drive to the Dock, open a **Finder** window. Enter ⇧⌘G (shift+command+G) to open the **Go to the folder** dialog box. Enter the following and click **Go**.

```
/System/Library/CoreServices/Finder.app/Contents/Applications/
```

Locate **iCloud Drive** in this folder and drag and drop it where you want it on the Dock.

Modify the Sidebar

The **Finder** Sidebar offers one-click access to items that you use the most, organized into five categories – **Favorites**, **iCloud**, **Shared**, **Devices**, and **Tags**.

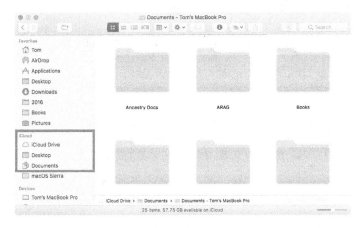

The **Favorites** category provides quick, single-click access to folders and files that you access frequently. Your **Home** folder, denoted by a house, **All My Files**, and **AirDrop** are listed first. You can add any folder to Favorites by locating the folder in Finder and then dragging it into the Sidebar.

The order of the items listed under favorites can be rearranged by dragging them until the list is arranged the way you want it. Any item in the Favorites list can be removed by dragging it off the Sidebar until a gray circle containing an **X** appears underneath its title. Simply release and the item disappears.

Secondary clicking on an item in the **Favorites** list opens a submenu allowing you to **Open in New Tab**, **Show in Enclosing Folder**, **Get Info**, **Rename** the folder, **Remove from Sidebar**, or **Add to Dock**.

The iCloud section lists the contents of your iCloud Drive. Secondary clicking on an item in the **iCloud** list opens a submenu allowing you to **Open in New Tab**, **Show in Enclosing Folder**, **Get Info**, **Rename** the folder, **Remove from Sidebar**, or **Add to Dock**. Like the Favorites, you can rearrange items under iCloud by dragging them.

The **Shared** category includes other computers, network drives, or shared devices on your network.

The **Devices** category includes internal drives, external drives, or other devices connected to your Mac. A secondary click on items in the list of **Devices** provides a different set of options allowing you to **Open in New Tab**, **Show in Enclosing Folder**, **Eject**, **Get Info**, **Decrypt**, **Rename**, **Remove from Sidebar**, or **Add to Dock**.

The **Tags** category lists the Finder Tags. Clicking on a Tag populates the Finder window with all files tagged with the selected tag. Secondary clicking offers options to **Open in New Tab**, **Remove from Sidebar**, **Delete Tag**, or change its color.

Choose Which Items Appear in Sidebar

macOS lets you customize the Sidebar, choosing which items you want to display. To customize the Sidebar, select **Finder > Preferences...** or enter ⌘, (command+comma).

Once the preference pane appears, make sure **Sidebar** is selected from the set of four icons at the top of the pane. Using the checkboxes, check and uncheck items until you have configured the Sidebar to your liking.

Checked items are displayed in Sidebar, while unchecked items are hidden. Hidden items can be unhidden later by again accessing the Finder preferences and checking their associated checkbox(es).

Hiding Sidebar Lists

Hovering your mouse over any of the Sidebar categories reveals a **Hide/Show** toggle switch to the right of the category name. Clicking **Hide** collapses the category while clicking **Show** expands it.

Add Trash to the Sidebar

Missing from the **Finder** Sidebar is one of the most often used folders on macOS, the **Trash**. It only takes a couple of steps to add the Trash to the Sidebar.

First, open a Finder window. Enter ⇧⌘G (shift+command+G) to open the **Go to the folder** dialog box. Enter the following and click **Go**.

~/Trash

Next, switch to **Column** view. The Trash folder will be highlighted, but it will be grayed to indicate that it is a hidden folder. Drag it into the Sidebar. I recommend placing it at the bottom as shown, but its location is your choice.

You now can use the Trash folder in the Sidebar to drop files into the Trash. However, the Sidebar Trash folder doesn't quite operate like the Trash in the Dock. Besides the fact that the icon is wrong (it's a folder instead of a trash can), you cannot empty the Trash by secondary clicking. If you want to empty the trash from Finder, click on the Trash folder in the Sidebar and then click the **Empty** button in the upper right.

Remove a Folder from the Sidebar

To delete any folder from the Sidebar, drag it off the Sidebar until an **X** appears below its name and release your hold.

Rename Sidebar Items

Any folder added to the Finder **Sidebar** can be renamed by secondary clicking on it to display a contextual menu. From that menu, you can **Open in New Tab**, **Show in Enclosing Folder**, **Get Info**, **Rename**, **Remove from Sidebar**, or **Add to Dock**. Renaming an item in the Sidebar not only renames the Sidebar shortcut, but also renames the original folder as well.

Change the Sidebar Icon Size

By default, macOS sets the size of the icons in the Sidebar to medium. If you have a lot of items in the Sidebar, you may want to set the icons to a smaller size to avoid having to scroll. Conversely, you may like the Sidebar to display larger icons to make the items easier to read.

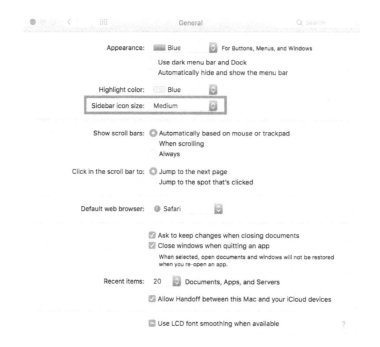

To change the icon size in Sidebar, open the **General** preference pane in the System Preferences application. Use the drop-down menu next to **Sidebar icons size** to choose **Small**, **Medium**, or **Large**.

Hide the Side Bar

To hide the Sidebar, choose **View > Hide Sidebar** or enter ⌥⌘S (option+command+S). The Sidebar can be toggled back on by selecting **View > Show Sidebar** or by entering ⌥⌘S (option+command+S).

Another method is to hover your pointer over the dividing line between the Sidebar in the right-hand pane until the resizing pointer appears. Sliding the resizing pointer left or right will make the Sidebar width smaller or larger, respectively. The resizing pointer can also be used to hide the Sidebar by moving it all the way to the left until the Sidebar disappears.

Show the Finder Bars

macOS offers a number of features in Finder to make navigating through the macOS file system much easier or to provide additional information. These features consist of various bars can be toggled on or off as needed. You can choose to show or hide the **Path Bar**, **Status Bar**, and **Tab Bar**. With the exception of the Sidebar, these three bars are disabled by default. Let's enable them and see what they do.

Show the Path Bar

There are a number of ways to view the path taken to arrive at the folder currently displayed in Finder. You could press and hold the **Back** button in the upper left of the toolbar to display the path taken to reach the folder. Another method is the hold the ⌘ (command) key down while clicking on the folder name in the Title Bar. This will reveal the path taken to reach the folder displayed. Yet another method is to display the Finder **Path Bar**. When the Path Bar is enabled, every Finder window will display it at the bottom of the window.

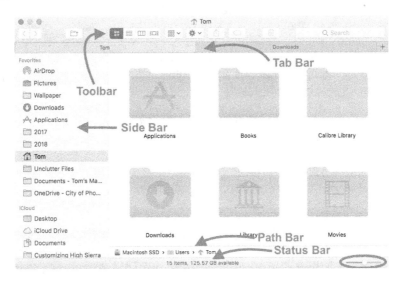

The **Path Bar** is located below the main Finder pane and displays the path from the folder shown to the top of your file system. To enable the Path Bar, select **View > Show Path Bar** or enter ⌥⌘P (option+command+P). To turn the Finder Path Bar off, select **View > Hide Path Bar** or enter ⌥⌘P (option+command+P). The Path Bar can be toggled on and off with the ⌥⌘P (option+command+P) keyboard shortcut.

Path Bar Tips & Tricks

You can drag files into any folder listed in the **Path Bar** to move them. If you want to copy the file instead, hold down the ⌥ (option) key while dragging. To create an alias, hold down ⌥⌘ (option+command) keys while dragging. A folder can even be dragged within the Path Bar to move it to a new location. You can even drag between different Finder windows. While dragging, hover the pointer over the Path Bar of the inactive Finder window and it will become active after a few moments.

If you change your mind while dragging, press the **esc** key to cancel. If you change your mind after completing the move, copy, or alias creation, select **Edit > Undo** or enter ⌘Z (command+Z) to undo.

You can see the contents of any folder in the **Path Bar** by double-clicking on it. Its contents will replace the items displayed in the current Finder window. If you hold down the ⌘ (command) key while double-clicking, the folder will open in a new tab. Holding down the ⌥ (option) key while double-clicking opens the folder in a new Finder window while simultaneously closing the source window or tab.

Sometimes a path is so long that it cannot fit in the Path Bar. In that case, macOS will truncate the folder names. Simply hover your pointer over a truncated folder name will expand it so you can read it.

Shorten the Path Bar

macOS lists the path from the root of the disk drive to the current directory, which, depending on the depth of your directory structure, can result in ridiculously long paths and truncated, difficult to read folder names in the path. If most of your file browsing is done in your **Home** directory, it would be better if the path was shortened to reflect your location as it relates to your Home directory.

To shorten the path shown in the **Path Bar**, open Terminal and enter the following commands. This change takes effect immediately.

```
defaults write com.apple.finder PathBarRootAtHome -bool TRUE

killall Finder
```

To revert to the macOS default and show the longer path, enter the following commands.

```
defaults delete com.apple.finder PathBarRootAtHome

killall Finder
```

Show the Path in the Title Bar

If you prefer to not use the Path Bar, macOS allows you to configure Finder's Title Bar to display the path. By default, the Title Bar simply shows the name of the current folder. If you would like to show the path instead, open Terminal and enter the following commands. This change takes effect immediately.

```
defaults write com.apple.finder _FXShowPosixPathInTitle -bool TRUE

killall Finder
```

To revert back to the macOS default, enter the following commands.

```
defaults delete com.apple.finder _FXShowPosixPathInTitle

killall Finder
```

Show the Status Bar

The Finder **Status Bar** shows the number of items contained within a folder and the amount of free space left on the drive in which the folder is located.

To turn the Finder Status Bar on, select **View > Show Status Bar** or enter ⌘**/** (command+/). When the Status Bar is enabled, every Finder window will display the Status Bar at the bottom, below the Path Bar.

Another handy feature of the Finder Status Bar is that it provides a slider in the lower right corner that you can use to change the size of the icons displayed in the Finder window. Slide the slider left or right to make the icons smaller or larger, respectively.

To hide the Finder Status Bar, select **View > Hide Status Bar** or enter ⌘**/** (command+/).

Show the Tab Bar

The **Tab Bar** appears just below the Finder Toolbar. Once multiple tabs are opened, macOS will automatically display the Tab Bar. If you prefer to see the Tab Bar all the time, select **View > Show Tab Bar** or enter ⇧⌘**T** (shift+command+T). When the Tab Bar is enabled, every Finder window will display the Tab Bar below the Finder Toolbar.

The Tab Bar will automatically unhide when a second tab is opened. To hide the Tab Bar, select **View > Hide Tab Bar** or enter ⇧⌘**T** (shift+command+T). Note that you can only hide the Tab Bar when Finder is displaying a single tab. Whenever multiple Finder tabs are open, the Tab Bar will automatically appear and the option to hide it will be grayed out in the **View** menu.   Hiding the Tab Bar when you have a single tab open makes the Finder interface appear cleaner.

Show the File Preview Panel

The **File Preview Panel** comes in handy when you want to see a preview of a file or image without having to use Quick Look. The Preview Panel also shows the file name, size, date created, date modified, date last opened, and tags. You can even add tags directly from the Preview Panel. The Preview Panel comes in quite handy when looking for a file misplaced in the Trash folder since the Trash folder will not allow you to open files.

To show the Finder Preview Panel, select **View > Show Preview** or enter ⇧⌘P (shift+command+P). Select any file to see it in the Preview Panel. Once you have enabled the Preview Panel, it is enabled for any new Finder window. To hide the Preview Panel, select **View > Hide Preview** or enter ⇧⌘P (shift+command+P).

Customize the Toolbar

The Finder **Toolbar**, located at the top of the Finder window, provides a number of tools to manipulate the contents of folders displayed in the Finder window's right-hand pane. The picture below shows the default Finder Toolbar.

From left to right, the Toolbar provides forward and back buttons to navigate through folders similar to navigating forward and back in Safari.

The next set of four icons change how the contents of a folder are viewed – by **Icon**, by **List**, by **Column**, or by **Cover Flow**.

The **Arrange** button offers a drop-down list where you choose how to sort files in the Finder window. The sorting options are: by **Name**, **Kind**, **Application**, **Date Last Opened**, **Date Added**, **Date Modified**, **Date Created**, **Size**, or **Tag**. The final option, **None**, leaves the folder unsorted.

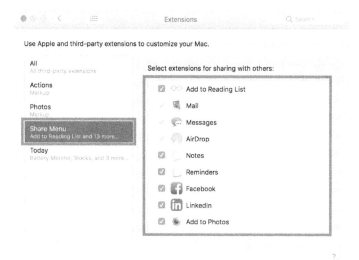

The **Action** button provides a contextual drop-down menu that changes based on the item that is selected.

The **Share** button lets you share an item via Mail, Messages, Airdrop, or through a number of third party extensions. macOS will list your recent shares under **Recents**, allowing you to quickly share an item. To configure the third party extensions available in the **Share Menu**, click the Share button and select **More...** or open the **Extensions** preference pane in the System Preferences app. Select **Share Menu** in the left column if not already selected. Use the checkboxes to select which third party extensions you wish to make available in the Share drop-down menu.

Back to the Finder toolbar, the **Edit Tags** button allows you to add, change, and remove tags. Finally, at the upper right corner of the Finder window is a Spotlight search field that we will cover later in this chapter.

macOS allows you to customize the Finder **Toolbar**, adding, removing, and rearranging tools as you see fit. Secondary click in any open area of the Toolbar to reveal a contextual menu. This menu allows you to choose how the tools appear. Tools can be displayed using both their **Icon and Text**, **Icon Only**, or **Text Only**. The current setting has a checkmark next to it. An option to completely hide the toolbar is also available.

The final option, **Customize Toolbar...** allows you to add, rearrange, and remove tools using the drop-down tools palette with the entire selection of available tools. You can also access this palette by selecting **Customize Toolbar...** from the **View** menu. Simply drag and drop the tools from the palette into the Toolbar. Rearrange as you see fit. You can choose how the tools will be displayed – **Icon and Text**, **Icon Only**, or **Text Only**. Click the **Done** button when finished.

The additional tools that are available include the **Path** tool, which displays the full path to the location shown in Finder's right-hand pane. You can also see the path by holding down the ⌘ (command) key while clicking on the title shown at the top of the toolbar.

The **Eject** tool will eject optical media from the optical drive and will unmount any drive whose contents are displayed in Finder's right-hand pane. The **Burn** tool is used to burn files and folders to optical media such as a CD or DVD.

The **Space** and **Flexible Space** tools are used to space out the tools in the toolbar by adding a blank space between them.

The **New Folder** tool does what its name implies, creating a new folder in the current folder displayed in the right-hand pane.

The **Delete** tool sends the selected items to the Trash.

The **Connect** tool is used to connect to network servers and shared drives.

The **Get Info** tool opens the Get Info window which displays information about the selected file such as its tags, kind, size, location, date created, date modified, its file extension, Spotlight comments, the default application which opens the file, and a file preview. The Get Info tool can be used on multiple files.

The **Quick Look** tool opens a preview of the selected file without launching the application in which it was created. Quick Look allows you to preview a file before deciding to open it. The Quick Look window provides a **Open with** button, allowing you to launch the application that created the file, as well as a **Share** button. You also can open Quick Look by clicking on a file and pressing the spacebar.

The **Share** button allows you to share a selected item using the third party extensions configured in the **Extensions** preference pane in System Preferences.

To add a tool to the Toolbar, drag it from the palette and drop it onto the toolbar. Existing tools located on the Toolbar can be rearranged by dragging them. A tool is removed by dragging it off the Toolbar and back on to the tools palette. Click the **Done** button when finished customizing your toolbar.

Tools located on the Toolbar can be rearranged without having to use the drop-down tools palette. To move a tool, hold the ⌘ (command) key down while dragging the tool to its new location. You can also use the ⌘ (command) key to remove a tool. Hold down the ⌘ (command) key while dragging the tool off the Toolbar. The tool will disappear.

To revert back to the default set of tools, drag the default set on to the Finder Toolbar and click **Done**.

Tag Files & Folders

Tagging files is a major shift in the way you work with the macOS file system. Files no longer need to be saved in a specific folder in order to create a relationship between them. Tags remove the need to have deeply nested folders within the file system in order to create relationships between different files. It doesn't matter where files are saved because Tags can be used to relate them to each other. The macOS search capabilities in both Finder and Spotlight allow you to immediately locate files based on their Tags regardless of where they reside in the file system.

Tagging files with a color and name is a convenient way to organize related files, such as files from a project, without having to create a special folder or modify the locations of the files. You can customize the name to "Kitchen Remodel Project" or "Budget" instead of categorizing only by color.

To tag a file that is open, move the pointer to the right of the filename in the Title Bar, click on the drop-down arrow, and click on the Tags field. You can choose a tag from the list or create a new one. This method does not work on all applications, most notably the Microsoft Office productivity suite.

There are several methods to tag an item in Finder. The first is to select the item, click the **Edit Tags** button in the toolbar, and select the appropriate tag. Another method is to select the file, secondary click on it, and add a Tag. Files can be tagged with one or more tags as needed. A third method is to select the file or files you want to Tag and select a Tag from the bottom of the Finder **File** menu. The fourth method is to select the files in Finder and click on the appropriate Tag in the Sidebar. The fifth method is to choose a Tag when saving a file for the first time.

To change or remove a Tag from an open file, click on the arrow next to the file name in the title bar to reveal the drop-down menu. Remove or modify any existing Tags.

To change or remove a tag from an item in Finder, select the file and click the **Edit Tags** button in the Toolbar. Remove or modify any existing Tags. An alternate method is to secondary click on an item and remove or change any existing Tags from the contextual menu. A third method is to use **File > Tags...** to remove existing Tags.

Customize Tags

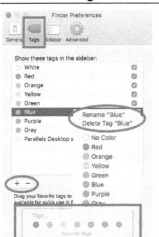

You can rename **Tags** in the Finder preference pane. Select **Preferences...** from the **Finder** menu. You can also access the preferences by entering ⌘, (command+comma). Once the Finder preferences appear, make sure **Tags** is selected from the set of four icons at the top of the pane.

To rename a tag, click on its name and rename it. The tag will appear under **Tags** in the Sidebar if its checkbox is checked. Drag the Tags to rearrange their order.

To add a new Tag, click the **+** button. To remove a Tag, click the **−** button or secondary click on the Tag and choose **Delete**. You can also rename a tag by secondary clicking on it and choosing **Rename**.

The bottom section of this pane is used to configure which tags appear in Finder menus. To remove a Tag, drag it off the preference pane. To add a Tag, drag it from the list at the top into the **Tags...** box at the bottom.

A quicker way to create a Tag is to click the **Edit Tags** button in the toolbar to reveal an option to enter the name of a new Tag. Begin typing in the field, and you will be given the option to create a new Tag. Press **return** when finished.

Create a Keyboard Shortcut for Tags

To tag a file in macOS, secondary click on it in a Finder windows to reveal the **Tags** option in the contextual menu. If you prefer to use keyboard shortcuts, you can create a keyboard to assign a tag to a file.

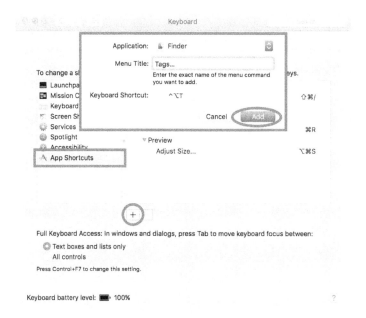

Open the **Keyboard** preference pane from System Preferences and select **Shortcuts** from the choices at the top of the pane. Next choose, **App Shortcuts** from the list at the left and then click the **+** to reveal a drop-down configuration sheet. Using the drop-down menu next to **Application:**, select **Finder**. For the **Menu Title** enter **Tags…**. To get the ellipsis (the three periods after the word "Tags"), enter ⌥**;** (option+;). Enter your desired keyboard shortcut in the **Keyboard Shortcut:** field and then click the **Add** button.

Search for Tags

All files associated with a Tag can be easily and quickly retrieved using the Sidebar in Finder. However, there is no easy way to find files and folders tagged with multiple Tags in the Sidebar. The only method is to perform a tag search using Spotlight.

To search for a file that is tagged with both a blue and a purple tag, open Spotlight and enter the following search.

```
tag:blue tag:purple
```

You can also search for tagged files by the Tag name. For example, if I rename the blue tag "macOS" and the purple tag "Apple." The following Spotlight search will return the same result as the search above.

```
tag:macOS tag:Apple
```

Create a Smart Folder

macOS offers several ways to create a Smart Folder. The first is to execute a search using Spotlight, selecting **Show all in Finder…** and then clicking **Save**. Other methods include selecting **File > Find**, using the **⌘F** (command+F) keyboard shortcut, or typing search criteria into the **Search** field of an open Finder window. Another method is to select **File > New Smart Folder** or use the shortcut ⌥⌘N (option+command+N) when Finder is the active application.

After selecting **Show all in Finder…**, you can save your search by clicking the **Save** button located in the upper right of the Finder window below the Tabs. You are creating a **Smart Folder**, a dynamic list of items meeting your search criteria. By saving a search as a Smart Folder, you save time by not having to rebuild a search from scratch each time. When you click the **Save** button, a drop-down sheet will appear allowing you to name the Smart Folder, save it, and display it in the Sidebar. I recommend saving frequently used searches to the Sidebar so you can access them quickly.

Smart Folders are dynamically updated and remain current as you add and delete items matching the search criteria. All items are conveniently displayed in a Smart Folder as if they were located in a single folder regardless of where they actually reside in your file system. While the items only appear to be located in one folder, they remain safely tucked away in the folders in which you saved them.

To add additional search criteria, click the **+** button next to **Save**. You can choose the search scope with **This Mac** being the default. You also have the option of only searching within the current folder. That option is directly to the right of **This Mac**. Any search line can be removed by clicking the **–** button. Select **Other…** to reveal a list of over 100 attributes against which you can search.

Once you have perfected your search criteria, click the **Save** button to reveal a drop-down configuration sheet allowing you to name your Smart Folder, save it to a folder, and add it to Sidebar.

By default, all Smart Folders are saved to the **Saved Searches** folder, however, you can choose where to save your Smart Folder. The checkbox next to **Add to Sidebar** is checked by default. Uncheck it if you do not want your Smart Folder to appear in the Sidebar, otherwise your new Smart Folder will appear at the bottom of your list of Favorites.

Open a File & Close Finder

Holding down the ⌥ (option) key while double-clicking on a file or folder in a Finder window will open the file while simultaneously closing the Finder window. You can also accomplish the same thing with the keyboard shortcut ⌥⌘O (option+command+O).

Disable Opening Folders in Tabs

macOS opens all folders in a new tab by default. It is sometimes more convenient to have multiple tabs available, particularly if you are copying or moving files between them. In the past you would have had to open multiple Finder windows, cluttering your desktop. However, if you prefer not to open folders in Tabs, you can disable this feature.

To change the macOS default to open a folder in a new Finder window instead of a new tab, open the **Finder** preferences by selecting **Finder > Preferences...** or by entering **⌘,** (command+comma). Next, select **General** if not already highlighted. Uncheck the checkbox next to **Open folders in tabs instead of new windows**.

Changing how folders are opened in Finder does not disable the Finder Tabs feature. You can still open a new Tab with **⌘T** (command+T) or by choosing **File > New Tab**.

When you disable opening folders in tabs, you also change another macOS behavior. Double clicking to open a folder while holding down the ⌘ (command) key will open the folder in a new Finder window. Holding down the ⌘ (command) key when tabs are enabled opens the folder in a new Tab.

Merge Multiple Finder Windows into Tabs

If you have multiple Finder windows open, you can merge them all into a single window with each Finder window becoming its own Tab. To merge all windows, click on any Finder window then select **Window > Merge All Windows**.

Make a New Finder Window from a Tab

Any of the Tabs in a Finder window can be used to create a separate Finder window. Secondary click on the tab you want to move to a new window and select **Move Tab to New Window**. Alternately, you can drag and drop a tab out of a Finder window onto the desktop to make it open in a new Finder window.

The contextual menu revealed when secondary clicking on a Tab also allows you to create a **New Tab**, **Close Tab**, **Close Other Tabs**, or **Move Tab to New Window**.

Change the Icon Size, Spacing, Arrangement, & Sort

The default icon size in macOS is 64 x 64 pixels. While this is good for most applications, you may find it too small when trying to view documents, pictures, or movies in Finder. macOS allows you to change the default icon size to make it smaller or larger.

To change the default icon size, secondary click any open space in a Finder window to reveal a contextual menu. Choose **Show View Options**. You can also select **View** >

Show View Options or enter ⌘J (command+J). The Finder View Panel appears with the name of the folder located in the Title Bar at the top of the window. If the checkbox next to **Always open in icon view** is checked, this folder will always open in icon view.

The next section allows you to change the arrangement of the icons and how they are sorted. Use the drop downs to choose your desired arrangement and sorting methods.

In the next section, you can change the icon size using the slider. Icons can be made as small as 16 x 16 pixels or as large as 512 x 512 pixels. The macOS default is 64 x 64. The largest size is handy when sorting through a folder containing pictures or movies.

The next section allows you to change the text size for the label shown at the bottom of files and folders. The default text size is 12 points. Supported text sizes are 10, 11, 12, 13, 14, 15, and 16 points. The default label position is at the bottom of files and folders. macOS lets you display the label at the bottom or to the right of an item.

The next section contains two checkboxes. The first, **Show item info**, will display the size of the file or the number of items a folder contains. The second checkbox, **Show icon preview**, is checked by default and will render a preview of the file content. If you uncheck it, macOS will display only default icons rather than rendering file content previews.

The next section allows you to change the background upon which icons are displayed. The default is white but you have the choice of choosing a color or a picture.

Clicking on the **Use as Defaults** button located at the bottom of the window makes your selections the default for the current folder and all of its sub-folders.

Show the User Library Folder

macOS allows you to toggle a switch to make the **Library** folder, which is normally hidden, visible. To make the **Library** folder visible, open **Finder** and navigate to your **Home** directory. Secondary click any open space in the Finder window showing your Home directory. Choose **Show View Options**. You can also select **Show View Options** from under Finder's **View** menu or enter ⌘J (command+J). Check the checkbox next to **Show Library Folder**.

Once your Library folder is visible, you can use the keyboard shortcut ⇧⌘L (shift+command+L) to go directly to it from any Finder window.

If you do not want to permanently make your Library folder visible and need only temporary access, hold down the ⌥ (option) key while selecting the **Go** menu. The

Library folder will appear while you are holding down the ⌥ (option) key. Select **Go > Library**.

Show Hidden Files

macOS hides any file or folder when its name begins with a "." If you need to show hidden files, you can quickly see them with the keyboard shortcut ⇧⌘. (shift+command+period). Hidden files and folders will now be visible in every Finder window. To revert back to the macOS default, enter the keyboard shortcut ⇧⌘. (shift+command+period) again to hide the files.

You can also enter the following commands in Terminal to show hidden files and folders.

```
defaults write com.apple.finder AppleShowAllFiles TRUE
```

```
killall Finder
```

To revert back to the default where hidden files and folders remain invisible in Finder windows, enter the following commands in Terminal.

```
defaults write com.apple.finder AppleShowAllFiles FALSE
```

```
killall Finder
```

Change the Spring Load Delay

Try dragging a file or folder onto another folder, pausing for a moment without releasing your hold on the file. Suddenly the folder will spring open to reveal its contents. This is a macOS feature called spring-loaded folders. Once a spring-loaded folder opens, you can repeat to drill down through the directory structure until you reach your desired destination folder. The delay, the amount of time you must pause on a folder before it springs open, can be tweaked or turned off all together.

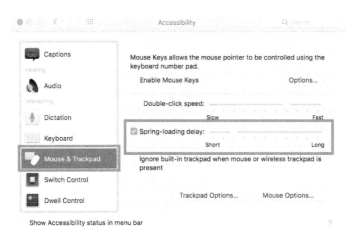

To adjust the spring load delay, open the **Accessibility** preference pane in the System Preferences application. Next, select **Mouse & Trackpad** in the left-hand pane. Adjust the spring load **Delay** using the slider located next to **Spring-loading delay**. If you want to disable the spring load delay feature entirely, uncheck the checkbox next to **Spring-loading delay**.

The **Tab Bar** appears just below the Finder toolbar. Like macOS folders, Finder tabs are spring-loaded meaning the tab will expand if you drag a file or folder and hover over it until the spring load delay timer expires.

If you are in a hurry and don't want to wait for the spring load delay timer to expire, hit the **spacebar** to bypass the spring load delay to open a folder or tab immediately.

Select the Folder Displayed in New Windows and Tabs

macOS displays the **All My Files** view when new **Finder** windows and tabs are opened. If you prefer new windows and tabs display another folder, such as your **Home** directory, you can set this attribute in the Finder preferences.

Launch the Finder preferences by selecting **Finder > Preferences...** or by entering ⌘, (command+comma). Next, select the **General** tab. Use the drop-down menu under **New Finder windows show** to set your desired location.

Close All Finder Windows

Sometimes you'll end up with a lot of open Finder windows. Wouldn't it be great if there was an easy and quick way to close all of them? Hold down the ⌥ (option) key while clicking the red **Close** window control in the upper left-hand corner of any Finder window. All Finder windows will close. Another option is to enter ⌥⌘W (option+command+W) to close all Finder windows. By the way, this trick works for any application.

You can also minimize all open windows of an application by holding down the ⌥ (option) key while clicking the yellow minimize window control in the Title Bar.

Show File Extensions

For those of you switching from a Microsoft Windows PC to a Mac and are worried because you miss the comfort of seeing those 3- and 4-letter file extensions after every filename, macOS allows you to turn on file extensions. They are disabled in macOS by default.

To have macOS show the file extensions, open the Finder preferences by selecting **Finder > Preferences...** or by entering **⌘,** (command+comma). Next, select the **Advanced** tab if not already highlighted. Check the checkbox next to **Show all filename extensions**.

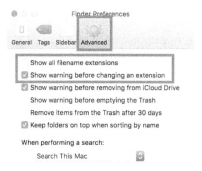

Note that macOS will also warn you if you change a filename extension. To disable this warning, uncheck the checkbox next to **Show warning before changing an extension**. However, changing a file extension could make a file unusable.

Quickly Duplicate a File

macOS offers a number of methods to duplicate a file. You can select a file in Finder, secondary click to reveal the contextual menu and choose **Duplicate**. Or you could select **File > Duplicate**. A quicker method is the hold down the ⌥ (option) key and drag the file to a blank space in the Finder window and release.

Backspace & the Delete Key

There are a few things that freak out Microsoft Windows users who are moving to a Mac. First, there is no right mouse button. There isn't a left mouse button either. Second, the **delete** key on a Mac keyboard acts like the backspace key on a PC. So how do you delete? On a Mac, the **delete** key works both ways. Hold down the **fn** key while pressing **delete**. Third, macOS doesn't display file extensions by default, proving that learning the difference between all of those 3- and 4-letter extensions was a terrible waste of your time. Fourth, windows do not have scroll bars. You'll see what to do about that soon.

Cut & Paste Files

If you are moving to a Mac from a PC, you'll notice that the **Cut** command and **⌘X** doesn't work in Finder. OMG! How do you cut and paste a file?

No need to panic. Since macOS is based on the Unix operating system, there is no concept of cut and paste. Cut and paste is equivalent to a move in macOS. To accomplish a cut and paste in macOS, you would simply move a file by dragging and dropping it in its new location.

If you really, really can't live without cut and paste, there is a workaround. Select the file in Finder, then copy it by selecting **Edit > Copy** or by entering **⌘C** (command+C). Navigate to the file's new location and hold down the ⌥ (option) key while selecting the **Edit** menu. When the ⌥ (option) key is held down, **Paste Item** will become **Move Item Here**. You can also enter ⌥⌘V (option+command+V) to move the file. This effectively is the same thing as cut and paste in the PC world. That said, it so much easier to simply drag and drop a file in macOS.

Rename a Group of Files

macOS features the ability to rename a list of files using a batch rename tool in Finder. Launch **Finder** and select the documents you want to rename. Next, secondary click on one of the files in the group and choose **Rename**. The number of items will be listed as in **Rename 10 Items...** in the contextual menu.

The drop-down configuration sheet offers several renaming options: **Replace Text**, **Add Text**, or **Format**.

Replace Text is used when the files all have a common element within their name. For example, files from a digital camera may be named "img" followed by a number. You could replace "img" with something more descriptive like "2017 Vacation."

The **Add Text** option allows you to add text before or after the existing file name.

The **Format** option lets you completely change the file name to one of three different formats: **Name and Index**, **Name and Counter**, or **Name and Date**. For example a group of files could be renamed "2017 Vacation" with an index, counter, or date appended.

For all options, click the **Rename** button when finished.

Delete a File Immediately

To delete a file immediately, highlight the file you want to delete in Finder and hold down the ⌥ (option) key while selecting **File > Delete Immediately...** or enter ⌥⌘delete (option+command+delete). A dialog box will appear to confirm the deletion and warn that this action cannot be undone. Click the **Delete** button to delete the file immediately or **Cancel**.

Note that the Delete Immediately option will only appear in the **File** menu when you are holding down the ⌥ (option) key. When the ⌥ (option) key is held down, **Move to Trash** will change to **Delete Immediately**.

Change the Scroll Bar Behavior

Scroll bars only appear when you are actually scrolling. This is very different from Microsoft Windows where scroll bars are a permanent and ugly blight on the right and bottom edge of every window. If you are a former Windows PC user and really miss your scroll bars, macOS can be configured so those ugly scroll bars are permanently tacked to the right and bottom edges of every macOS window.

To change the behavior of the scroll bars, open the **General** preference pane in System Preferences. When set to **Automatically based on mouse or trackpad**, scrollbars will not appear unless the document requires scrollbars and you have placed either one finger on the mouse or two fingers on a trackpad in preparation to scroll. This is the macOS default. If you like your scroll bars hidden until you are actually scrolling, choose **When scrolling**. Once you're done scrolling, the scrollbars will hide themselves. If you are a former Windows user suffering from scroll bar separation anxiety, select **Always**.

You have two options for clicking within a scroll bar – **Jump to the next page**, which is the default behavior, or **Jump to the spot that's clicked**. When **Jump to the next page** is selected, clicking within the scroll bar will page up or page down a single page at a time.

When **Jump to the spot that's clicked** is selected, clicking within the scroll bar will take you to that spot in the document. For example, clicking the very bottom of the scroll bar will take you to the end of a document. Clicking ¼ of the way down the scroll bar, will allow you to jump about a quarter way through your document. This feature is quite handy when you need to navigate quickly through a long document.

Disable Scrolling Inertia

macOS mimics the scrolling experience of iOS devices where a flick of your fingers causes the window to scroll rapidly. This feature is called **Scrolling Inertia** and is enabled by default. Flicking your fingers across your trackpad will cause the window to scroll rapidly. Compared to normal scrolling, it appears the window was scrolling about 100 mph. If you don't like Scrolling Inertia, macOS allows you to disable it.

To disable Scrolling Inertia, open the **Accessibility** preference pane in the System Preferences application. Next, select **Mouse & Trackpad** in the left-hand pane. To turn off Scrolling Inertia on a trackpad, click **Trackpad Options...**. **Do not uncheck** the box next to **Scrolling** as it will turn off scrolling. That's a very bad thing. Instead, use the drop-down menu next to **Scrolling** to select **without inertia**. Click **OK** when finished.

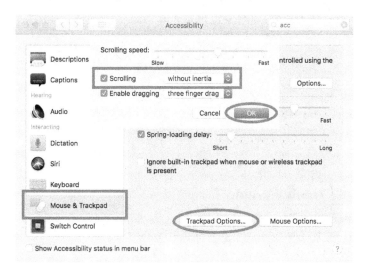

Rubberband scrolling lets you scroll a little further past the end of a file or webpage, and then bounces back to the end of the content. The rubberband animation lets you know you've reached the end. This is the same animation used by iOS on the iPhone and iPad.

Change the Scrolling Speed

If you find macOS' default scrolling speed too slow or too fast, you can tweak the scrolling speed until you get it just right. To change the scrolling speed, open the **Accessibility** preference pane in the System Preferences application. Next, select **Mouse & Trackpad** in the left-hand pane. Click **Trackpad Options...** or **Mouse Options...** to configure the scrolling speed on each.

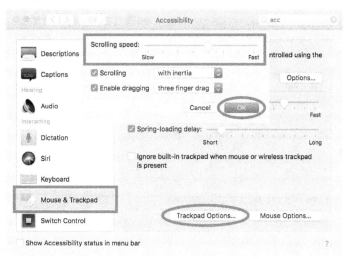

Both the trackpad and mouse options will reveal a drop-down configuration sheet. Use the slider at the top to adjust the scrolling speed. Click **OK** when finished.

Change the Search Scope

When searching in Finder, macOS searches your entire Mac. You can change the search scope to limit it to the current folder or a previous search scope.

To change the search scope, open Finder preferences by selecting **Finder > Preferences...** or by entering ⌘, (command+comma). Next, select the **Advanced** tab if not selected already. Use the drop-down list under **When performing a search** to select your desired search scope.

Remove the Empty Trash Warning

Every time you empty the **Trash**, macOS asks you if you are sure you want to permanently erase the items in the Trash. If you find this warning unnecessary, you can disable it.

To tell macOS to stop confirming that you want to empty the Trash, open Finder preferences by selecting **Finder > Preferences...** or by entering ⌘, (command+comma). Next, select the **Advanced** tab if not already highlighted. Uncheck the checkbox next to **Show warning before emptying the Trash**.

Remove the Warning when Deleting from iCloud Drive

macOS will warn you if you delete a file from iCloud Drive. This feature is useful if you enabled iCloud Desktop and Documents. However, if you feel this warning is unnecessary, macOS lets you disable it.

To disable this warning, open the Finder preference pane by selecting **Finder > Preferences...** or by entering ⌘, (command+comma). Next, select the **Advanced** tab if not already highlighted. Check the checkbox next to **Show warning before removing from iCloud Drive**.

Remove Items in the Trash After 30 Days

macOS can automatically delete items that have been in the Trash folder for 30 days. This is a handy feature that ensures old files you put in the Trash are not left hanging around indefinitely.

To enable this feature, open the Finder preference pane by selecting **Finder > Preferences...** or by entering ⌘, (command+comma). Next, select the **Advanced** tab if not already highlighted. Check the checkbox next to **Remove items from the Trash after 30 days**.

Quiet the Trash

macOS makes a sound that sounds like the crinkling of paper when emptying the **Trash**. This can be annoying if you're working in a quiet office environment or are listening to music. The sound of the trash emptying can disturb your concentration or the concentration of others.

To quiet the Trash when emptying, open Terminal and enter the following commands. This change takes effect immediately.

```
defaults write com.apple.finder FinderSounds -bool FALSE
```

```
killall Finder
```

Enter the following commands in Terminal to revert to the macOS default. This change takes effect immediately.

```
defaults delete com.apple.finder FinderSounds
```

```
killall Finder
```

Display Folders on Top

You can configure macOS to display folders at the top of the directory when sorting by name in a Finder window. This feature ensures that files and folders are better organized.

To enable this feature, open the Finder preference pane by selecting **Finder > Preferences…** or by entering ⌘, (command+comma). Next, select the **Advanced** tab if not already highlighted. Check the checkbox next to **Keep folders on top when sorting by name**.

When enabled, Finder will sort folders by name, placing them all at the top of the list. Files will be sorted next and placed after the list of folders. I feel this is a far better way to manage folders and files, however, if you prefer the folder and file sorting behavior of previous releases of macOS, uncheck the checkbox.

Change the Columns Displayed in List View

macOS displays the following three columns in the **Finder List View**: **Date Modified**, **Size**, and **Kind**. The Finder List View also supports other attributes such as **Date Created**, **Date Last Opened**, **Date Added**, **Version**, **Comments**, and **Tags**.

To change the columns shown in the Finder List View, select **View > Show View Options** from the Finder View menu or enter **⌘J** (command+J) to display the View Options preference pane. Check the checkboxes next to the items you want to display. Be sure your Finder window is in list view otherwise you will not see these options.

Multiple Item Inspector

The Get Info feature provides information about a file. If you select multiple files and choose **File > Get Info** or enter **⌘i** (command+i), macOS will open a Get Info pane for each file. That is not what you intended if you wanted to see the combined size of a group of files.

To launch the **Multiple Item Inspector**, hold down the ⌥ (option) key while selecting **File > Show Inspector** or use the keyboard shortctut **⌥⌘i** (option+command+i). Additional files can be added to an open Multiple Item Inspector window by holding down the ⌘ (command) key while clicking on them. The Multiple Item Inspector will dynamically update as new files are added.

Change the Title Bar Font Size

macOS allows you to change the size of the Title Bar font. To change the font size, enter the following commands in Terminal. The number equals the font size. In the example, the new font size is 14 points.

```
defaults write com.apple.finder NSTitleBarFontSize 14
```

```
killall Finder
```

To revert back to the macOS default, enter the following commands.

```
defaults delete com.apple.finder NSTitleBarFontSize
```

```
killall Finder
```

Calculate Folder Sizes

When you're viewing items in **List View** in **Finder**, you will notice that only files have an entry under the **Size** column. macOS does not calculate the size of folders by default. Therefore, you will see a pair of dashes in the size column.

If you would like to see the amount of disk space your folders are using, you need to tell macOS to **Calculate all sizes**. To enable this feature, select **View > Show View Options** from the Finder View menu or enter **⌘J** (command+J) to display the View Options preference pane. Check the checkbox next to **Calculate all sizes**.

This attribute is set on a per-folder basis. So if you would like to make this the default for all folders click the **Use as Defaults** button at the bottom of the preference pane. However, be careful to ensure that the other attributes on the preference pane are set to properly display folders the way you want to see them.

Increase the Window Resize Area

Any application window can be resized by hovering your pointer over any of its borders until the pointer changes to the resizing pointer, which is a double headed black arrow. Dragging the resizing pointer allows you to resize the window. The area in which the pointer changes to the resizing pointer is quite thin and it is sometimes difficult to get the pointer in exactly the right spot to make the resizing pointer appear.

This tweak increases the size of the area in which the pointer will change into the resizing pointer. Open Terminal and enter the following command. You will need to logout and log back in for the change to take effect.

```
defaults write -g AppleEdgeResizeExteriorSize 15
```

Feel free to try different numbers at the end of the command to make the area larger or smaller as you see fit.

To revert back to the macOS default, enter the following command. You will need to logout and log back in for the change to take effect.

```
defaults delete -g AppleEdgeResizeExteriorSize
```

Add a Quit Command

Finder is the one application that you can't quit. The reason for this is that Finder is responsible for managing the macOS file system and must run all the time. If you check out the **Finder** menu you will not find a **Quit** command. That is because other than relaunching Finder through **Force Quit** or with a **killall Finder** command, Finder must run continuously.

So why would you want to add a Quit command to the Finder menu? Having a Quit command in the Finder menu is a quick and easy way to execute the **killall Finder** command or to restart Finder.

Open Terminal and enter the following commands to add a Quit command to Finder.

```
defaults write com.apple.finder QuitMenuItem -bool TRUE
```

`killall Finder`

To revert back to the macOS default and remove the Quit command from the Finder menu, enter the following commands.

`defaults delete com.apple.finder QuitMenuItem`

`killall Finder`

14

Window Snapping

There is only one feature I truly miss when switching between my Windows PC at work and my MacBook Pro at home – Microsoft's window snapping feature. Drag a window to the right edge of the screen and it will snap to exactly half the size of your desktop. Drag another window to the left edge and it will snap to the other half. This feature is great when you need to compare two documents side-by-side. While macOS supports Split View mode, it just isn't quite the same as the window snapping functionality of Windows.

Another feature I miss is the ability to maximize a window by dragging it to the top of the desktop. I know I can maximize a window with the green Full-Screen button, but doing so hides the Menu Bar and the Dock. Often it's more productive to not wait for the Menu Bar or the Dock to unhide when you need them.

Luckily there are a couple of great, low-cost apps in the Mac App Store that offer window snapping functionality, and like everything on a Mac, window snapping is more powerful and more fully featured than Microsoft's implementation. Let's take a look.

Magnet

The first application I'd like to introduce to you is my favorite window snapping app, **Magnet**. Magnet is simple, easy to use, and highly intuitive. It supports window snapping by dragging, using a keyboard shortcut, or through a drop-down menu on its Menu Extra. Magnet keeps your desktop organized by letting you snap windows to use a quarter, third, half, two-thirds, or your entire desktop. Neatly aligning your windows side-by-side eliminates having to constantly switch apps. I especially like the capability to maximize a window to full screen without losing the Menu Bar and Dock. This is particularly important when you want to access the Application Menu without having to wait for it to unhide itself in native macOS Full-Screen mode.

If you are looking for Windows-like snapping features, Magnet delivers them in a powerful, customizable, and easy to use application. Because Magnet packs so many powerful features in a simple to use package, it is my recommended window snapping app for macOS. As I write this sentence, all versions of this app have 6,455 five-star ratings. Magnet is available from the Mac App Store for 99¢ at the time of this writing at: https://itunes.apple.com/us/app/magnet/id441258766?mt=12.

Set the Security & Privacy Settings

The first time you launch Magnet, you will be asked to authorize the application in the **Security & Privacy** preference pane of System Preferences. Click on the **Privacy** tab and select **Accessibility** from the left panel. Unlock the pane by clicking on the lock at the lower left and enter your credentials. Check the checkbox next to **Magnet** to authorize the application.

Launch Magnet at Start Up

To ensure you can always take advantage of Magnet's powerful window snapping capabilities, verify that Magnet is configured to launch when you start your Mac.

From the Magnet Menu Extra, select **Preferences...** to open the Magnet preference pane. Ensure that the checkbox next to **Launch at login** is checked.

If you prefer to launch Magnet each time your Mac restarts, uncheck this checkbox. However, it is more convenient to leave it checked so Magnet will always launch when you restart your Mac.

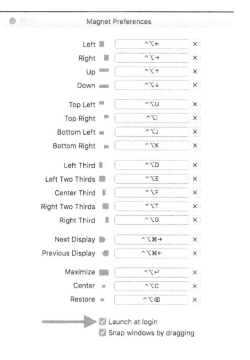

Sides do Halves

The simpliest method of rearranging and resizing the windows on your desktop is to drag them. Window snapping is accomplished by simply dragging a window to a location at the edge of your desktop.

Let's say you want to compare two documents side-by-side. Drag one document to the left edge of your desktop. The left half of your desktop will dim, previewing the result of the window snap. Release your hold on the window and it will resize to the left half of your desktop. Drag the other document to the right edge and the right half of your desktop will dim. Release and the window will resize to the right half of your desktop. Simple!

Perhaps you'd prefer to compare the documents with one occupying the top half of your desktop and the other the botton half. To snap a window to the top half of your desktop, drag it to the left or right side, just below either of the top corners. The top half of your desktop will dim to preview the snap. Release your hold on the window and it will resize to the top half of your desktop.

For the bottom half, drag the window to the left or right side, just above either of the bottom corners. The bottom half of your desktop will dim to preview the snap. Release your hold on the window and it will resize to the bottom half of your desktop.

You just learned the first rule of Magnet. Sides do halves.

If you prefer to use keyboard shortcuts, the default shortcut to snap a window to the left half of the desktop is **^⌥left** (control+option+left arrow). To snap a window to the right half, use **^⌥right** (control+option+right arrow).

A window can be snapped to the top half of the desktop with the keyboard shortcut **^⌥up** (control+option+up arrow). Use the keyboard shortcut **^⌥down** (control+option+down arrow) to snap to the lower half.

If you need another option, Magnet features a Menu Extra with a drop-down menu from which you can select **Left**, **Right**, **Up**, or **Down**.

Corners for Quarters

Dragging a window to any of the four desktop corners will snap it to that corner and resize it to a quarter of the desktop.

The second rule of Magnet is corners for quarters.

If you prefer to use keyboard shortcuts, the default shortcuts for the four corners of the desktop – top left, top right, bottom left, or bottom right are **^⌥U** (control+option+U), **^⌥i** (control+option+i), **^⌥J** (control+option+J), and **^⌥K** (control+option+K), respectively.

From the Magnet Menu Extra, select **Top Left**, **Top Right**, **Bottom Left**, or **Bottom Right**.

Bottom makes Thirds

Drag a window to the bottom of your desktop and it will snap to the left, center, or right third. Move your pointer across the bottom edge of your desktop without releasing your hold to preview your options. When you do so, you'll notice you have the option of resizing to a third or to two-thirds of your desktop.

The third rule of Magnet is bottom makes thirds.

If you prefer to use keyboard shortcuts, the default shortcut to snap a window to the left third is **^⌥D** (control+option+D). Need the window bigger? The **^⌥E** (control+option+E) shortcut will snap a window to the left two thirds of your desktop. Use the keyboard shortcut **^⌥F** (control+option+F) to snap a window to the center third. The shortucuts for the right two-thirds and right third are **^⌥T** (control+option+T) and **^⌥G** (control+option+G), respectively.

From the Magnet Menu Extra, select **Left Third**, **Left Two Thirds**, **Center Third**, **Right Two Thirds**, or **Right Third**.

Top Edge to Maximize

Magnet supports a full screen mode, called **Maximize**, which differs from the native macOS Full-Screen mode discussed in the Mission Control chapter. With Magnet, you can take a window to full screen without hiding the Menu Bar and Dock, which is the default behavior when using the native macOS Full-Screen mode. This feature comes in handy when you're using an application that has many controls in the Application Menu and you don't want to wait for it to unhide itself when using macOS Full-Screen mode. Similarly, Magnet's Maximize feature does not hide the Dock, allowing you to access it without waiting for it to unhide itself. To maximize a window, drag it to the top edge of your desktop.

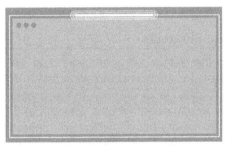

The final rule of Magnet is top edge to maximize.

If you prefer to use keyboard shortcuts, the default shortcut to maximize a window is **^⌥return** (control+option+return).

From the Magnet Menu Extra, select **Maximize**.

Center a Window

Magnet features a **Center** option, which will center the active window on the desktop. It's accessible only through the Magnet Menu Extra or by using the keyboard shortcut **^⌥C** (control+option+C).

Restore a Window

To restore a snapped window to its original size and location, simply drag it away from the edge of the desktop, use the keyboard shortcut **^⌥delete** (control+option+delete), or select **Restore** from Magnet's Menu Extra.

Move a Window to Another Display

If you have multiple displays, you can use Magnet to move a window to another display. The keyboard shortcut of **^⌥⌘right** (control+option+command+right arrow) will move the active window to the next display. Use the **^⌥⌘left** (control+option+command+left arrow) keyboard shortcut to move the window back to the previous display.

From the Magnet Menu Extra, select **Next Display** or **Previous Display**.

Magnet supports up to six external displays.

Ignore an Application

An **Ignore** option, accessible from Magnet's Menu Extra, lets you tell Magnet to ignore the currently active application. This is handy if you are manipulating an application's windows and don't want Magnet's snapping features to engage.

Change the Default Keyboard Shortcuts

If you want to change any of the default keyboard shortcuts, select **Preferences**... from the Magnet Menu Extra to open the Magnet preference pane. Click on the **X** next to the keyboard shortcut you want to change or click on the keyboard shortcut itself to reveal **Type New Shortcut**. Enter your desired keyboard shortcut in this field. To return to the previous entry, click the circular restore button, which will replace the **X** shown to the right of the keyboard shortcut once the default shortcut has been changed.

Disable Window Snapping by Dragging

Magnet lets you disable window snapping by dragging if you prefer to use only Magnet's keyboard shortcuts or its drop-down menu in the Magnet Menu Extra.

Next Display ▶	^⌥⌘→	×
Previous Display ◀	^⌥⌘←	×
Maximize	^⌥↵	×
Center ■	^⌥C	×
Restore ■	^⌥⌫	×

☑ Launch at login
Snap windows by dragging

To disable windows snapping by dragging, launch the Magnet preference pane by selecting **Preferences**... from the Magnet Menu Extra. Uncheck the checkbox next to **Snap windows by dragging**.

If you change your mind, check the checkbox next to **Snap windows by dragging** to enable this feature.

BetterSnapTool

If you require more customization capability than provided by Magnet, I recommend **BetterSnapTool**, which is a full featured, highly customizable window snapping tool available for $2.99 on the Mac App Store. As I write this sentence, all versions of this app have 3,642 five-star ratings. Written by Andreas Hegenberg, BetterSnapTool's standout feature is the ability to create your own custom snap area. Like Magnet, BetterSnapTool allows you to instantly change the size of your windows by dragging them to the top, left, or right edge, or the 4 corners of your desktop. BetterSnapTool goes a little further by allowing you to customize the appearance of the preview, the snap delay, and the space between window edges.

Similar to Magnet, you can snap a window to the left edge and another to the right edge of your desktop to compare two documents side-by-side. Windows can be maximized by dragging them to the top edge of the desktop. This differs from macOS's Full-Screen mode since the Menu Bar and Dock do not hide when using BetterSnapTool.

BetterSnapTool lets you create your own custom Snap Areas anywhere on your desktop and supports 19 different window resizing and snapping options. It also allows you to create keyboard shortcuts to move and resize windows. BetterSnapTool is available from the Mac App Store at:
https://itunes.apple.com/us/app/bettersnaptool/id417375580?mt=12.

Set the Security & Privacy Settings

The first time you launch BetterSnapTool, you will be asked to authorize the application in the **Security & Privacy** preference pane of System Preferences. Click on the **Privacy** tab and select **Accessibility** from the left panel. Unlock the pane by clicking on the lock at the lower left and enter your credentials. Check the checkbox next to **BetterSnapTool** to authorize the application.

Launch BetterSnapTool at Start Up

To ensure you can always take advantage of BetterSnapTool's powerful window snapping features, verify that Magnet is configured to launch when you start your Mac. To open the BetterSnapTool preference pane, click on its Menu Extra in the Menu Bar and select **Preferences**. Click on **General Settings**, if not already highlighted.

Check the two checkboxes at the bottom of the pane. **Start BetterSnapTool everytime your Mac starts up** ensures that BetterSnapTool is available for you every time you restart your Mac. If you uncheck this box, you'll have to manually launch the BetterSnapTool each time you want to use it.

The checkbox next to **Show menubar icon** toggles the Menu Extra on and off. The Menu Extra provides quick access to the BetterSnapTool preference pane. Once you have completely configured BetterSnapTool to your liking, you can uncheck this box to remove the Menu Extra. To access the preferences again, launch BetterSnapTool from Launchpad, Spotlight, or from your Applications folder or stack.

Enable Snap Areas

BetterSnapTool is pre-configured to snap to 7 locations on your desktop. Snapping a window to the top maximizes it without hiding the Menu Bar and Dock. Snapping a window to the left or right edge of the desktop, snaps the window to the selected edge and resizes it to half the desktop. Snapping a window to any of the desktop's four corners snaps it to the corner and resizes it to a quarter of the desktop.

BetterSnapTool will provide a preview of how the window will resize when the pointer touches the corner or edge of the desktop. Drag and hold a window to one of the snap areas. Releasing your hold will cause the window to resize. If you don't release your hold, you can drag the window off the edge or corner and release to cancel.

The top part of the preference pane shows the seven snap locations with a check in each checkbox indicating they are active. Uncheck any checkbox next to a snap location you do not want to use.

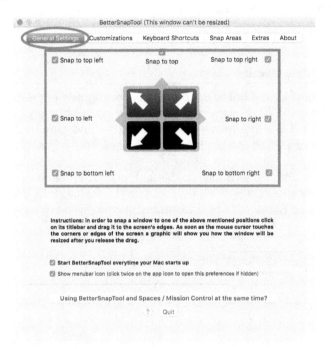

Do not press the **Quit** button at the bottom of the preference pane as it quits the application. To close the preference pane, click on the red close button in the upper left.

Clicking the button labeled **Using BetterSnapTool and Spaces / Mission Control at the same time?** opens a window with instructions on how to adjust the drag delay when dragging windows to another desktop space located to the left or right of your active desktop space. The issue here is that too small a delay will interfere with BetterSnapTool's ability to snap to the left or right edge. If the delay is too small, the Desktop Space will change as macOS assumes you want to move the window to another space. The recommendation is to set the window edge delay between desktop spaces to 2 seconds, giving you sufficient time to drag a window to the left or right edge and release your hold to resize. If you want to drag the window to an adjacent desktop space, simply hold the window along the edge until the window edge delay timer expires and the desktop space changes. BetterSnapTool will preview the window resize, but will not resize the window unless you release your hold.

To adjust the drag delay between spaces, open Terminal and enter the following commands to adjust the delay timer to 2 seconds.

```
defaults write com.apple.dock workspaces-edge-delay -float 2
```

```
killall Dock
```

I've used BetterSnapTool for a long time and I found a 1 second delay works fine for me. You can adjust the time by changing the number after **–float** in the first command to find delay that works best for you. Decimals are allowed so you can try 1.5 or 2.5 seconds. Setting the number to 0 completely removes the workspace edge delay and effectively eliminates the edges of your desktop as snap areas for BetterSnapTool.

For more information on the workspace edge delay timer, see the section "Move a Window to Another Desktop."

Customizing the Preview Overlay

When you drag a window to one of the snap locations configured in the **General Settings** tab, BetterSnapTool provides a preview overlay to show you what the window will look like when resized. If you don't like the default of a white border and gray background, you can change these settings as well as the border width, corners, and animation.

Select **Preferences** from the BetterSnapTool Menu Extra in the Menu Bar. If you chose to not show the Menu Extra, launch BetterSnapTool from Launchpad, Spotlight, or from your Applications folder or App Stack. Click on **Customizations** if it is not already highlighted.

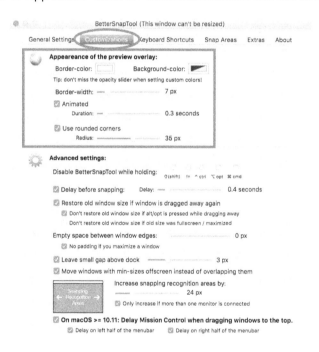

Clicking the white box next to **Border-color** launches a color wheel that lets you change the color of the border around the preview overlay. To change the preview overlay background from the default, click the black/gray box next to **Background-color**. Similarly, you will be presented with a color wheel to select your desired background color.

You can customize the width of the preview overlay border using the slider next to **Border-width**. Valid widths are from 0 to 50 pixels with the default being 7 pixels. You can also click on **7 px** to directly enter the width in the box provided.

The preview overlay's animation duration can be adjusted from 0 to 2 seconds with the default being 0.3 seconds. The duration is how long it takes the preview overlay to expand to show you how the window will resize. Unchecking the checkbox next to **Animation** disables the preview overlay animation. In this case, BetterSnapTool will instantly show you how the window will resize when you drag a window to a snap location.

The corners of the preview overlay border are rounded with a default radius of 35 pixels. You can use the slider next to **Use rounded corners** to change the radius to any value between 0 and 60 pixels. Similar to the border width, you can click on **35 px** to directly enter the width in the box provided. Unchecking the checkbox changes the preview overlay corners to 90-degree angles.

Temporarily Disable Window Snapping

You can configure a modifier key or combination of modifier keys to temporarily disable BetterSnapTool. This is handy if you intend to drag a window to another desktop space and don't want BetterSnapTool to engage. You can choose any one or a combination of the following modifier keys: ⇧ **fn** ⌃ ⌥ ⌘ (shift, function, control, option, command).

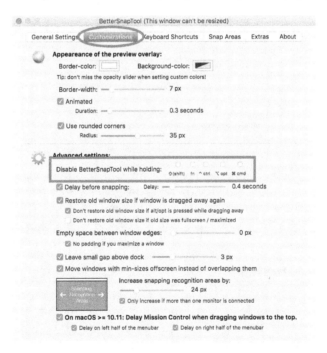

To configure modifier keys to temporarily disable BetterSnapTool, open the BetterSnapTool preference pane and click on **Customizations**, if not already highlighted. Check the checkboxes above your desired modifier keys in the **Advanced settings** section.

Configure the Snap Delay

BetterSnapTool displays the preview overlay animation the moment your pointer touches a defined Snap Area. If you would like to add a delay before the preview overlay is displayed, open the BetterSnapTool preference pane and click on **Customizations**, if not already highlighted. Check the checkbox next to **Delay before snapping** to reveal a slider that supports values between 0 and 2 seconds. You can also click on the **second** box to directly enter the delay.

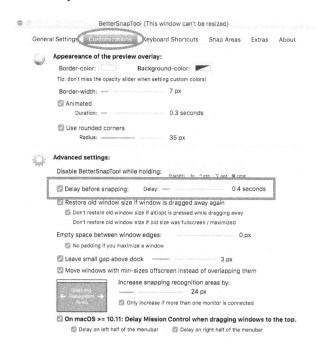

Be careful setting this delay timer as it can conflict with the workspace edge delay between Desktop Spaces. If the workspace edge delay is set to a smaller delay than the snap delay, BetterSnapTool will never display the preview overlay. The workspace edge delay timer will expire and your window will be moved to the adjacent Desktop Space.

Disable Window Size Restoration

After resizing a window with BetterSnapTool, you can resize it back to its original size by dragging it away from the Snap Area. For example, if you resized a window to occupy half your desktop by dragging it to the right edge, dragging it away will restore the window to its original size. This function is enabled by default.

To disable window size restoration, open the BetterSnapTool preference pane and click on **Customizations**, if not already highlighted. Uncheck the checkbox next to **Restore old window size if window is dragged away again.**

Another available option is to disable window size restoration when the original window size was Full Screen or maximized. To enable this feature, check the checkbox next to **Don't restore old window size if old size was fullscreen / maximized.**

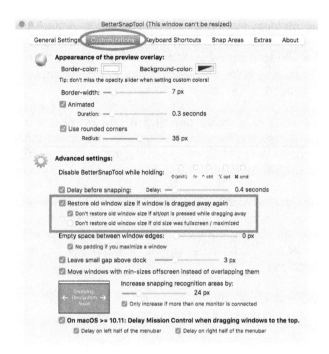

Add Padding Around Windows & the Dock

BetterSnapTool leaves no space between the edge of the desktop and the window when resizing. However, you can configure the amount of padding around a window after it is resized.

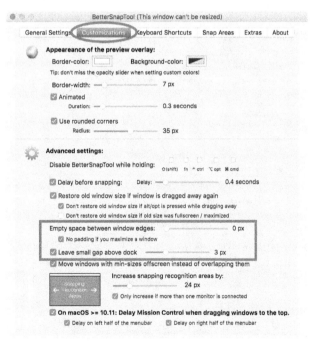

If you would like some padding around a window, open the BetterSnapTool preference pane and click on **Customizations**, if not already highlighted. Use the slider next to **Empty space between window edges** to select a value between 0 and 100 pixels. You can click on the **0 px** to directly enter the padding size in the box provided. Note that the padding will be applied around all four sides of the window.

You can check the checkbox next to **No padding if you maximize a window** to avoid adding padding around maximized windows. If you do not check this option and have padding configured, windows will not fully maximize as they will be surrounded on all sides by the padding configured by the slider.

BetterSnapTool will not resize a window over the Dock. You can increase the separation between the bottom edge of a window and the Dock by checking the box next to **Leave small gap above dock** and moving the slider to your desired gap. Valid entries are 0 to 10 pixels. Similar to other configuration items, you can click the setting and directly enter a value into the configuration box.

A final option is to ensure windows with minimum sizes do not overlap. When this option is enabled, minimum sized windows will be pushed off screen.

Increase the Snap Recognition Area

BetterSnapTool will play the preview overlay animation or resize a window the moment your pointer reaches an active Snap Area. You can increase the snap recognition area up to 100 pixels (the default is 0). The increased snap recognition area means that you will no longer have to move your pointer all the way to the edge of an active Snap Area. You only have to move your pointer near it.

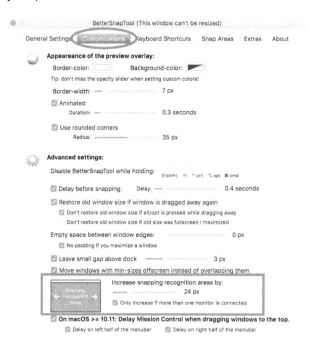

To increase the snap recognition area, open the BetterSnapTool preference pane and click on **Customizations**, if not already highlighted. Use the slider next to **Increase snapping recognition areas by** to select a value between 0 and 100 pixels.

If you have a multiple monitor system, you will have to configure a larger snap recognition area in order for BetterSnapTool to resize windows dragged to the edge of the desktop. In a dual monitor setup, you will notice that only one edge resizes windows. Dragging a window to the opposite edge of the desktop moves the window to the other monitor. By increasing the snap recognition area, BetterSnapTool will resize the window without the pointer actually having to touch the edge of the desktop.

You can configure larger snap recognition areas to enable only when more than one monitor is connected. This is handy if you have a MacBook, MacBook Air, or MacBook Pro and are using it in a dual monitor setup. When docked in dual monitor mode the larger snap recognition area is enabled. When undocked, the larger snap recognition area is disabled. Check the box next to **Only increase if more than one monitor is connected** to enable this option.

Delay Mission Control

macOS lets you simultaneously open Mission Control and drag a window to another desktop by dragging a window to the very top of your screen. Unfortunately, this interferes with BetterSnapTool's ability to snap a window to full size when dragging it to the top of the screen. The solution is to configure a delay before Mission Control launches. This can be done in the BetterSnapTool preference pane.

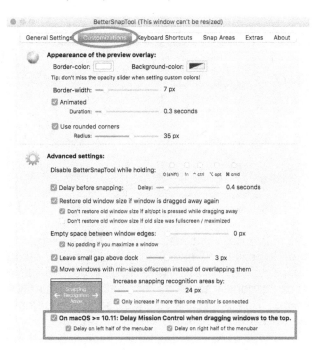

To delay Mission Control, open the BetterSnapTool preference pane and click on **Customizations**, if not already highlighted. Check the checkbox next to **On macOS High Sierra: Delay Mission Control when dragging windows to the top**.

You can configure delays for the entire screen or for only the left or right half of the Menu Bar. Check the checkboxes next to **Delay on left half of the menubar** or **Delay on the right half of the menubar** to configure a delay for only half the screen. This allows you to take advantage of both the Mission Control feature and the BetterSnapTool's full screen window snap.

Create a Pop-up Window Resizing Menu

BetterSnapTool supports a total of 20 window resizing options. Only 7 of the options are available by dragging a window to a snap recognition area. The additional 13 window resizing options can only be accessed by configuring BetterSnapTool to display its pop-up resizing menu using a keyboard shortcut. You can also configure keyboard shortcuts for each resizing option.

To access the 13 additional resizing options, open the BetterSnapTool preference pane and click on **Keyboard Shortcuts**, if not already highlighted. Choose your desired keyboard shortcut in the **Click to record shortcut** box next to **show menu with all selected actions**. You can optionally check the box next to **also duplicate the menubar preferences to this menu**. This option lets you access this menu from BetterSnapTool's Menu Extra under **Change Window Position / Size**.

To use the pop-up menu to resize a window, hover your pointer over the window you want to resize and enter the keyboard shortcut you configured. The pop-up resizing menu will appear. All you need to do is select your desired resizing choice.

BetterSnapTool lets you configure which resizing options are displayed on the pop-up resizing menu. Uncheck the options you don't want to appear. You can optionally assign keyboard shortcuts to any or all of the resizing options.

Create Custom Snap Areas

If 20 resizing options and 7 Snap Areas aren't enough for you, BetterSnapTool offers virtually limitless resizing and Snap Area options through an advanced feature called **Snap Areas**. This feature lets you define a specific window size and a customized snap recognition area.

Creating a custom Snap Area is a multi-step process.
1. Resize an arbitrary window to the desired position and size. Make sure this window is the active window.
2. Click on the BetterSnapTool Menu Extra and select **Snap Areas (Advanced Feature)**.
3. Select **Create New Snap Area (Use Active Window As Template)**.
4. BetterSnapTool will enter editing mode. The active window will be grayed out and bordered by a dotted red line. A dialog box will appear in the center of your monitor instructing you to click the box to define a new Snap Area.

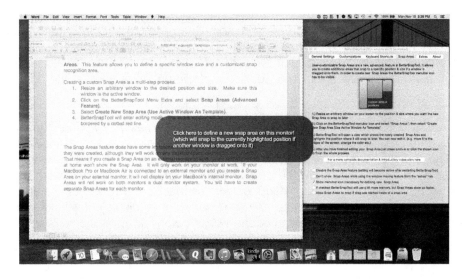

5. The light blue Snap Area box shown below will appear on your desktop. Resize it using the resizing handles and move it to the area of your desktop where you want your Snap Area to be located.

6. There are four tools under the Snap Area. From left to right, the first tool (the one that looks like a gear) allows you to require one or more of the following modifier keys: ⇧ **fn** ⌃ ⌥ ⌘ (shift, function, control, option, or command) to be held down to show the custom Snap Area. Configuring this option will prevent the Snap Area from displaying every time you move a window. You can also configure BetterSnapTool to display the Snap Area only when a window from a specific application or set of applications are being moved.

7. The color wheel allows you to select the background and border colors. You can also configure border type and width and corner radius if you do not like the defaults. There is also an option to make the Snap Area invisible. When invisible, the Snap Area will only appear when you hover over it with your pointer. Finally, the tool lets you configure the length of the preview overlay animation.

8. You can add custom text to your Snap Area with the text tool. Note that clicking the **X** in the last tool will delete the Snap Area and exit edit mode without creating your custom Snap Area.

9. Once you have finished configuring the Snap Area options, enter ⌘**W** (command+W) or click the gray box in the center of your desktop to exit edit mode. Your custom Snap Area is now ready to use.

To use your custom snap area, simply drag the window you want to resize to your custom snap area. Release your hold on the window after the preview and the window will snap and resize.

To access a video showing how to create a custom Snap Area, open the BetterSnapTool preference pane and click on **Snap Areas**, if not already highlighted. Click the introductory video button. Your default browser will open and will navigate to the page containing the video. There are also 5 additional configuration options at the bottom of this tab.

The Snap Areas feature does have some limitations. Snap Areas only work on the display where they were created, although they will work on any desktop space defined on that display. That means if you create a Snap Area on an external display at work, your external display at home won't show the Snap Area. The Snap Area will only work on your monitor at work. If your MacBook, MacBook Air, or MacBook Pro is connected to an external monitor and you create a Snap Area on your external display, it will not work on your MacBook's internal display. Snap Areas will not work on both monitors in a dual monitor system. You will have to create separate Snap Areas for each monitor.

Edit or Delete a Custom Snap Area

To edit or delete a previously configured custom Snap Area, click the BetterSnapTool Menu Extra and select **Snap Areas (Advanced Feature) > Edit Snap Areas**. Click on the custom Snap Area you want to edit and make your desired changes. To delete a Snap Area, click the **X** and confirm you want to delete. When finished enter ⌘**W** (command+W) or click the gray box in the center of your desktop to exit edit mode.

Define the Window Control Buttons

BetterSnapTool has a feature that lets you define a resizing option for the window control buttons in the upper left of a window when you secondary click on them or use a mouse with a middle button. You have 19 different resizing options to choose from.

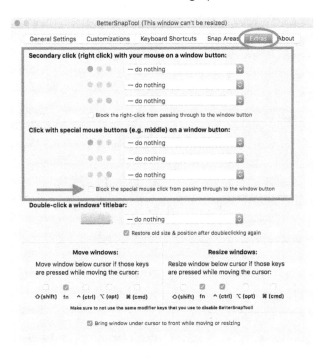

To define resizing options for the window control buttons, open the BetterSnapTool preference pane and click on **Extras** if not already highlighted. Select options for each window control for a secondary click, or middle button if your mouse has one. You will need to check the checkbox next to **Block the right-click from passing through to the window button**. If you fail to do so, you will be disappointed. BetterSnapTool will execute the resize command and immediately afterward macOS will execute the command associated with the window control.

Resize by Double-Clicking the Title Bar

You can configure BetterSnapTool to resize a window when you double-click on the window's title bar. Similar to the window controls, you have 19 different resizing options from which to choose.

To configure resizing by double-clicking the title bar, open the BetterSnapTool preference pane and click on **Extras**. Choose the desired resizing action. If you have already configured macOS to minimize a window by double-clicking the title bar, a dialog box will warn you of the conflict. You can choose to **Cancel** or have BetterSnapTool open the **Dock** preference pane so you can resolve the conflict.

If you want a second title bar double-click to restore the window's original size and location, check the box next to **Restore old size & position after doubleclicking again**.

Move & Resize Windows with a Modifier Key

The macOS default is that a window must be active for you to move or resize it. Not with BetterSnapTool. All you have to do is hover your pointer over the window you want to move or resize, hold down the configured modifier key, and move your pointer to move or resize it. It doesn't matter if the window is active or not.

To configure modifier keys to move and resize a window, open the BetterSnapTool preference pane and click on **Extras**, if not already highlighted. Select the desired modifier keys for each action. Optionally, you can configure BetterSnapTool to make the window active while moving or resizing it. Check the checkbox next to **Bring window under pointer to front while moving or resizing** to configure this option.

15

Keyboard

In this chapter, we'll cover the keyboard. I know what you are thinking. "Why a chapter on the keyboard?" "Everyone knows how to use a keyboard." Before you skip this chapter, let me show you a few keyboard customization tricks. macOS let's you change the behavior of the keys and allows you to create custom keyboard shortcuts to boost your productivity.

Disable the Caps Lock

Why should you disable the caps lock? Because things like thiS HAPPEN WHEN YOU ACCIDENTALLY HIT THE CAPS LOCK. If your Mac's caps lock is driving you nuts, macOS allows you to disable it.

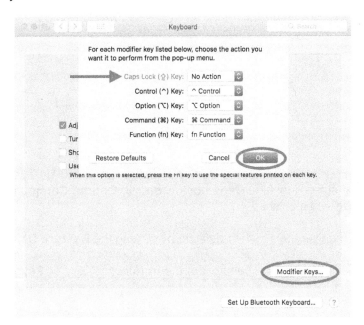

To disable the caps lock key, open the **Keyboard** preference pane in System Preferences. Select **Keyboard**, if not already highlighted. Next, click the **Modifier Keys...** button to reveal the Modifier Keys configuration sheet. Choose **No Action** from the drop-down list next to **Caps Lock**. You can enable the caps lock key by choosing **Caps Lock** from the drop-down list.

Change the Behavior of the Modifier Keys

macOS allows you to change the behavior of the modifier keys – ^ ⌘ ⌥ **fn** – control, command, option, and function, respectively. Why would you want to change the behavior of the modifier keys? If you are familiar with a keyboard layout that is different than the one on your Mac, you may want to modify the layout.

To change the default behavior of the modifier keys, open the **Keyboard** preference pane from the System Preferences application. Click on the **Keyboard** tab if it is not already highlighted. Next, click the **Modifier Keys...** button at the lower right of the preference pane. A configuration sheet will appear from under the title bar. If you have multiple keyboards, select the keyboard from the drop-down menu.

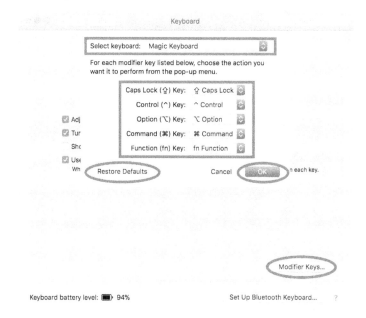

Choose the new modifier key mapping from the drop-down menu next to each of the modifier keys. Your choices include **Caps Lock**, **Control**, **Option**, **Command**, **Escape**,or **No Action**. Click **OK** when finished.

You can return the modifier keys to their defaults by clicking the **Restore Defaults** button.

Note that you can only change the behavior of the **fn** (function) key on keyboards that do not have a Touch Bar.

Turn Keyboard Backlight Off When Idle

One of the great features of a MacBook, MacBook Pro, and MacBook Air is that keyboard backlighting is standard on all models. Anyone who has fumbled around in dim light on a cheap PC keyboard knows the value of keyboard backlighting. Keyboard backlight is on by default and does not turn off even if your Mac is idle.

If you would like to dim your keyboard lighting when your Mac has been idle for a period of time, open the **Keyboard** preference pane in the System Preferences application. Click the **Keyboard** tab if not selected already.

Check the checkbox next to **Turn keyboard backlight off after** and select **5**, **10**, **30 seconds**, or **1** or **5 minutes** from the drop-down menu.

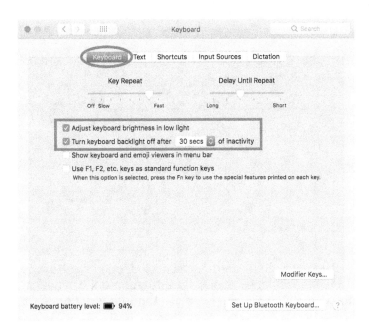

Precisely Adjust the Keyboard Backlight

Sometimes it seems you never can get the keyboard backlight adjusted to your liking. One segment more is too much. One less is too little. Wouldn't it be awesome if you could adjust the keyboard backlight in smaller increments? macOS has a solution for you!

Hold down the ⇧ ⌥ (shift+option) keys while adjusting the keyboard backlight to adjust it in quarter-segment increments. This feature allows you to precisely adjust the brightness exactly to your liking. This trick also works when adjusting the display brightness and volume.

Make the Function Keys Act Like Function Keys

When you press an **F** (function) key, it will execute the command associated with it (i.e., Mission Control, Launchpad, Play/Pause, Volume Up, Volume Down, Mute, etc.). On a Mac you need to hold down the **fn** (function) key in order to use an **F** key as a standard **F** key, which is the opposite of how Windows PC keyboards work.

If you want to press **F12** and have it execute the keyboard shortcut configured in the **Keyboard** preference pane instead of increasing the volume, you have to hold down the **fn** (function) key while pressing **F12**. This is particularly confusing for former Windows PC users switching to a Mac. If you'd like the **F** keys to work like they do on a PC, macOS allows you to configure the **F** keys so that they act like standard function keys.

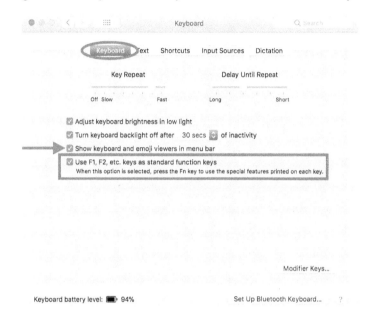

To make the **F** keys perform like standard function keys, open the **Keyboard** preference pane in the System Preferences application. Click **Keyboard** if it is not already selected. Check the box next to **Use all F1, F2, etc. keys as standard function keys**.

How do you increase the volume and use the other special features? Hold down the **fn** key while pressing an **F** key to use the special features when the **F** keys are configured as standard function keys.

Show Keyboard and Character Viewer

For quicker access to the **Keyboard Viewer** and the **Character Viewer**, you can add a drop-down menu in the Menu Bar. From the Keyboard preference pane, select **Keyboard** if it is not already highlighted, then check the checkbox next to **Show keyboard and emoji viewer in menu bar**.

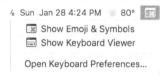

The Keyboard Viewer shows you where characters for other languages, symbols, and special characters are located on the keyboard.

The Character Viewer shows you a huge selection of emoji and symbols including math and currency symbols, flags, bullets and stars, arrows, letter symbols, parentheses, pictographs, and punctuation.

Enable Key Repeat

By default, holding down a key in macOS does not activate key repeat as you might expect, particularly if you are used to Windows PCs. Instead, a contextual menu appears, which allows you to insert diacritic characters (i.e., accented and other non-English characters). Unless you often write in a foreign language, you may find this feature to be an annoyance. macOS allows you to make key repeat operate as you expect it to when holding down a key.

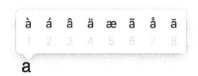

To enable key repeat, open Terminal and enter the following command. You will need to log out and log back in for this change to take effect.

```
defaults write -g ApplePressAndHoldEnabled -bool FALSE
```

To revert back to the macOS default, enter the following. You will need to log out and log back in for the change to take effect.

```
defaults delete -g ApplePressAndHoldEnabled
```

Automatically Add a Period

macOS can automatically add a period when you enter two spaces. To enable this feature launch the Keyboard preference pane and select the **Text** tab. Check the checkbox next to **Add period with double-space**.

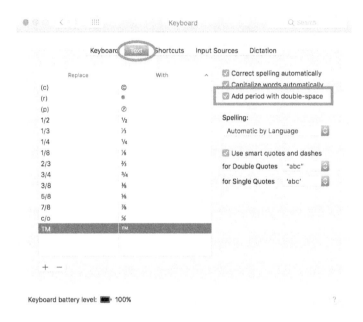

Create a Text Replacement

You can create text replacements in the **Text** tab in the **Keyboard** preference pane. The **Replace List** lets you create shortcut phrases or text that can be replaced with longer text. This allows you to use text shortcuts that macOS will automatically replace with longer phrases.

To create a text replacement, open the **Keyboard** preference pane from the System Preferences application and click the **Text** tab. Next, click the **+** at the lower left of the left pane. Enter a text shortcut in the **Replace** column and the phrase you want to replace it with in the **With** column.

In the example below, I have created two text replacements. The first is **lwn** which will be replaced by **Leaving work now**. The second, **omw**, will be replaced with **On my way!**

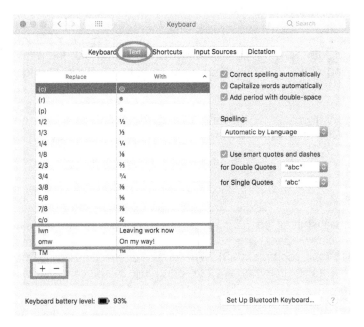

Text replacement works across Apple applications with iCloud keeping your replacements up to date across your Apple devices. Note that iCloud Drive must be enabled for this feature to work.

Enable Desktop Shortcuts

If you created new Desktops in Mission Control, macOS automatically created a keyboard shortcut for each new Desktop Space. Each keyboard shortcut allows you to jump directly to a Desktop and are in the form of ^ (control key) followed by the Desktop number. However, these keyboard shortcuts are disabled by default.

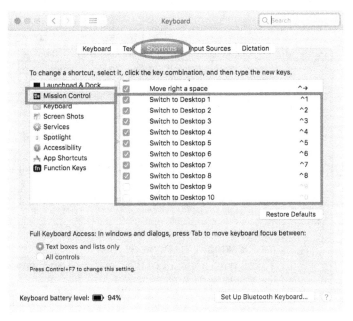

To enable or change the Desktop keyboard shortcuts, open the **Keyboard** preference pane and click **Shortcuts**. Next, select **Mission Control** from the left pane. Scroll down in the right pane and check the checkbox next to each Desktop shortcut you want to enable.

To change the shortcut, click on the shortcut in the right pane and enter your new keyboard shortcut. Click the **Restore Defaults** button to restore a keyboard shortcut to its default value.

Take a Screenshot

You can take a screenshot of your entire desktop, an area of your desktop, a window using, and even the Touch Bar using a keyboard shortcut. To take a screenshot of your desktop, enter ⇧⌘3 (shift+command+3). To capture a specific area of the desktop or a window, enter ⇧⌘4 (shift+command+4) to bring up a set of crosshairs. Drag the crosshairs across the desired area and release when done.

To take a screenshot of a window, press ⇧⌘4, move the crosshairs over the window you want to take a screenshot of, press the **spacebar** to change the crosshairs to a camera, and click your mouse or trackpad. Your Mac will take a screenshot of the entire window. The window does not have to be the active window. If you own a MacBook Pro with a Touch Bar, you can take a screenshot of the Touch Bar by pressing ⇧⌘6 (shift+command+6).

Change Screenshot Keyboard Shortcuts

macOS has a number of predefined keyboard shortcuts to take screenshots as shown in the table. Note that ⇧⌘6 (shift+command+6) and ^⇧⌘6 (control+shift+command+6) will only work if you have a MacBook Pro with a Touch Bar.

⇧⌘3	Takes a screenshot of the desktop and saves it to the Desktop or designated folder.
^⇧⌘3	Takes a screenshot of the desktop and saves it to the Clipboard.
⇧⌘4	Takes a screenshot of a user-defined area and saves it to the Desktop or designated folder.
^⇧⌘4	Takes a screenshot of a user-defined area and saves it to the Clipboard.
⇧⌘4 + space	Takes a screenshot of a window and saves it to the Desktop or designated folder.
^⇧⌘4 + space	Takes a screenshot of a window and saves it to the Clipboard.
⇧⌘6	Takes a screenshot of the Touchbar and saves it to the Desktop or designated folder.
^⇧⌘6	Takes a screenshot of the Touchbar and saves it to the Clipboard.

If you want to change the default screenshot keyboard shortcuts, you can redefine them in the **Keyboard** preference pane. You can also disable them if you have no need to take screenshots.

Open the Keyboard preference pane in System Preferences and click the **Shortcuts** tab. Next, select **Screen Shots** in the column at the left. The default shortcuts are listed in the right pane. Click on the existing shortcut to change it. Uncheck a shortcut if you want to disable it.

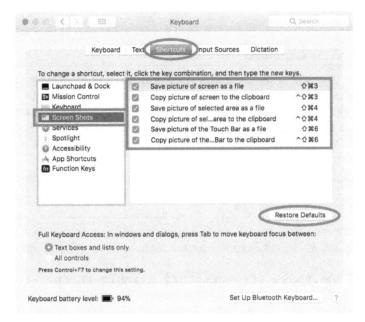

Click the **Restore Defaults** button to restore the default keyboard shortcuts.

Change the Screenshot Destination Folder

macOS saves screenshots to the **Desktop** folder by default. If you take a lot of screenshots, your Desktop can quickly fill up with clutter. macOS lets you change the default destination folder to something other than the Desktop.

First, determine where you want to save your screenshots. For this example, I'll first create a folder called **Screenshots** in my **Documents** folder. The path I'll need to enter in the command to change the destination folder is:

`~/Documents/Screenshots/`

To change the default destination for screenshots, launch Terminal and enter the following commands. Note that the first two lines are one command. Do not press the **return** key until you have entered the entire command. There is a space after location. Replace **~/Documents/Screenshots/** with the path to your desired folder.

```
defaults write com.apple.screencapture location
~/Documents/Screenshots/
```

```
killall SystemUIServer
```

Enter the following commands to revert back to the macOS default of saving screenshots to the Desktop.

```
defaults write com.apple.screencapture location ~/Desktop/
```

```
killall SystemUIServer
```

Save Screenshots to the Clipboard

Saving screenshots to a file is handy if you need to annotate the screenshot, however, sometimes you just need to copy the screenshot directly into a document. In this case, it is much easier to save a screenshot to the **Clipboard**. Add the ^ (control) key to the screenshot keyboard shortcuts and macOS will save your screenshot to the Clipboard. All you have to do is to paste the screenshot into your document using **Edit > Paste** or ⌘**V** (command+V).

Remove Shadows from Screenshots

macOS inserts a gray shadow around an image captured by a screenshot. If you would like to remove the shadow, launch Terminal and enter the following commands.

```
defaults write com.apple.screencapture disable-shadow -bool TRUE
```

```
killall SystemUIServer
```

To revert back to the macOS default, enter the following commands in Terminal.

```
defaults write com.apple.screencapture disable-shadow -bool FALSE
```

```
killall SystemUIServer
```

Change the Screenshot File Format

macOS saves screenshots in Portable Network Graphics (PNG) format, an open extensible image format supporting lossless data compression. PNG was created as an improved, non-patented replacement for Graphic Interchange Format (GIF). macOS supports the ability to save screenshots in other graphics formats as well.

If you would prefer to save your screenshots in **jpg** format, launch Terminal and enter the following commands.

```
defaults write com.apple.screencapture type jpg
```

```
killall SystemUIServer
```

macOS also supports **tiff**, **PDF**, **bmp**, and **pict** formats.

To change the default file format for screenshots, replace **jpg** in the above command with your desired format.

To revert back to the macOS default, enter the following commands in Terminal.

```
defaults write com.apple.screencapture type png
```

```
killall SystemUIServer
```

Custom Keyboard Shortcuts

Veteran Mac users know that keyboard shortcuts are a huge productivity booster, allowing you to quickly perform routine and repetitive tasks more efficiently. Keyboard shortcuts are an alternative to executing a command through a drop-down menu using your mouse or trackpad. For example, you can quit a running application using the keyboard shortcut ⌘Q (command+Q), which is much faster than using your mouse or trackpad to select **Quit** from the Application Menu.

I'm sure you noticed some drop-down menu items that you use frequently in various applications do not have an associated keyboard shortcut. This forces you to access the drop-down menu using your mouse or trackpad. If you find yourself using a particular command that does not have a keyboard shortcut, macOS allows you to create your own custom keyboard shortcut.

While I have covered various keyboard shortcuts throughout this book, I'll show you how to create your own custom keyboard shortcuts. You can use keyboard shortcuts to speed up common tasks, to open applications, and execute commands within applications. I'll also show you how to modify existing macOS keyboard shortcuts. If you are looking for a productivity boost, keyboard shortcuts are a very efficient method for you to do most things faster with a few keystrokes.

Create a Keyboard Shortcut

Let's walk through the creation of a custom keyboard shortcut for a specific application. First, open the **Keyboard** preference pane and click the **Shortcuts** tab. Next, click on **App Shortcuts** in the left hand pane. The **Show Help menu** keyboard shortcut will be listed under **All Applications** in the right hand pane. Any existing application specific keyboard shortcuts will be listed in the right pane. To create a new keyboard shortcut, click the **+** below the right pane.

A configuration sheet will appear from under the title bar. To create a keyboard shortcut that works in all applications choose **All Applications** from the drop-down menu next to **Application**. An **All Applications** keyboard shortcut will work in any application that has the menu item as an option.

If you want to create a keyboard shortcut for a specific application, select the application from the drop-down menu next to **Application**. In the example below, I am creating a keyboard shortcut for the **Mail** application.

259

Next, enter the **Menu Title** exactly as it appears in the drop-down Application menu in the application. In the example below, I will create a keyboard shortcut for the command to **Synchronize All Accounts** in the Apple Mail application. This command is available in the **Mailbox** menu. Therefore, I entered the menu and sub-menu hierarchy in the **Menu Title:** field. The menu hierarchy is **Mailbox > Synchronize All Accounts**, which you would enter as:

`Mailbox->Synchronize All Accounts`

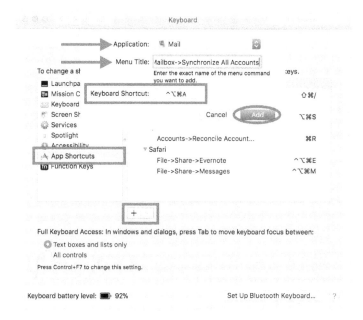

Note the **->** (hyphen+greater than sign) between the top menu item, **Mailbox**, and the submenu item, **Synchronize All Acounts**. Be sure to not enter any spaces between the menu and submenu items.

Lastly, enter you desired keyboard shortcut in the field next to **Keyboard Shortcut**. In the example above, my new keyboard shortcut for the Synchronize All Accounts command in Mail is **^⌥⌘A** (control+option+command+A).

Click the **Add** button when finished. Note that macOS will add the shortcut you created to the Application Menu.

If the command has an ellipsis (three periods) appended to it, enter the three periods (...) or use the shortcut **⌥;** (option+;) as in the following example for a command available in the Microsoft Word.

`File->Save As Template...`

Sometimes the command is buried three or four levels in a menu hierachy. In this case, the **->** (hyphen+greater than) becomes even more important. For example, I will often find an interesting article on the web that I want to share via a text Message and it would be cool if I had a keyboard shortcut so I could share the article more quickly.

In this case, the menu hierarchy is three levels and I entered the following in the **Menu Title:** field, seperating each level with a **->** (hyphen+greater than). Be sure you do not enter any spaces between the menu and submenu items.

`File->Share->Messages`

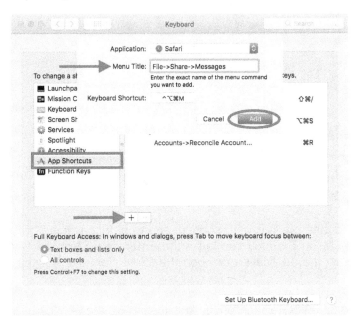

Next, I entered my custom keyboard shortcut, **^⌥⌘M** (control+option+command+M), in the **Keyboard Shortcut:** field as shown below.

Reviewing the **File > Share** submenu in Safari shows my newly created keyboard shortcut to share via the Messages, **^⌥⌘M** (control+option+command+M).

As you can see from the menu to the right, I also created another keyboard shortcut to share via Evernote using the keyboard shortcut **^⌥⌘E** (control+option+command+E).

To remove a custom keyboard shortcut, click to highlight it and click the **–** button at the bottom of the right pane.

Create Keyboard Shortcuts to Launch Applications

HotKey is a nifty little utility by Peter Vorwieger that lets you define keyboard shortcuts to quickly launch applications or open folders in Finder. The app features a Menu Extra allowing you to quickly launch an app or open a folder from its drop-down menu.

To configure your own custom shortcuts in HotKey, open the HotKey preference pane by selecting **Preferences...** from the HotKey Menu Extra. Next, click the **+** button, which will open your Applications folder. If you are creating a keyboard shortcut to launch an app, select the app and click the **Choose** button. To create a keyboard shortcut to open a folder, navigate to your desired folder using this Finder window, select the folder, and click **Choose**. Lastly, enter your new shortcut in the **Enter new Shortcut** field.

If you do not want to create a keyboard shortcut and want a convenient way to launch an application from the Menu Bar, you can leave the **Enter new Shortcut** field blank. You will be able to launch the application or open the folder from the HotKey Menu Extra's drop-down menu.

To remove a shortcut, click to highlight it and then click the **−** button. Shortcuts can be disabled by unchecking the checkbox next the them. Keyboard shortcuts that unchecked will be not been shown in the HotKey drop-down menu.

HotKey comes with a pre-configured keyboard shortcut to **Show Clipboard**, which will display the contents of the clipboard on your Desktop when you enter ⇧⌘**space** (shift+command+space). Pressing ⇧⌘**space** (shift+command+space) again will dismiss the clipboard. To disable this shortcut, uncheck the checkbox next to it. Note that HotKey will not allow you to remove the **Show Clipboard** keyboard shortcut.

Other options you should configure include ensuring the checkbox next to **Start at Login** is checked to ensure HotKey is available everytime you restart or log in to your Mac. The checkbox next to **Hide Dock Icon** does exactly what you would expect it to do. When unchecked, the HotKey icon will appear in your Dock. When checked, the HotKey icon will not appear in the Dock. The checkbox next to **Big Menu Icons**, toggles between small icons when unchecked and bigger icons when checked.

HotKey allows you to import and export your keyboard shortcuts if you want to share them or to make a backup. To export your keyboard shortcuts, select **Import/Export...** from the HotKey Menu Extra, then select **Import...** or **Export...** from the submenu.

HotKey App was available for free in the Mac App Store at the time of this writing at: https://itunes.apple.com/us/app/hotkey-app/id975890633?mt=12

16

Touch Bar

Some models of the Apple 13" MacBook Pro and all 15" models feature a 2170 x 60-pixel touchscreen display called the **Touch Bar** where the function keys are normally located. The Touch Bar is a dynamic input device with a strip of vitual keys that automatically change based on the running application and what you're doing. The far right corner features a Touch ID that allows you to unlock your MacBook Pro, unlock apps that require a password, or authorize Apple Pay with your fingerprint. The **Control Strip**, which contains four controls, is located at the right quarter of the Touch Bar with the **esc** key located on the far left.

By default, the Control Strip contains four controls for brightness, volume, mute, and Siri, from left to right. Tapping the arrow located at the left of the Control Strip reveals the full set of controls normally found on the top row of a physical keyboard – brightness, Mission Control, Launchpad, keyboard backlight, media playback, and the volume controls as shown below. When expanded, the Control Strip is called the **Expanded Control Strip**.

Holding down the **fn** key reveals the standard set of function keys, **F1** to **F12**.

| esc | F1 | F2 | F3 | F4 | F5 | F6 | F7 | F8 | F9 | F10 | F11 | F12 |

The Touch Bar is a virtual keyboard that offers quick access to common tools and other functionality that would normally require the Application Menu to access. These tools are displayed between the **esc** key and the **Control Strip** in an area called **App Controls**. The tools shown in App Controls change with the running application.

macOS lets you customize the controls that appear on the Touch Bar. You can change the the controls shown in the Control Strip, Expanded Control Strip as well as the App Controls available in various applications. On the next few pages, I'll show you how to customize the Touch Bar to make it more useful and increase your productivity.

Let's first start with Touch ID and Apple Pay and then move on to basic customization of the Touch Bar controls.

Setup Up Touch ID

Touch ID allows you to log into your user account using your fingerprint rather than typing your password. You can use Touch ID to make purchases from the App Store, iBooks, and iTunes. You can also use Touch ID to make purchases on websites that support Apple Pay. If you share your MacBook Pro with other family members, the macOS Touch ID feature supports multiple users' fingerprints.

To setup Touch ID, open the **Touch ID** preference pane in System Preferences.

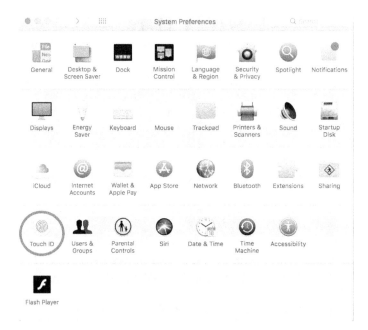

Next, click the **+** in the Touch ID preference pane to add your fingerprint. Enter your password when prompted. Place your finger on the Touch ID button and follow the instructions to lift and rest your finger to capture your fingerprint. Ensure that your finger is clean and dry for best results.

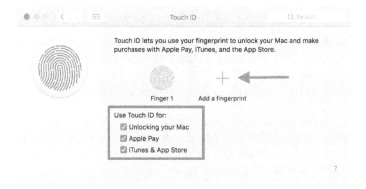

Repeat to add addition fingerprints. macOS will allow you to enter up to three fingerprints per user account.

To delete a fingerprint, hover over an existing fingerprint with the pointer until an **X** button appears. Click the **X** button to delete.

Touch ID can be used to unlock your Mac, use Apple Pay, and to make purchases from iTunes and the Mac App Store. Be sure the three checkboxes under **Use Touch ID for:** are checked.

Set up Apple Pay

If you did not set up Apple Pay when first setting up your MacBook Pro or if you need to make changes, open the **Wallet & Apple Pay** preference pane from System Preferences.

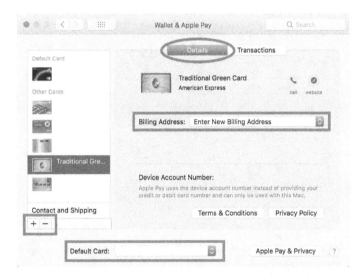

To add a new a credit card to Apple Pay, click the **Details** tab if not already highlighted. Next, click the **+** at the bottom of the left pane to add a new credit card. If you have multiple credit cards, select the default card from the drop-down menu next to **Default Card**.

If you have to change your billing address, you can do so by selecting **Enter New Billing Address** from the drop-down menu next to **Billing Address**.

To delete an existing credit card, click the **–** button at the bottom of the left pane. Click the **Delete** button on the configuration sheet.

Make the Expanded Control Strip the Default

By default, the Control Strip is collapsed to the right side of the Touch Bar, requiring you to tap the expand arrow to expand it to access the other tools available in the **Expanded Control Strip.** You can configure the Expanded Control Strip to always be available in the Touch Bar so that the macOS system tools are at your fingertips just like they are on a MacBook Pro without a Touch Bar.

Note that App Controls will no longer be available if you configure the Touch Bar to display the Expanded Control Strip at all times.

To permanently display the Expanded Control Strip on the Touch Bar, open the the **Keyboard** preference pane from System Preferences. Click the **Keyboard** tab if it is not already highlighted. Select **Expanded Control Strip** from the drop-down menu next to **Touch Bar shows**.

To return to the macOS default, select **App Controls with Control Strip** from the drop-down menu next to **Touch Bar shows**.

Make App Controls the Default

If you want to remove Control Strip entirely from the Touch Bar, macOS lets you configure the Touch Bar to show only the App Controls.

To configure the Touch Bar to display only the application controls, open the **Keyboard** preference pane from System Preferences. Click the **Keyboard** tab if it is not already highlighted. Select **App Controls** from the drop-down menu next to **Touch Bar shows**.

To return to the macOS default, select **App Controls with Control Strip** from the drop-down menu next to **Touch Bar shows**.

Make the Function Keys the Default

If you prefer the function keys to be the default, open the **Keyboard** preference pane from System Preferences. Click the **Keyboard** tab if it is not already highlighted. Select **F1, F2, etc. Keys** from the drop-down menu next to **Touch Bar shows**.

To return to the macOS default, select **App Controls with Control Strip** from the drop-down menu next to **Touch Bar shows**.

Switch between the Control Strip and Function Keys

When you press the **fn** (function) key, the Control Strip will change to show a set of function keys from **F1** to **F12** as shown below.

If you configured macOS to always display the strip of function keys, you may want to change the role of the **fn** (function) key so that it switches to the Expanded Control Strip when pressed. Launch System Preferences and open the **Keyboard** preference pane. Click **Keyboard** if not already highlighted. Select **Expand Control Strip** from the drop-down menu next to **Press Fn key to**.

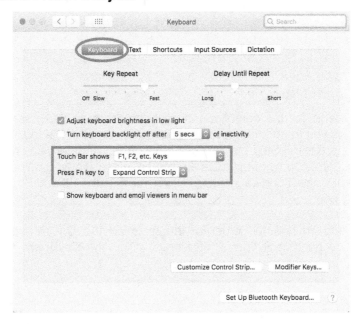

Use the fn Key to Show the Expanded Control Strip

By default, pressing the fn key toggles the Touch Bar to the function keys, **F1** through **F12**. If you do not have a need for the function keys, you can configure the Touch Bar to expand the Control Strip when you hold down the fn key. Often this is quicker than tapping the left arrow on the Control Strip to expand it.

To configure the **fn** key to toggle to the Expanded Control Strip, open the **Keyboard** preference pane from System Preferences. Click on the **Keyboard** tab if it is not already highlighted. Select **Expand Control Strip** from the drop-down menu next to **Press Fn key to**.

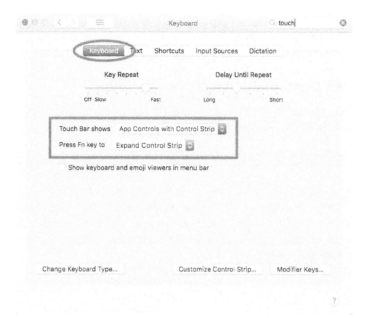

Customize the Control Strip

You don't have to settle for the default set of tools on the macOS **Expanded Control Strip**. macOS allows you to add, remove, and change the order of the tools, allowing you to put the tools on the Control Strip that you use most often. Another reason to customize the Control Strip is that a couple of the tools already have associated trackpad gestures to invoke them, Mission Control and Launchpad, which frees up the F3 and F4 keys for other tools you commonly use.

To add, remove, and change the order of the tools on the Control Strip, open the **Keyboard** preference pane in System Preferences. Click the **Keyboard** tab if it is not already highlighted.

Next, click the **Customize Control Strip...** button to reveal a pallette of tools, which will appear at the bottom of your desktop. The icons on your Touch Bar will jiggle similar to the way apps on an iPhone jiggle when editing them.

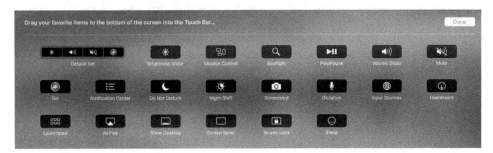

The next part is going to seem a little weird at first. To add a tool to the Touch Bar, click, hold, and drag the tool from the palette to the Touch Bar. This means you will drag it to the bottom of your screen and on to the Touch Bar. The tool will appear highlighted on the Touch Bar. Drag it left or right on the Touch Bar. Other tools will move out of the way. When the tool is in your desired location, release your hold. What seems a little weird at first is the fact that you can control icons on the Touch Bar, which is off your desktop with with your trackpad or mouse.

Removing a tool from the Touch Bar is equally weird the first time you try it. Move your pointer to the bottom of your desktop and keep going until a tool on the Touch Bar becomes highlighted. Move left or right to highlight the desired tool. Click, hold, and drag the tool up from the Touch Bar and back on to the tools palette and release.

To rearrange the tools on your Touch Bar, move your pointer to the bottom of your desktop and keep going until a tool on the Touch Bar becomes highlighted. Move left or right until the tool you want to move is highlighted. Click, hold, and drag the tool to your desired location and release.

Tap **Done** on the Touch Bar or click **Done** on the tools palette when finished.

Customize Safari App Controls

A number of applications allow you to customize the tools on the Touch Bar, allowing you to add, remove, and rearrange them to your liking. Check the application's **View** menu to see if it allows you to customize the Touch Bar. The default Safari App Controls are shown below with the Control Strip in its usual spot on the right side of the Touch Bar.

To customize the Safari tools on the Touch Bar, launch Safari and select **View > Customize Touch Bar...** to reveal the Safari tool palette.

To add a tool to the Touch Bar, click, hold, and drag the tool from the Safari tools palette to the Touch Bar until the tool appears highlighted on the Touch Bar. Drag it left or right until the tool is in your desired location then release your hold. Note that you cannot drag an application tool to the minimized Control Strip on the right of the Touch Bar.

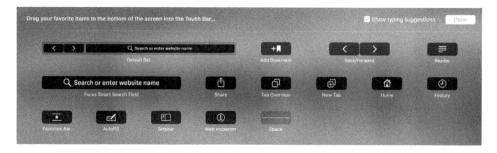

To remove a tool from the Touch Bar, move your pointer to the bottom of your desktop and keep going until a tool on the Touch Bar becomes highlighted. Move left or right until the tool you want to remove is highlighted. Click, hold, and drag the tool up from the Touch Bar and back on to the Safari tools palette and release.

To rearrange the tools on your Touch Bar, move your pointer to the bottom of your desktop and keep going until a tool on the Touch Bar becomes highlighted. Move left or right until the tool you want to move is highlighted. Click, hold, and drag the tool to your desired location and release.

To return to the default Safari Touch Bar, drag and drop the **Default Set** from the Safari tool palette on to the Touch Bar.

Tap **Done** on the Touch Bar or click **Done** on the Safari tools palette when finished.

Customize Mail App Controls

To customize the Mail tools on the Touch Bar, launch Mail and select **View > Customize Touch Bar...** to reveal the Mail tool palette. The default Mail App Controls are shown below.

To add a tool to the Touch Bar, click, hold, and drag the tool from the Mail tools palette to the Touch Bar until the tool appears highlighted on the Touch Bar. Drag it left or right until the tool is in your desired location then release your hold. Note that you cannot drag an application tool to the minimized Control Strip on the right of the Touch Bar.

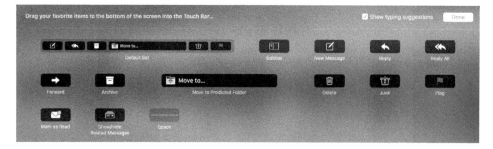

To remove a tool from the Touch Bar, move your pointer to the bottom of your desktop and keep going until a tool on the Touch Bar becomes highlighted. Move left or right until the tool you want to remove is highlighted. Click, hold, and drag the tool up from the Touch Bar and back on to the Mail tools palette and release.

To rearrange the tools on your Touch Bar, move your pointer to the bottom of your desktop and keep going until a tool on the Touch Bar becomes highlighted. Move left or right until the tool you want to move is highlighted. Click, hold, and drag the tool to your desired location and release.

To return to the default Mail Touch Bar, drag and drop the **Default Set** from the Mail tool palette on to the Touch Bar.

Tap **Done** on the Touch Bar or click **Done** on the Mail tools palette when finished.

Configure the Touch Bar to show the Function Keys in a Specific App

If you have an application that utilizes the **F1** to **F12** function keys, macOS lets you configure the Touch Bar to display the function keys when running that application. This is a handy feature that eliminates the need to press the **fn** (function) key to toggle between the Control Strip and the **F** keys.

To configure the Touch Bar to show the function keys in a specific application, open the **keyboard** preference pane from System Preferences. Click on the **Shortcuts** tab if it is not already highlighted. Select **Function Keys** from the left pane. Click the **+** at the bottom of the right pane. Choose the application from the list.

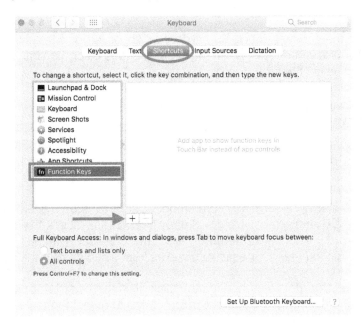

The Touch Bar will always show the strip of function keys when you run that application.

To delete an application, click the **–** button at the bottom left of the right pane.

Enable Touch Bar Zoom

If you are having difficulties seeing the tools on the Touch Bar, you can enable Touch Bar zoom. Touch Bar zoom will display a zoomed Touch Bar on your desktop.

Open the **Accessibility** preference pane in System Preferences. Scroll down to **Zoom** in the left pane. Check the checkbox next to **Enable Touch Bar Zoom**.

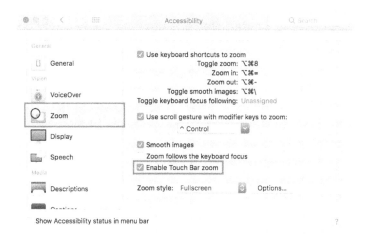

To zoom the Touch Bar, hold a finger on the Touch Bar instead of tapping. To increase or decrease the zoom, press and hold the ⌘ (command) key while pinching two fingers open or closed on the Touch Bar.

To select a tool on the zoomed Touch Bar, slide your finger left or right until the circle on the desktop is on your desired tool. When the circle changes color, you can lift your finger off the Touch Bar to select the tool.

Lock Your Mac with the Touch Bar

If you're tired of your roommate or kids posting stupid stuff on Twitter or Facebook when you leave the room with your Mac on, you can customize the Touch Bar to add a tool to quickly lock your Mac.

First, open the **Security & Privacy** preference pane in the System Preferences application. Click the **General** tab if it is not already highlighted. Check the checkbox next to **Require password**. Choose **immediately** from the drop-down menu. Enabling this feature will require you to enter your password wakes from sleep or from the screen saver.

Next, open the **Keyboard** preference pane, click the **Keyboard** tab if not already highlighted. Click the **Customize Control Strip...** button to reveal the tools palette. Drag the **Screen Lock** tool onto the Control Strip or Expanded Control Strip. Tap **Done** on the Touch Bar or click **Done** on the tools palette when finished.

Now you can lock your Mac by simply tapping the Screen Lock tool on the Touch Bar.

17

Safari

 For most users, **Safari** requires little customization and can be operated in an "out-of-the-box" mode. But if you have made it this far, you and I both know that you are not like most users. There is a lot of customization that can be done to fine tune Safari, change its appearance, and make it perform better.

Customize the Toolbar

The **Toolbar**, located at the top of the Safari window, provides a number of tools to enhance your web browsing experience. You can customize the **Toolbar**, adding, removing, and rearranging the tools as you see fit. Secondary click in any open area of the Toolbar to reveal a contextual menu with a single option to **Customize Toolbar...**, which reveals a drop-down tools palette with the entire selection of tools available.

The tools palette allows you to add additional tools to the Toolbar by dragging and dropping them onto the Toolbar. Any extensions that offer their own tool will also be shown on the tools palette. To add a tool to the Toolbar, drag and drop it. Existing tools located on the Toolbar can be rearranged by dragging them. A tool is removed by dragging it off the Toolbar and onto the drop-down tools palette.

The tools are available include the **iCloud Tabs** tool, which displays the websites open in tabs on other devices associated with your iCloud account including your iPhone and iPad.

The **Share** button lets you share an item via Mail, Messages, Airdrop, or through a number of third party extensions. macOS will list your recent shares under **Recents**, allowing you to quickly share an item. To configure the third party extensions available in the **Share Menu**, click the Share button and select **More...** or by opening the **Extensions** preference pane from System Preferences. Select **Share Menu** in the left column if not already selected. Use the checkboxes to select which third party extensions you wish to make available in the Share drop-down menu.

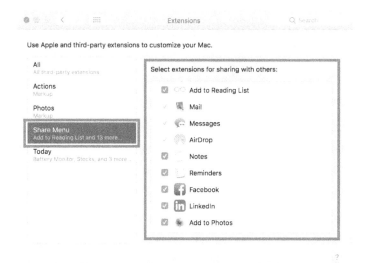

Back to the Safari toolbar, the **Show/Exit Tab Overview** button allows you to view all the pages open in Safari as tabs, small thumbnails of the pages. This lets you quickly jump to a page simply by clicking on it. The **Top Sites** tool shows you your Top Sites, which are websites you frequently visit. The **Home** tool will take you to the Home page configured in Safari's General preferences.

The **History** tool displays a history of webpages you have previously visited. The **Sidebar** tool toggles the Safari sidebar on and off. Safari's sidebar displays your bookmarks, reading list, and shared links. The **Favorites Bar** tool toggles the Safari's favorites bar on and off. The Favorites Bar conveniently lists the websites in your Favorites bookmark folder in a bar just below the Safari toolbar.

The **Autofill** tool tells Safari to automatically fill website forms with data such as your name, address, email, and phone number. The **Zoom** tool does what you would expect it to do – zooming in and out. The **Mail** tool lets you share a webpage via Mail. The **Print** tool lets you print a webpage.

Any third party tools that you have added are located after the search bar. In the picture of the toolbar palette, you will see that I have added tools for **1Password** and **Evernote**. The **Flexible Space** tool is used to space out the tools in the toolbar by adding a blank space between them. Click the **Done** button when finished customizing your Safari toolbar.

To revert back to the default set of tools, drag the default set onto the toolbar and click **Done**.

Tools located on the Toolbar can be rearranged without having to use the drop-down tools palette. To move a tool, hold the ⌘ (command) key down while dragging the tool to its new location. You can also use the ⌘ (command) key to remove a tool. Hold down the ⌘ (command) key while dragging the tool off the Toolbar.

Change the Default Browser

Safari is the default browser in macOS High Sierra. The default browser is the browser that is launched when you click on a link in an email or another application. While it may seem odd, Apple allows you to choose another browser installed on your Mac as the default. If you want to change the **Default web browser**, open the **General** preference pane in the System Preferences application.

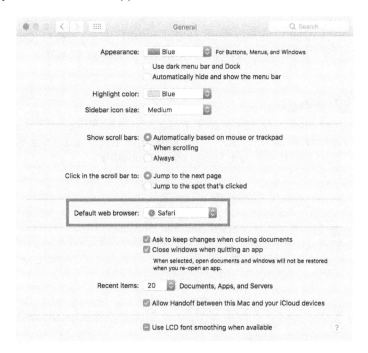

Note that you will have to install other browsers first. Firefox and Chrome are the usual suspects. Both are available at no cost. Firefox is available at https://www.mozilla.org and Chrome can be downloaded at https://www.google.com/chrome/. Once you have other browsers installed on your Mac, they will be listed in the menu next to **Default web browser**.

Configure Your Home Page

Your **Home Page** is the page your browser will navigate to when you click the **Home** button in Safari's toolbar. You also can configure Safari to open new windows and tabs using your Home Page. To configure your Home Page, browse to the site you want as your home page. Next, open the Safari preferences by choosing **Safari > Preferences...** or enter ⌘, (command+,). Click the **General** icon at the top of the pane if it is not already selected.

Safari is configured with Apple's home page as the default. Click **Set to Current Page** or type the URL of your desired Home Page in the field next to **Homepage**.

Choose How Safari Opens

From the General tab of the Safari preference pane, you can configure Safari to start with **A new window**, **A new private window**, or **All windows from last session**. Make your selection from the drop-down menu next to **Safari opens with**.

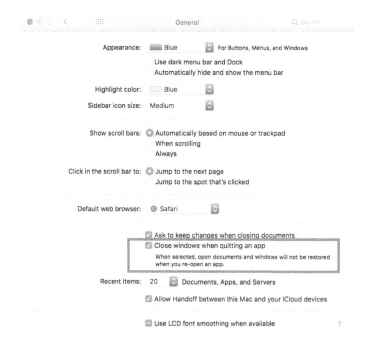

If this option is not shown, you have disabled the feature **Close windows when quitting an application**. To enable, open the **General** preference pane in the System Preferences application and check the box next to **Close windows when quitting an application**.

Choose How New Windows & Tabs Open

Safari offers a number of choices with which to open new windows. To configure how Safari opens new windows and tabs, open the Safari preferences by choosing **Safari > Preferences...** or enter ⌘, (command+,).   Click the **General** icon at the top of the pane.

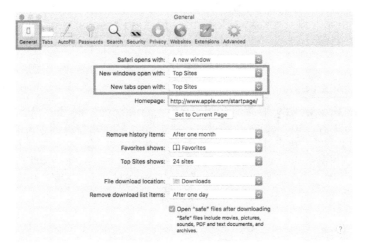

The drop down menu next to **New windows open with** allows you to choose from **Favorites**, a **Homepage** of your choosing, an **Empty Page**, the **Same Page** which you most recently viewed, with **Tabs for Favorites**, or a set of tabs using a **Tabs folder** of your choosing. The default is for Safari to open new windows with Favorites from your Favorites bookmarks folder.

The drop down menu next to **New tabs open with** allows you to choose from **Favorites**, a **Homepage** of your choosing, an **Empty Page**, or the **Same Page** which you most recently viewed. By default, Safari opens new windows and new tabs with your Favorites.

Add a Website to your Favorites

To add a website to your Favorites, click on the URL search bar to reveal your Favorites list. Drag and drop the website into your Favorites.

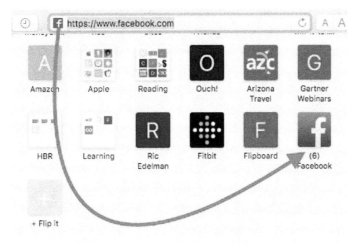

Manage Bookmarks

To manage your **Bookmarks**, select **Bookmarks > Edit Bookmarks** or enter ⌥⌘B (option+command+B) to launch the Bookmarks Editor. From the Bookmarks Editor, you can drag, drop, rearrange, delete, and add Bookmarks or Bookmark folders. To hide the Bookmark Editor when finished, select **Bookmarks > Hide Bookmarks Editor**, enter ⌥⌘B (option+command+B), click on a Bookmark to go to a website, or enter a URL in the address and search field.

Hide Frequently Visited Sites

Safari collects your **Frequently Visited** websites automatically, keeping track of the sites you visit most frequently and displaying them under your **Favorites**. If you do not want to see your most frequently visited sites, you can hide them by selecting **Bookmarks > Show Frequently Visited in Favorites**. When there is a checkmark next to this option in the drop-down menu, your Frequently Visited sites will be shown underneath your Favorites.

Show the Favorites Bar

Safari displays your Favorites when opening a new window or tab. What if you want quick access to your Favorites without having to open a new window or tab? If you want your Favorites available at all times, select **View > Show Favorites Bar** or enter ⇧⌘B (shift+command+B). The Favorites Bar will appear directly below the Safari toolbar. Enter ⇧⌘B (shift+command+B) to toggle the Favorites Bar off.

Select Your Favorites Source

Safari sources the websites for **Favorites** from the Favorites folder in your Bookmarks. You can change the default source for Favorites to any of your other Bookmark folders. This comes in handy if you configured Safari to display the Favorites Bar and want a Bookmarks folder to be used as your Favorites when opening a new window or tab.

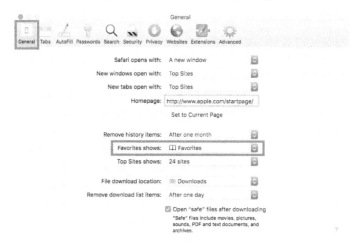

To change the folder used for Favorites, open the Safari preferences by choosing **Safari >
Preferences...** or enter ⌘, (command+,).   Click on the **General** tab if it is not already
highlighted. Select your desired Bookmarks folder using the drop-down menu next to
Favorites shows.

Configure Top Sites

Top Sites is another method Safari uses to collect sites that you visit most often. You can
configure Safari to keep 6, 12, or 24 sites in the Top Sites list.

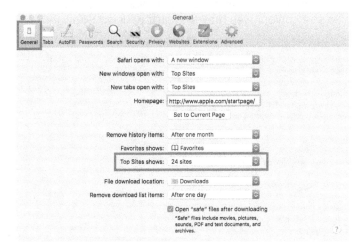

To configure the number of sites in the Top Sites list, open the Safari preferences by
choosing **Safari > Preferences...** or enter ⌘, (command+,).   Click the **General** icon at
the top of the pane if it is not already selected. Choose 6, 12, or 24 sites in the drop-down
list next to **Top Sites show**.

Add a Top Site

Adding a website to the **Top Sites** list is accomplished by dragging the website from the
address and search field to the Top Sites tool on the Safari toolbar as shown below.
When the big green **+** appears release your hold.

Organize your Top Sites

To rearrange, organize, and delete your Top Sites, click on the **Top Sites** button from the
Safari Favorites view.

Drag and drop the website thumbnails to rearrange them. To pin them permanently, click and hold until you see a blue stick pin appear in the upper left corner of the thumbnail. Click on the stick pin to pin the website to your Top Sites list. Click the **X** to delete a site.

Remove Your Browsing History

Safari will maintain a history of all websites you have visited. This is a handy feature if you want to return to a website but didn't bookmark it. You can view your browsing history by date in Safari by selecting **History > Show History** or by entering ⌘Y (command+Y). Select **History > Hide History** or enter ⌘Y (command+Y) to hide your web browsing history. You can also search your web browsing history using Spotlight.

The length of time Safari will keep your history is configurable to one day, one week, two weeks, one month, one year, or manually. Make your selection from the drop-down list next to **Remove history items** in the **General** tab of the Safari preference pane.

Choose Where to Save Downloaded Files

Safari saves downloaded files to the **Downloads** folder by default. You can change this location to any folder by choosing **Other...** in the drop-down list next to **Save downloaded files to**. Navigate to your desired location and press the **Select** button. You can also configure Safari to ask you for the save location each time you download a file. Choose **Ask for each download** to select this option.

Safari maintains a list of all files downloaded. By default, this list is cleared after one day. You can configure Safari to remove this list when Safari quits, upon successfully downloading the file, or manually in the drop-down list next to **Remove download list items**.

Safari will automatically open movies, pictures, sounds, PDF files, text documents, and archives upon downloading. You can change this behavior by unchecking the checkbox next to **Open "safe" files after downloading** in the General tab in the Safari preference pane.

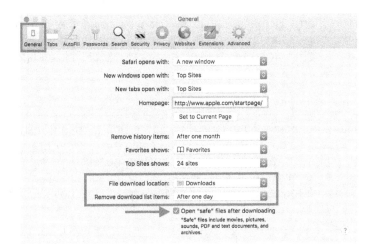

Open Web Pages in New Windows

Safari opens new pages in tabs unless the page is designed for a specially formatted window. To configure how Safari opens new pages, open the Safari preferences by choosing **Safari > Preferences...** or enter **⌘,** (command+,). Click the **Tabs** icon at the top of the pane if it is not already selected.

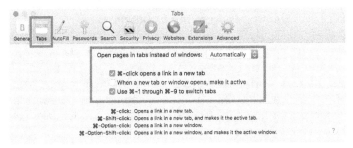

Open pages in tabs instead of windows is set to **Automatically** by default. Two other configuration options are available – **Never** or **Always**. **Never** will open all pages in a new Safari window. If you choose **Always**, Safari will create a new tab even if a website requests a window of a particular size.

Holding down the ⌘ (command) key while clicking on a link opens a new tab. To turn this feature off uncheck the checkbox next to **⌘-click opens a new link in a new tab**. Holding the ⇧⌘ keys (shift+command) when clicking on a link opens a new tab and makes it the active tab. Holding the ⇧⌥ keys (shift+option) while clicking a link opens it in a new window. Holding the ⇧⌥⌘ keys (shift+option+command) while clicking a link opens it in a new window and makes it active.

You can choose to make a new tab or new window active when it opens by checking the checkbox next to **When a new tab or window opens, make it active**. This feature is disabled by default.

A new option in High Sierra is the ability to switch tabs using the ⌘ (command) key combined with the numbers 1 through 9. This option is enabled by default. Uncheck the checkbox next to **Use ⌘-1 through ⌘-9 to switch tabs** to disable this feature.

Edit Autofill

Safari's **Autofill** feature automatically inserts data into online forms including your name, address, user name, password, credit card, or other information you previously entered into a web form. If you need to change this information because you moved, changed your login credentials, or received a new credit card, you can edit the information saved in Autofill from the Safari preference pane. Click on the **Autofill** tab if not selected already.

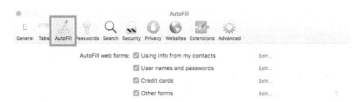

Safari will autofill information from your contacts card, which consists of your name, address, city, state, zip code and phone number. This feature is handy when filling out shipping information when making an online purchase. To edit your contact information, click the **Edit** button next to **Using info from my Contacts card**.

Safari securely saves your login credentials and will automatically enter your user name and password when you revisit a website. To edit your login credentials, click the **Edit** button next to **User names and passwords**. The tab will immediately jump to the **Passwords** tab and list all websites for which user names and passwords have or have not been stored. Double-click any item to edit your stored credentials. Enter your user name and password when challenged.

Safari securely saves your credit card number, expiration date, and cardholder name and automatically enters this information when needed to complete a purchase. To edit your credit card information, click the **Edit** button next to **Credit cards**. Double-click on a stored credit card to edit it. Enter your user name and password when challenged. You can also **Add** new credit cards or **Remove** old ones. Click **Done** when finished.

The **Other forms** attribute allows Safari to save information entered on web forms and automatically enters the information when you revisit the same webpage. To view or edit, click the **Edit** button next to **Other forms**. Safari will provide a list of all websites where you filled out a webform of some type. You can **Remove** any site or **Remove All**. Click **Done** when finished.

If you use **iCloud Keychain**, the information stored by Safari is available to your iOS devices and other Macs using the same Apple ID. Information modified on any device is updated in iCloud. Similarly, if you change your address or phone number in the **Contacts** application in either macOS or iOS, the changes will be updated through iCloud to all your Apple devices. This is the reason why it is very important to use only a single Apple ID for all your Apple devices.

Turn Off Autofill

Autofill automatically fills online web forms with your name, address, user name, password, credit card, or other information. All of these options are enabled by default. Any option can be disabled by unchecking the checkbox next to the category. Uncheck all the checkboxes to completely disable autofill.

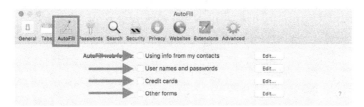

Manage Login Credentials

Safari securely saves your user names and passwords, automatically entering your login credentials the next time you visit a website.

Open the Safari preferences by choosing **Safari > Preferences...** or enter ⌘, (command+,). Click the **Passwords** tab at the top of the pane if it is not already selected. The **Passwords** tab lists all websites for which login credentials have been stored. Highlight any site to edit the user name or password or to **Remove** your credentials. Enter your user name and password when challenged. You can also use the search field to find websites, user names, or passwords.

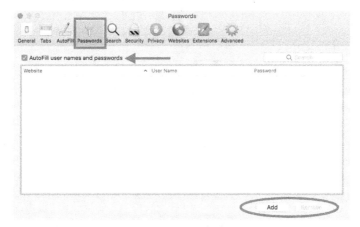

To add credentials for a website, click the **Add** button. Enter the website address, user name, and password in the fields provided.

To see the password for any site, check the checkbox next to **Show passwords for selected websites**. Click on any site to see the password.

Stop Safari from Saving Login Credentials

Safari saves user names and passwords you enter on websites. If you do not want Safari to save your login credentials, uncheck the box next to **AutoFill user names and passwords** to disable this feature.

Recall a Forgotten Password

If you cannot recall a password for a particular website, you can retrieve your lost password from the Passwords tab of the Safari preference pane. Enter your user name and password when challenged. When you click on any of the websites, Safari will display your password.

Change the Search Engine

You can choose the search engine Safari uses for web searches. Open the Safari preferences by choosing **Safari > Preferences...** or enter ⌘, (command+,). Click the **Search** tab at the top of the pane if it is not already selected.

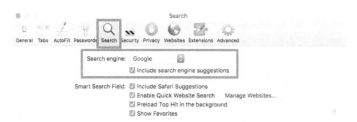

Choose your preferred search engine from the drop-down list next to **Search engine**. You can choose from **Google**, **Yahoo**, **Bing**, or **DuckDuckGo**.

Checking the checkbox next to **Include search engine suggestions** allows Safari to query your chosen search engine for suggestions as you type your search terms. When the checkbox next to **Include Safari Suggestions** checked, Safari will suggest news, Wikipedia articles, iTunes music, weather, sports, stocks, and help from Apple as you type in Safari's Smart Search field.

Enable Quick Website Search lets Safari record information about your searches to speed up future searches. With this feature enabled, you can search within a website by entering the site's name followed by the search term in Safari's search field. You can see and remove a site for which Safari recorded search information by clicking the **Manage Websites...** button. Click on any website to highlight it and click **Remove.** You have the option of removing all websites by clicking **Remove All.** Click **Done** when finished.

When **Preload Top Hit in the background** is enabled, Safari will begin to load the top search hit.

Disable Favorites View

The **Favorites View** is enabled by default and will display your favorite websites as icons below Safari's address and search field. Simply click the address and search field to display your favorite and frequently visited sites. Safari can also be configured to open all of your Favorites in tabs when opening a new Safari window. This feature is enabled in the General tab of the Safari preference pane using the drop-down list next to **New windows open with** and selecting **Tabs for Favorites**.

To disable the Favorites View, open the Safari preference pane by choosing **Safari > Preferences...** or enter ⌘, (command+,). Click the **Search** tab at the top of the pane if it is not already selected. Uncheck the box next the **Show Favorites**.

Block Fraudulent Websites

Safari warns you if a website you are attempting to visit is suspected to be a fraudulent website running a phishing scam. Phishing is an attempt by cyber criminals to trick you into divulging personal information such as your user name, password, social security number, credit card numbers, or banking information.

Most phishing attempts start as a fake email that appears to be from a bank, credit card company, or major retailer alerting you that you must take care of something immediately otherwise your account will be suspended or closed. The links in the email direct you to a fraudulent website that appears to be the real thing. If you enter your login credentials or other personal information, it will be captured by a cyber criminal, who will use your information to make fraudulent purchases, steal money from your accounts, or steal your identity.

Safari will warn you if you visit a website that has been reported as fraudulent when the checkbox next to **Warn when visiting a fraudulent website** is checked. I strongly recommend you do not disable this security feature.

Allow Pop-Up Windows

Safari blocks annoying pop-up windows by default. However, some websites use pop-up windows to display essential content. If you want to allow pop-up windows, open the Safari preference pane by choosing **Safari > Preferences...** or enter ⌘, (command+,). Click the **Search** tab at the top of the pane if it is not already selected. Uncheck the box next to **Block pop-up windows** when you want to view pop-up windows from certain websites.

Check the checkbox when you want Safari to again block pop-up windows.

Prevent Website Tracking

Safari version 11 in macOS High Sierra introduced Intelligent Tracking Prevention to help protect your privacy. Intelligent Tracking Prevention makes it more difficult for advertisers to gather data about your browsing habits in order to deliver targeting advertising to you. As you would expect advertisers are furious. Thank you Apple.

With **Prevent cross-site tracking** enabled, website tracking data is periodically deleted, making it harder for an advertiser to track you across different websites. When **Ask websites not to track me** is enabled, Safari will ask websites and their third-party content providers to not track you. Each time you visit a website, Safari will send a request to not track you. However, it is up to the website to honor this request.

Block Website Cookies

Safari allows you to block websites, third parties, and advertisers from storing cookies on your Mac. Cookies are small amounts of data that a website sends and stores on your Mac. Every time you go back to a website that sent Safari a cookie, Safari will send the cookie back. Cookies can be used to compile records of your browsing activity and can store passwords and credit card information and are therefore, a privacy concern. Safari allows you to remove and block cookies that websites and third parties use to track you.

You have the option to **Block all cookies** n the **Privacy** tab in the Safari preference pane, which will stop websites, third-party content providers, and advertisers from storing cookies on your Mac. However, doing so often prevents many websites from not working properly. For example, your bank's website will not recognize you and ask you challenge questions to verify your identity and may not work at all.

You probably already have cookies stored on your Mac. Safari will let you see which websites have stored cookies on your Mac and remove some or all of them. Click **Manage Website Data...** to see which websites have stored cookies on your Mac. To remove individual website cookies, select the website and click **Remove**. You also have the option to **Remove All**. Click **Done** when finished.

Disable Apple Pay

You can use Apple Pay to pay for purchases you make online. By default, Safari will **Allow websites to check if Apple Pay is set up**. The Apple Pay feature requires your Mac to have a Touch ID. If your Mac does not have a Touch ID, the website will check to see if you have Apple Pay set up on an iPhone or Apple Watch. If you want to disable this feature and stop websites from checking to see if Apple Pay is set up, open the Safari preference pane and select the **Privacy** tab. Uncheck the checkbox next to **Allow websites to check if Apple Pay is set up**.

Browse the Web in Private

If you prefer to browse the web in private, you can enable Safari's **Private Browsing** mode by selecting **File > New Private Window** or by pressing ⇧⌘N (shift+command+N) to open a new Private Browsing window. Safari will not save your browsing history and asks all websites you visit to not track you.

When Private Browsing is enabled, the address and search field will change to white letters on a dark background. When in Private Browsing mode, each tab is isolated from the others, so a website in one tab cannot track your browsing in another tab. Note that Autofill does not work when in Private Browsing mode and Safari will not store open webpages in iCloud or save your browsing history.

To stop using the Private Browsing feature, close the Private Browsing window and open a new Safari window by selecting **File > New Window** or by entering ⌘N (command+N).

Safari Push Notifications

Websites supporting Apple's push notification service can send notifications of breaking news, sports, a new post, or other relevant info. These notifications will appear on your desktop and in Notification Center. Before a website can send you push notifications, you must choose to opt in. If a website supports push notifications, you'll be asked if you would like to receive notifications when browsing to the website in Safari. Click **Allow** to opt in or **Don't Allow** to opt out. Don't worry, you can always change your mind later. You can configure how you receive these notifications in the Notifications preference pane in System Preferences.

If you no longer find notifications from a particular website useful, you can opt out. Similarly, if you opted out, you can opt back in.

To change your Safari notification choice, open the Safari preference pane and select the **Websites** tab. The websites that have asked for permission to send you push notifications will be listed. Next to each website is a drop-down menu with two choices: **Allow** and **Deny** with the current status displayed.

If you wish to delete a website from the list, highlight it and click the **Remove** button. If you would prefer that websites not ask you to opt in to their push notification service, uncheck the checkbox next to **Allow websites to ask for permission to send push notifications**. Checking this checkbox stops websites from asking you if you want to receive notifications from them.

Stop Websites from Snooping on Your Location

Websites can spy on your location. This can be quite handy if location information is necessary to deliver relevant content like the local weather or news. However, sometimes there is absolutely no reason for a particular website to know your location. Safari can be configured to ask your permission before providing your location information to a website that asks for it.

To change your location setting, open the Safari preference pane by selecting **Safari > Preferences...** or enter ⌘, (command+,). Click on **Location** in the left pane, which will populate a list in the right pane of currently open websites and those for which you have configured a location policy. **Allow** or **Deny** will be listed in the right pane for each website. You can change the action for any website using the drop-down menu.

To stop websites from snooping on your location, select **Deny** from the drop-down menu next to **When visiting other websites:** at the lower right corner of the preference pane. You also have the option of **Ask** or **Allow**. When **Ask** is selected, Safari will ask you if you want to provide your location each time a website asks for your location.

Display Web Articles without Annoying Ads

Nothing is more annoying than a web page filled with obnoxiously large amounts of advertising. Safari can be configured to default to **Safari Reader**, which removes the annoying advertising to display a clean, readable version of a website article.

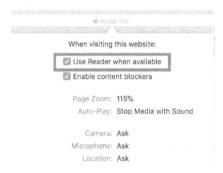

To force a website to use Safari reader, hold down the ^ (control) key while clicking on the URL in the Safari Smart Search field. Next, click on **Settings for This Website...** from the contextual menu to reveal the website settings. Check the checkbox next to **Use Reader when available.** Once you have made your selection, click anywhere to make this dialog box disappear.

To configure websites to default to Safari Reader view, open the Safari preference pane by selecting **Safari > Preferences...** or enter ⌘, (command+,). Click on the **Websites** tab and then select **Reader** in the left pane. The right pane will populate with a list of currently open websites and their Safari Reader configuration. Select **On** or **Off** in the drop-down menu next in the column to the right of each website. **On** configures the website to use the Safari Reader by default for all content on the website.

To configure Safari to always default to the Safari Reader view, select **On** from the drop-down list next to **When visiting other websites**. Website articles will automatically use Safari Reader allowing you to enjoy the article sans advertising.

Configure Website Content Blocking

A content blocker blocks annoying advertisements and third-party tracking scripts in order to protect your privacy and enhance your web browsing experience.

To see enable your content blocker for a website, hold down the ^ (control) key while clicking on the URL in the Safari Smart Search field. Next, click on **Settings for This Website...** from the contextual menu to reveal the website settings. Check the checkbox next to **Enable content blockers.** Once you have made your selection, click anywhere to make this dialog box disappear.

To ensure your content blocker is enabled for all websites, open the Safari preference pane by selecting **Safari > Preferences...** or enter ⌘, (command+,). Click on the **Websites** tab and then select **Content Blockers** in the left pane. The right pane will populate with a list of currently open websites and their content blocker setting.

To change a setting for a currently open website, select **On** or **Off** from the drop-down menu next to the website name. On blocks ads and other unwanted content from appearing on the website. Off will not block ads and other unwanted content.

To enable your content blocker for all websites, select **On** from the drop-down menu next to **When visiting other websites:** in the lower right corner of the preference pane.

Stop Obnoxious Auto-Play Videos

There is nothing worse than opening a bunch of tabs in Safari and then being assaulted by a cacaphony of video advertising blaring out of your speakers. You don't have to hunt down each one to kill or mute the annoying advertisement. A feature in Safari 11.0 allows you to selectively block auto-play videos.

To block website videos from auto-playing, hold down the ^ (control) key while clicking on the URL in the Safari Smart Search field. Next, click on **Settings for This Website...** from the contextual menu to reveal the website settings. From the drop-down menu next to **Auto-Play**, make your selection from the the available options of **Allow All Auto-Play**, **Stop Media with Sound**, or **Never Auto-Play**. Once you have made your selection, click anywhere to make this dialog box disappear. Note that you still can watch the videos by clicking the video play button if you chose **Stop Media with Sound** or **Never Auto-Play**.

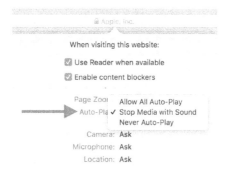

macOS allows you to preemptively block video auto-play for all websites. To block auto-play video for all websites, open the Safari preference pane by selecting **Safari > Preferences...** or enter ⌘, (command+,). Click on the **Websites** tab and then select **Auto-Play** in the left pane. The right pane will populate with a list of currently open websites and their auto-play settings.

To block auto-play video for all websites, select **Never Auto-Play** from the drop-down menu next to **When visiting other websites:** in the lower right corner of the preference pane.

To change any individual setting, use the drop-down menu to the right of the website name. You have the choice of **Allow All Auto-Play**, **Stop Media with Sound**, and **Never Auto-Play.**

Set Website Page Zoom

You can set the page zoom in Safari so that text and images appear larger (or smaller). Page zoom can be set individually by website or you can set a default page zoom for all websites.

To set the page zoom for a website, hold down the ^ (control) key while clicking on the URL in the Safari Smart Search field. Next, click on **Settings for This Website...** from the contextual menu to reveal the website settings. From the drop-down menu next to **Page Zoom**, make a selection from the the available zoom options. Once you have made your selection, click anywhere to make this dialog box disappear.

To set the page zoom for websites, open the Safari preference pane by selecting **Safari > Preferences...** or enter ⌘, (command+,). Click on the **Websites** tab and then select **Page Zoom** in the left pane. The right pane will populate with a a list of currently open websites and those for which you have configured a page zoom policy. To change any individual setting, use the drop-down menu to the right of the website name. You have the choice of **50%, 75%, 85%, 100%, 115%, 125%, 150%, 175%, 200%, 250%,** and **300%**.

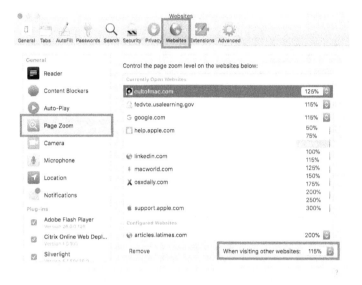

To change the page zoom for all websites, select your desired page zoom setting from the drop-down menu next to **When visiting other websites:** in the lower right corner.

Control Camera and Microphone Access

Safari version 11 allows you to control the access to your Mac's camera and microphone.

To set the camera and microphone preferences for a website, hold down the ^ (control) key while clicking on the URL in the Safari Smart Search field. Next, click on **Settings for This Website...** from the contextual menu to reveal the website settings. From the drop-down menu next to **Camera** and **Microphone**, make a selection from the the available zoom options of **Ask**, **Deny**, or **Allow**. Once you have made your selection, click anywhere to make the dialog box disappear.

To set the camera and microphone settings for websites, open the Safari preference pane by selecting **Safari > Preferences…** or enter ⌘, (command+,). Click on the **Websites** tab and then select **Camera** or **Microphone** in the left pane. The right pane will populate with a list of currently open websites and their settings. To change an individual setting, use the drop-down menu to the right of the website name. You have the choice of **Ask**, **Deny**, or **Allow**.

To change the camera and microphone settings for all websites, select your desired setting zoom from the drop-down menu next to **When visiting other websites:** in the lower right corner of the preference pane.

Set a Policy for Internet Plug-Ins

You can control whether Safari will show plug-in content on websites. Plug-ins are used to show pictures, music, videos, animation, and other interactive features. To see which plug-ins have been installed and which websites are using them, open the Safari preference pane by selecting **Safari > Preferences...** or by entering ⌘, (command+,). Select the **Websites** tab at the top of the pane if it is not already selected. Next, scroll down to the **Plug-ins** in the left pane and choose a plug-in. The right pane will populate with a list of currently open websites and those for which you have configured a plug-in policy. To change any individual setting, use the drop-down menu to the right of the website name. You have the choice of **Ask**, **Off**, or **On**.

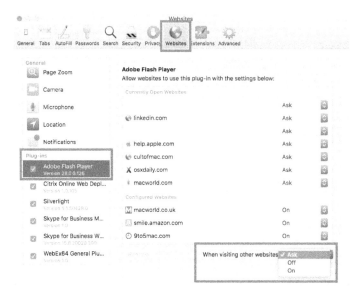

The **Ask** setting will configure Safari to ask you if the website can use the plug-in. When **Off** is set, Safari will display a placeholder instead of the plug-in content. Clicking on the placeholder will allow the website to use the plug-in. **On** lets the website use the plug-in unless it has been blocked by macOS File Quarantine.

To configure a global policy for an Internet plug-in, select **Ask**, **Off**, or **On** from the drop-down list next to **When visiting other websites**: in the lower right corner of the preference pane.

Manage Third Party Extensions

Extensions are small applications created by third party developers to enhance your web browsing experience.

The **Extensions** tab in the Safari preference pane allows you to selectively enable or disable an extension, configure them if they have options, or uninstall them. Until you have installed Extensions, this pane will be empty.

The Extensions list in the left column shows which extensions have been installed. You can select an extension to show any available options or to **uninstall** it.

The checkbox next to **Automatically update extensions from the Safari Extensions Gallery Updates** is checked by default. Apple recommends that automatic updates be enabled so that your extensions are kept up to date with the latest release.

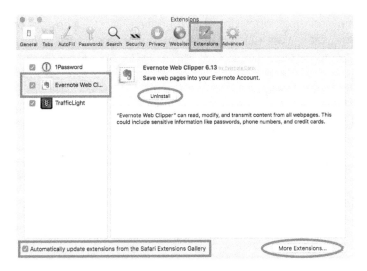

The **More Extensions...** button at the lower right opens the **Safari Extension Gallery** website at https://extensions.apple.com, where you can find extensions to add new features to Safari. Extensions can be installed with one click and there is no need to restart Safari.

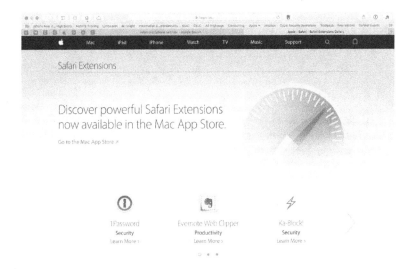

Make Safari Show the URL

One of the default features of Safari's streamlined design is that it does not show the full URL (website address) in its address and search field. Instead Safari only displays the domain name, such as apple.com. Clicking on the address and search field forces Safari to show the full URL, but what if you want the full URL to always be displayed?

Before I show you how to change this feature, a word of caution. Cyber criminals have figured out that we are so used to seeing incredibly long URLs, that we no longer pay much attention to them. Therefore, it is easy for a cyber criminal to trick us into thinking their fake website is actually the real thing. By displaying only the top level domain name,

Safari makes it plain and clear what website you have visited. Also, the padlock, which indicates you are on a secure site using HTTPS, is front and center.

To configure Safari to permanently display the full URL, select **Safari > Preferences...** or by entering ⌘, (command+,) to open the Safari preference pane. Click the **Advanced** tab at the top of the pane if it is not already selected. Check the box next to **Show full website address** next to **Smart Search Field**.

If you only need the URL so that you can copy or share it, clicking in the Safari Smart Search field will reveal the entire URL, already highlighted to make it easier to copy.

Show the Develop Menu

The **Develop Menu** allows you to access commands for developing websites with Safari. By default, the Develop Menu is hidden. To unhide the Develop menu, click **Show Develop menu in menu bar** in the **Advanced** tab of the Safari preference pane.

Pin a Web Site to the Tab Bar

The **Pinned Sites** feature allows you to pin your most frequently visited sites to the left side of the tab bar. Pinned sites refresh in the background, so they are always up to date.

This feature is especially useful if you have a few websites that you like to visit throughout the day, like Facebook or a news site.

To pin a site to the Tab Bar, open the website in a Safari tab. Secondary click on the tab and select **Pin Tab** from the contextual menu. The pinned site will move to the left to join your other pinned sites. Pinned sites can be rearranged by dragging them into place.

You can also pin a site by dragging the site's tab to the left to join your other pinned tabs and dropping it there. Once a site is pinned, you can quickly access it from any Safari window.

To unpin a site, secondary click on it and select **Unpin Tab**. The tab will move to the right to join your other unpinned tabs. You can also drag the pinned tab to the right. To permanently close a pinned tab, select **Close Tab**.

18

Mail

 The default mail client in macOS is an application simply called **Mail**. Other than configuration of mail accounts, Mail requires little customization and can be operated "out-of-the-box." There is a large amount of customization that can be done to fine tune Mail, change its appearance, and make it perform a little better to increase your productivitys.

Change the Mail Application

Mail is the default mail client in macOS. The default mail client is the application that launches when you want to send an email from another application or web link. If you prefer to use another email client Apple allows you to choose one. To change the default email client, open the Mail preference pane by choosing **Mail > Preferences...** or enter ⌘**,** (command+,). Click the **General** icon at the top of the pane if it is not already selected.

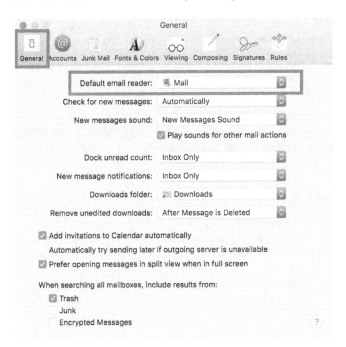

Choose your desired mail client from the drop-down list next to **Default email reader**. For email clients to populate the list, you will first need to download and install them. My favorite alternate mail client is Spark by Readdle. It is available for both macOS and iOS in their respective App Stores. Other options include Airmail 3, Microsoft Outlook, and Postbox. Choosing **Select...** will open a Finder window so you can locate your email application if it is not listed in the drop-down menu.

Change How Frequently Mail Checks for New Email

To change the frequency with which **Mail** checks for new email, open the Mail preference pane by choosing **Mail > Preferences...** or enter ⌘, (command+,). Click the **General** icon at the top of the pane if it is not already selected.

Your choices are **Automatically** (the default), **Every minute**, **Every 5 minutes**, **Every 15 minutes**, **Every 30 minutes**, **Every hour**, or **Manually**. If you select **Manually**, you will have to click the **Get Mail** button in the Toolbar to check for new email.

Change the New Mail Sound

The **New messages sound** allows you to select from a number of sounds to play when a new message arrives. Mail can also be configured to make no sound. Use the drop-down list in the General tab in the Mail preference pane to make your desired selection.

Uncheck the checkbox next to **Play sounds for other mail actions** if you want to disable sounds for other mail actions such as the sound when Mail sends email.

Control the Dock Badge

The **Mail** icon in the Dock displays a red badge showing the count of unread messages. The unread message count can be limited to those messages in the **Inbox Only**, unread messages received **Today**, or all unread messages across **All Mailboxes**.

Change How Mail Notifies You

When new email arrives, macOS will display a notification on your desktop. You can configure the Mail application to notify you when your receive new email in the **Inbox Only**, from **VIPs**, from your **Contacts**, **All Mailboxes** and email received **Today**. The Mail notification style must be configured to Banners or Alerts in the Notifications preference pane in System Preferences.

Choose Where to Save Downloaded Files

By default, Mail saves downloaded attachments to the **Downloads** folder. You can change this location to any folder by choosing **Other...** in the drop-down list next to **Downloads folder** in the General tab of the Mail preference pane. Navigate to your desired location and press the **Select** button.

Mail temporarily saves attachments to the Mail Downloads folder in the Library folder in your **Home** directory. By default, Mail will delete the attachments temporarily stored here when you delete the email containing the attachment. Two other options are **Never** or to delete attachments **When Mail Quits**.

Automatically Add Invitations to Calendar

Invitations you receive in email can be added to the **Calendar** application. To enable this feature, open the Mail preference pane by choosing **Mail > Preferences...** or enter ⌘, (command+,). Check the checkbox next to **Add invitations to calendar automatically**.

Send Later When the Mail Server is Unavailable

By default, Mail will open a dialog box and show other available mail servers if it cannot reach a mail server to send an email. If you prefer that Mail save outbound email messages in the Outbox until it can connect to a mail server at a later time, check the checkbox next **Automatically try sending later if outgoing server is unavailable**.

Open Messages in Split-View

By default, messages will open in Split-View mode when Mail is running in Full-Screen mode. If you do not like this behavior, you can disable it by unchecking the checkbox next to **Prefer opening messages in split view when in full screen**.

Change the Mail Search Scope

When searching mailboxes, you can choose to include results from the **Trash**, **Junk**, or **Encrypted Messages**. By default, only search results from inboxes and the Trash are included. Configure these attributes in the **General** pane of the Mail preferences.

Change Attachment Download Behavior

Mail will automatically download attachments by default. If you prefer to manually download attachments, open the Mail preference pane by choosing **Mail > Preferences...** or enter ⌘, (command+,). Click the **Accounts** tab at the top of the pane if it is not already selected. Next, click on **Account Information**.

Downloading of attachments is configured on a per mailbox basis. Select the mail account in the column at the left. Using the drop-down menu next to **Download Attachments:** select **All**, **Recent**, or **None**. Do the same for other email accounts, if desired.

Change Mailbox Behaviors

You can configure how you want the **Mail** to handle email drafts, sent email, junk email, and email you delete. To configure mailbox behaviors, open the Mail preference pane by choosing **Mail > Preferences...** or enter ⌘, (command+,). Click the **Accounts** icon at the top of the pane if it is not already selected. Next, click on **Mailbox Behaviors**.

Select an email account from the column at the left to configure its mailbox behavior. Draft messages are stored in the iCloud Drafts folder unless you select another folder using the drop-down list next to **Drafts Mailbox:**. The advantage of storing drafts in the iCloud Drafts folder is that draft messages will be available on your other devices. You can choose another folder in which to save draft messages or can choose to save them locally on your Mac. If you save drafts locally, they will not be available on your other devices.

Similarly, email that you have sent is stored in the iCloud Sent folder unless you select another folder using the drop-down list next to **Sent Mailbox:**. You can choose another folder in which to save sent messages or can choose to save them locally on your Mac. If you save sent mail locally, they will not be available on your other devices.

Junk Mail is also stored in iCloud, in the Junk folder unless you select another folder using the drop-down list next to **Junk Mailbox:**. You can choose another folder in which to save junk messages or can choose to save them locally on your Mac. If you save junk mail locally, they will not be available on your other devices.

You can configure Mail to periodically delete junk email messages after one day, one month, one year, when quitting Mail, or Never by selecting your desired option from the drop-down list under **Erase junk messages:**.

Your **Trash Mailbox** is stored in the **Deleted Messages** folder in iCloud unless you select another folder using the drop-down list next to **Trash Mailbox:**. You can choose another folder in which to save deleted email or can choose to save them locally on your Mac in the Mail **Trash** folder. If you save deleted mail locally, they will not be available on your other devices.

You can configure Mail to periodically delete trashed email messages after one day, one month, one year, when quitting Mail, or Never by selecting your desired option from the drop-down list under **Erase deleted messages:**. If you'd like to keep your deleted email, choose the never option. However, it's best to have Mail erase deleted messages automatically.

Mail allows you to archive old email, which is stored in the **Archive** folder in iCloud. Using the drop-down list next to **Archive Mailbox:**, you can choose another folder in which to save archived email.

Change the Mail Drop Threshold

When you try to send an email with an attachment larger than 20 MB, Mail will automatically send the attachment to your iCloud account. If the person you sent your email to is using the Mail application on macOS, the large attachment will be automatically downloaded and included in the email like any other attachment. For those using a different operating system or email client, a link is provided in the email along with its expiration date. The attachment will expire after 30 days.

Some organizations have some pretty draconian limits to attachments. I've seen some companies limit the size of email attachments to 10 MB and even 5 MB. macOS allows you to change the default threshold for **Mail Drop** to a lower threshold. To change the default threshold for Mail Drop, launch Terminal and enter the following commands.

```
defaults write com.apple.mail minSizeKB 10000
```

The 10000 at the end of the command is the Mail Drop threshold in KB. Since 1 MB equals 1,000 KB, 10 MB equals 10,000 KB.

To revert back to the macOS default of 20 MB, enter the following command in Terminal.

```
defaults write com.apple.mail minSizeKB 20000
```

Get Rid of Junk Email

Junk email is annoying and fills up your inbox. Mail has a number of configuration options to make junk email less of an annoyance. To configure junk mail handling rules, click on the **Junk Mail** icon in the Mail preference pane.

Junk email filtering is enabled by default. Uncheck the checkbox next to **Enable junk mail filtering**. You may wish to do so if your email provider already filters junk email or if you want to see all email, junk or not.

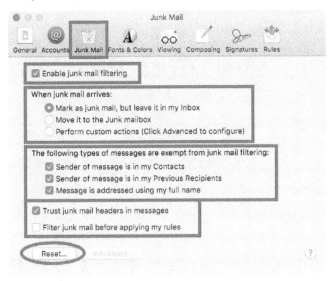

Junk email is left in your inbox where you are given a choice to mark an email as **Not Junk** if it was mistakenly identified as junk. Mail also gives you the option of moving junk email to the junk mailbox or configuring custom actions to identify and handle junk mail. To define custom actions, click the radio button next to **Perform custom actions**. Next, click the **Advanced...** button at the bottom of the preference pane to configure custom actions.

You can exempt email from being considered as junk if the sender is in Contacts, the sender is a Previous Recipient, or the email is addressed to your full name. Use the checkboxes to configure these options, which are all enabled by default.

Trust junk mail header in messages is enabled by default and uses any junk mail detection already present in email you receive to more accurately identify junk email.

You have the option of filtering out junk mail before applying any other mail filtering rules. Doing so, ensures that all email is first evaluated by the junk mail filter before being filtered by any email filtering rules you have created.

A **Reset...** button allows you to restore the default configuration.

Stop Squinting & Make Mail Fonts Bigger

Tired of squinting when trying to read email? There are two methods to increase the font size. You can temporarily increase the font size by using the ⌘+ (command +) keyboard shortcut. Conversely, the ⌘- (command -) decreases the font size.

If you desire a more permanent fix, open **Mail > Preferences...** or enter ⌘, (command+,). Click the **Fonts & Colors** icon at the top of the pane if it is not already selected. You can change the **Message list font**, **Message font**, and the **Fixed-width font**. Click the **Select...** button to change the font and font size.

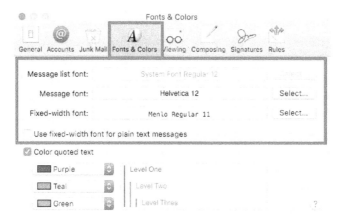

The message list font is used for viewing the list of messages when Mail is in classic layout with the message list above the messages. You can change to classic view by clicking the **Viewing** icon and checking the box next to **Use classic layout**.

The message font is the font used for viewing and writing email. Emails you receive will use this font unless the sender used a specific font in the message.

The fixed-width font is used for viewing and writing plain text email. Make sure you check the box next to **Use fixed-width font for plain text messages**.

You can also change the color of quoted text when replying to messages.

Switch to Classic View

By default, Mail will list messages in a column with the Mail preview pane to its right. Classic layout puts the message list at the top with the preview pane below. If you want to switch to classic layout, open **Mail > Preferences...** or enter ⌘, (command+,).

Click the **Viewing** icon at the top of the pane if it is not already selected. Check the checkbox next to **Use classic layout** to switch to the classic view. Uncheck to revert back to the default.

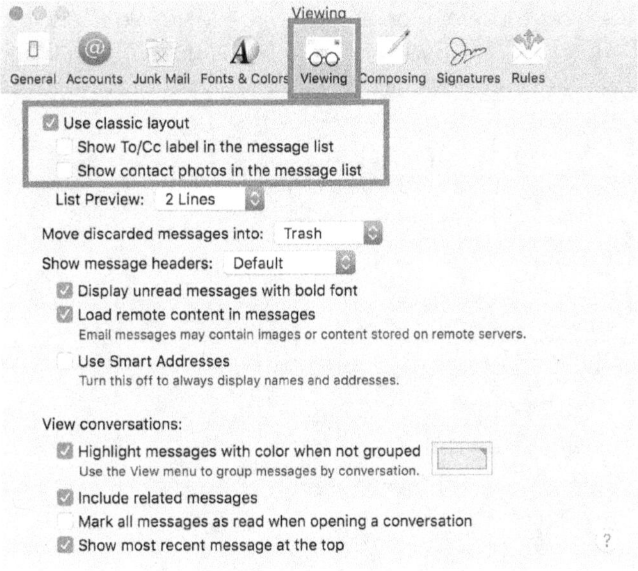

Show the To and CC Labels

You can configure Mail to display the **To** and **CC** labels. This allows you to see which messages were sent directly to you versus ones that you were copied. Check the box next to **Show To/Cc label in the message list** on the Viewing tab of the Mail preference pane to enable this feature.

Show Contact Photos in the Message List

You can configure Mail to display photos of your contacts in the message list. If the sender's photo is available, it will be shown to the left of the message in the message list. Check the box next to **Show contact photos in the message list** on the Viewing tab of the Mail preference pane to enable this feature.

Change the Number of Preview Lines

Mail can preview the first few lines of an email in the message list. This is a handy feature because you often can determine if you want to read or just trash and email message based on the preview. Your options are to show 1, 2, 3, 4, or 5 lines. Select the number of preview lines using the drop-down list next to **List Preview** on the Viewing tab of the Mail preference pane. To disable this feature, select **None** from the drop-down list.

Swipe Left, Swipe Right

A cool feature in Mail is the ability to swipe left and right with two fingers to take action on an email. Users of iOS will recognize this as a feature on their iPhone or iPad. Swiping right with two fingers will toggle the read/unread status of an email message. The action performed while swiping left is configurable in the **Viewing** tab of Mail preferences. You have the choice of trashing the email or archiving it. Make your choice from the drop-down menu next to **Swipe Left To**. Swipe left with two fingers to execute the command.

Show Smart Addresses

Mail will display the recipient's email address. When the **Smart Addresses** feature is enabled, Mail will only display the name. The recipient must be listed in the Contacts app, Previous Recipients List, or on a network server for the Smart Address to display. To enable this feature check the box next to **Use Smart Addresses Preview** on the **Viewing** tab of the Mail preference pane.

Configure Composing Options

The **Composing** tab of the Mail preference pane is used to configure the options for messages that you create.

You can choose to compose your outgoing messages using **Rich Text** (the default) or **Plain Text** from the drop-down list next to **Message Format**.

Mail checks the spelling of your outgoing email as you type it. You can choose to have Mail check your spelling when you click **Send** or **never** check your spelling from the drop-down list next to **Check spelling**.

You can also choose to have Mail copy or blind copy you by checking the box next to **Automatically myself** and selecting your choice from the drop-down list.

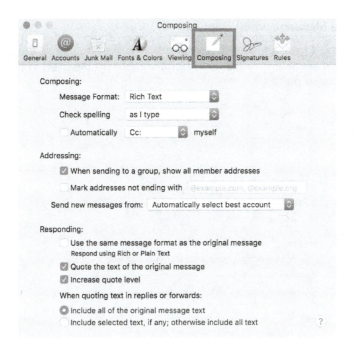

Select the Sending Email Account

If you have multiple Mail accounts configured, Mail will automatically select what it considers to be the best account to send from based on the currently selected email account and the email address of the first recipient in the message,

If you want your mail to originate from a specific Mail account, open **Mail > Preferences...** or enter ⌘, (command+,). Click the **Composing** tab at the top of the pane. Choose the account you want to use to send new email from the drop-down list next to **Send new messages from:**.

Configure Response Options

The **Responding** section on the **Composing** tab of the Mail preference pane controls the behavior of messages when replying and forwarding email.

You can choose to utilize the same message format as the original email by checking the box next to **Use the same message format as the original message**.

By default, Mail will quote the text of the original message when replying or forwarding an email, indenting all text included from the original email. Uncheck the boxes next to **Quote the text of the original message** and **Increase quote level** to disable these features.

Include the Original Message when Replying

Have you ever replied to an email and wondered why Mail truncated the original email, showing only part of a single line? This odd behavior can be disabled in the **Composing** tab of the Mail preference pane.

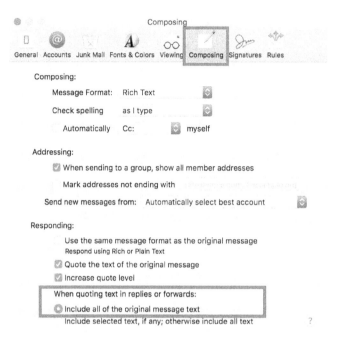

To include all of the original email in your reply, click the radio button next to **Include all of the original message text**.

Create a Signature

The **Signature** tab of the Mail preference pane allows you to create signatures for each of your Mail accounts. Mail automatically adds the signature to messages you create. You can have unique signatures for each mail account. To create, change, or delete a signature, open **Mail > Preferences...** or enter ⌘, (command+,). Click the **Signatures** icon at the top of the pane if it is not already selected.

Select the email account from the left column. To create a new signature click the **+** button at the bottom of the middle column. Enter your desired signature in the right pane. You can use the **Edit** and **Format** menus to change the font, layout, change text into links, or check spelling. If you want to add an image, drag it into the right pane. If you want to use your contact information from the Contacts application, drag your vCard into the right pane

To delete a signature, first select the email account. Highlight the signature you want to delete and click the **−** button at the bottom of the middle column.

If you want your signature to always use the message font you specified in the **Fonts & Colors** preferences, check the box next to **Always match my default message font**.

Create a VIP List

Not all email messages are created equal. You may want to highlight and prioritize messages received from certain people using Mail's VIP feature.

To add someone to the VIP list, first find an email message from them. Click the empty star next to their name in the email or secondary click on their name and select **Add to VIPs**. Once you have added one person to your VIP list, a new VIP mailbox will appear in the Mail Sidebar and in your Favorites Bar.

To remove someone from the VIP list, find an email message from them and click on the star next to their name or secondary click on their name and select **Remove from VIPs**.

Manage Email Overload

The best way to manage email overload is the create rules so that Mail can automatically process and take action based on various mail attributes. You can use mail rules to organize your mail and highlight mail that is important, separating it from the noise. For example, you could create a mail rule for email from your bank, move it to a special banking folder, play a sound, and bounce the Mail icon in the Dock to notify you. Mail supports 14 different pre-defined actions and 28 conditions, which you can combine to customize how you want your inbound email processed.

To create, modify, or delete mail rules, open **Mail > Preferences...** or enter ⌘, (command+,). Click the **Rules** icon at the top of the pane if it is not already selected. To modify, duplicate, or delete an existing rule, highlight it and click the **Edit**, **Duplicate**, or **Remove** button at the right. Click the **Add Rule** button to create a new mail rule.

Creating a new mail rule is easy. Rules have 2 components - the **conditions** and the **actions**. After clicking the **Add Rule** button, a configuration sheet will drop down. To create a new rule, first name the rule in the **Description** field.

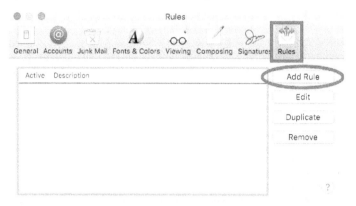

Next, choose whether **any** or **all** of the conditions have to be met to perform the selected actions. If you choose **any** the actions will be performed if only one of the conditions is met. **All**, as the name implies, requires that all conditions be met in order to perform the actions.

Now configure a condition from the more than two dozen conditions from the drop-down list. To add multiple conditions, click the **+** button. Use the **–** button to remove a condition. Under **Perform the following actions**, select the action you want Mail to perform. To add multiple actions, click the **+** button. Use the **–** button to remove an action. Click **OK** when finished.

Create a Rule to Play a Sound

Not all email messages are created equal. You can configure Mail to play a sound and bounce the Mail icon in the Dock to notify you when mail arrives from someone in your VIP list.

First, select **Mail > Preferences...** or enter ⌘, (command+,) to open the Mail preference pane. Select **Rules** if not already selected, and click on the **Add Rule** button. Enter a descriptive name in the **Description** field. In the conditions section, choose **Sender is**

VIP from the drop-down menu. In the **Perform the following actions** section, choose **Play Sound** from the drop-down menu and choose whatever sound you like from the next drop-down. Next, click the **+** button to create a new line. Select **Bounce Icon in Dock** from the drop-down menu. Click **OK** to finish and click **Apply** on the next dialog box.

When you receive email from someone in your VIP list, the Hero sound will play and the Mail icon located in the Dock will bounce.

To remove a rule, open the Mail preference pane, select **Rules**, highlight the rule you want to remove, and click the **Remove** button. Rules can also be disabled without deleting them. To do so, uncheck the box in the **Active** column next to the rule in the list to disable it. Check the box to enable the associated rule.

Create an Auto-Response Rule

Mail lets you set up an email response that will be automatically sent upon receiving new email. This is a handy feature to let those who sent you email know that you are out of the office, on vacation, in all day meetings, or that your response will be delayed. When Mail receives a new email, it can immediately respond with a message of your choice.

To set up an automated response, open **Mail > Preferences...** or enter ⌘, (command+,). Click the **Rules** icon at the top of the pane if it is not already selected. Click the **Add Rule** button to create a new mail rule.

Next, name your rule in the **Description** field. Under the **If any of the following conditions are met:** section, select **Every Message** from the drop-down menu. Then select **Reply to Message** in **Perform the following actions:** section.

Click the **Reply message text...** button to reveal a configuration sheet and enter your desired response message.

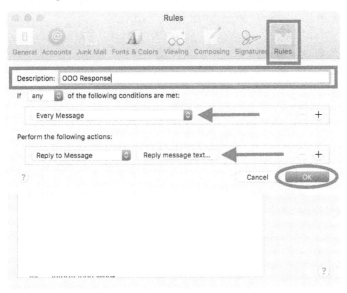

Click the **OK** button to save your message. Then click the **OK** button to enable your new auto-response rule. If you want to check your rule, send an email to yourself.

You can set up more complex rules so that Mail will automatically respond only to specific senders, like you customers or clients, other employees in your company, family, or friends.

To disable your auto-response rule, open **Mail > Preferences...** or enter ⌘, (command+,). Click the **Rules** icon at the top of the pane if it is not already selected. Uncheck the checkbox next to the name of your auto-response rule.

Customize the Toolbar

The **Toolbar**, located at the top of the Mail window, provides a number of tools to make you more productive. Mail allows you to customize the **Toolbar**, adding, removing, and rearranging tools as you see fit. Secondary click in any open area of the Toolbar to reveal a contextual menu with a single option to **Customize Toolbar...**, which reveals a drop-down tools palette with the entire selection of tools available.

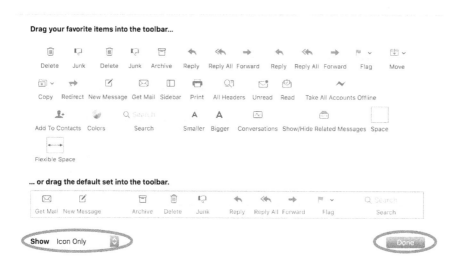

The tools palette allows you to add additional tools to the Toolbar by dragging and dropping them onto the Toolbar. Tools can be dragged off the Toolbar and dropped onto the palette to remove them. In addition, any tool can be removed from the Toolbar at any time by holding down the ⌘ (command) key and dragging it off. Tools can be rearranged at any time by holding down the ⌘ (command) key and dragging them.

To revert back to the default set of tools, drag the default set onto the Finder toolbar to replace the existing toolset.

Customize the Favorites Bar

Directly below the Toolbar is the **Favorites Bar**, another customizable component of the Mail window. At the extreme left is the **Mailboxes** button, which you can use to toggle the **Sidebar** on and off. The space to the right of the Mailboxes button is completely customizable.

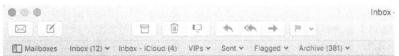

To customize your Mail **Favorites** bar, drag any item from the **Sidebar** on to the Favorites bar. You can drag individual mailboxes, section headings (i.e., **On My Mac**, **VIPs**, **Flagged**), a mail account, or a single flag. Practically anything in the Sidebar can be dragged on to the Favorites bar. Clicking on any item in the Favorites bar will change the Mail window to that view and the button will turn a darker shade of grey to denote that it has been selected.

If an item has sub-items, a small triangular caret will appear to its right. In this case, the button will both toggle the view on and off as well as displaying a drop-down menu. For example, clicking on **VIPs** in the picture above will display all the messages from everyone you have designated as a VIP. If you click the caret to the right of the **VIPs** button, a drop-down list will appear allowing you to select a specific VIP.

Drag any item to rearrange it. To remove an item from your Favorites bar, drag it off.

Embed Links in an Email

An embedded link allows the recipient of an email message to click on a link embedded within an email to go directly to a website, start a chat in Messages, or start a FaceTime call.

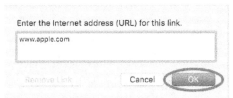

To embed a link into an email message, highlight the desired text in your email and then enter ⌘K (command+K). A drop-down dialog box will appear asking you to **Enter the Internet address (URL) for this link**.

To embed a link that will allow the recipient to start a chat session with you in **Messages**, enter the following followed immediately by your ten-digit phone number or email address.

`imessage://2025551234`

To embed a link that will allow the recipient to start a **FaceTime** call with you, enter the following followed immediately by your ten-digit phone number or email address.

`facetime://2025551234`

Links can also be embedded in other types of files, such as Word or Pages documents or Powerpoint or Keynote presentations by using **⌘K** (command+K).

Add Emoji

Emoji are those cute (or irritating depending on your point of view) little emoticons that originated in Japan in the late 1990s and have spread around the world since then. You can reveal the macOS emoji set in almost any application by pressing the **^⌘space** keys (control+command+space).

Not only will you have access to the emoji, but other special character sets are available. Click the icons at the bottom of the window to display the other character sets. Click on an emoji or special character to insert it into your document.

Use Natural Language Search

Like Spotlight, the **Mail** application supports natural language search capability. Therefore, you don't have to remember who sent you an email or the subject. For example, if you are interested in seeing emails that have a photo attached, you can enter "emails with a photo attached" in the Mail search field.

Markup an Email Attachment

Mail allows you to markup an image or PDF attachment. To markup a PDF attachment, attach an image to your email message by dragging it into the new message window. Hover over the image with your pointer until a small gray icon appears in the upper right corner of the image. Click on this icon and select **Markup**. The image will open in a new Markup window where you can edit the image similar to how you would annotate an image using the Preview application. Click **Done** when finished. The image, with your edits, will appear in the message window. The best part of this feature is that the original image remains untouched as the markups only appear on the attachment in Mail.

Sign a PDF Document

Another feature of Mail is the ability to sign PDF documents. First, attach the PDF requiring your signature to a new email message. Hover your pointer over the PDF in the message window until a small gray icon appears in the upper right corner. Click the icon and select **Markup**.

The PDF will open in a new Markup window. Click the **Signature** tool, click **Trackpad** if not already highlighted, **Click Here to Begin**, and sign your name using the Trackpad. Click **Done** when finished signing.

It is a little difficult to sign your name using your finger and the trackpad, so if you don't like the result, click **Cancel** and try again. Once you are satisfied, click the **Done** button in the upper right.

You can also use the camera to take a picture of your signature and add it to the PDF. Click **Camera** instead of **Trackpad** to use this option.

19

Security & Privacy

Control Which Apps Get Your Location

Location services are a handy feature of macOS that allows you to get the local weather, restaurant recommendations, use location-based reminders, and a host of other features that require knowledge of your current location. You can control which apps are allowed to get and use your location.

To control which apps get your location, open the **Security & Privacy** preference pane from System Preferences and select the **Privacy** tab. Note that you may have to unlock the preference pane by clicking the padlock in the lower left corner to make changes.

Uncheck the checkboxes next to apps that you do not want to receive your location information. You should not disable **Location Services** by unchecking the box next to **Enable Location Services.** Doing so prevents you from locating your Mac with the **Find My iPhone** feature.

See When Your Location is Accessed

Many services rely on your location to provide relevant information such as the weather, movie showtimes, and restaurant recommendations. If you want to know when macOS is using your location, you can configure it to display the location icon in the Menu Bar when your location is accessed. Similar to the iOS feature, a small location icon will appear in the Menu Bar whenever macOS is accessing your location.

To configure macOS to display the location icon in the Menu Bar, launch the **Security & Privacy** preference pane in System Preferences. Click the **Privacy** tab and select **Location Services** from the list at the left. Scroll down to the bottom of the list in the right-hand pane to **System Services** and click the **Details...** button.

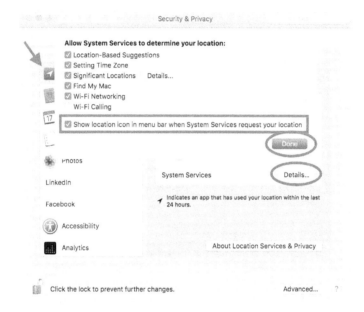

A drop-down configuration sheet will appear. Check the checkbox next to **Show location icon in menu bar when System Services request your location**. Click **Done** and then close the Security & Privacy preference pane.

When your location is requested, the location icon will appear in the Menu Bar on the far left of the Status Menu. The location icon will disappear automatically after your location data has been accessed.

Help Defeat the Evil Empire

You can help defeat the Evil Empire's plans for galactic domination by configuring Safari to not use Google as its search engine. Google gathers a tremendous amount of your personal information, more than you realize and most without your knowledge, in order to drive its evil advertising revenue. Seventy-five percent (75%) of all searches in the U.S. and 65% worldwide are done using Google's search engine. The Evil Empire tracks all of your searches, capturing detailed information on your search topics and which search results you clicked. Have you searched for information on a medical condition you'd like to keep private? Too late. The Evil Empire knows. Google states that its mission is "to organize the world's information and make it universally accessible and useful." That includes information that you may prefer to keep private.

If you prefer not to share information with Google, you can configure Safari to use a search engine that does not collect your personal information. Safari offers DuckDuckGo as an alternative search engine. Google's privacy policy, as of the writing of this book, is 8 pages long. DuckDuckGo's privacy policy is a mere 7 words, "We don't collect or share personal information." (https://duckduckgo.com/privacy)

To configure Safari to use DuckDuckGo as its search engine, select **Safari > Preferences...** or by entering ⌘**,** (command+comma). Click on **Search**, if it is not already selected. Using the drop-down menu next to **Search Engine**, select **DuckDuckGo.** Other options are Bing and Yahoo, however, both collect your personal data.

Stay Safe & Secure with VPN

If you have a MacBook, MacBook Pro, or MacBook Air, you probably use public Wi-Fi available at Starbucks, hotels, airports, and other businesses. Public Wi-Fi is horribly insecure. It doesn't matter if the service is free or if you have to pay a fee. When using public Wi-Fi, all of your traffic is sent in the clear, allowing anyone to capture the data you send or receive. Sometimes bad guys will camp out in public places and set up their laptops to mimic a legitimate public Wi-Fi service with a tantalizing name such as FREE Airport Wi-Fi. All they have to do is wait for victims to connect, capture private data, and use it to steal a victim's identity, drain bank accounts, or hack into your computer.

A Virtual Private Network (VPN) protects your data by encrypting it while it travels over public Wi-Fi. With identity theft dramatically on the rise, it is just plain reckless to use public Wi-Fi without a personal VPN. There are other reasons why you need a personal VPN account. A VPN makes you anonymous by hiding your Mac's actual IP address, replacing it with the IP address of the VPN service. This makes it more difficult for your Internet Service Provider, employer, the government, or others to track your online activity. If you are traveling in a foreign country, you may lose access to Netflix or to social media sites that the local government censors. A personal VPN will allow you to access services the government considers objectionable or are unavailable in foreign countries. If you want to protect your privacy and security when online, you should use a personal VPN service.

If your company provides a VPN for business use, you don't want to use it for personal use. Company VPNs are monitored for misuse. Do you really want your employer knowing your personal browsing habits? I think not. That's another reason why you should sign up for a personal VPN service. There are lots of choices available for fees ranging from free to $20 a month. Why not choose one of the free VPN services? The free services are more restrictive regarding maximum bandwidth, the ability to stream video, and are sometimes funded by obnoxious advertising. If you can live with these limitations, choose a free VPN service, otherwise better services without these limitations are available for a nominal monthly or yearly fee.

The VPN service I use is **NordVPN**, available at https://nordvpn.com/ and at the Mac App Store. NordVPN is a five-star *PCMag.com* Editor's Choice and Best of Year 2017. It features over 2,762 servers worldwide at the time of this writing. NordVPN has a no logs policy so you don't have to worry about your privacy. Six devices can be connected simultaneously so you can use NordVPN on your Mac, iPad, and iPhone concurrently. Unlike many VPN providers, NordVPN offers unlimited bandwidth. NordVPN offers four plans. A monthly plan costs $11.95 a month. A one-year plan is $5.75 a month and a 2-year plan is $3.29 a month. The best value is the 3-year plan at $2.75 a month. All plans come with a 30-day money back guarantee if you are not satisfied.

NordVPN performs well using the Ookla speed test available at http://www.speedtest.net/. A nice feature is that I can use the same account on my Mac, iPhone, and iPad. NordVPN even support Windows PCs in case you have to cross over to the dark side.

Disable the Guest User Account

The **Guest User** account is enabled by macOS by default. Selecting the Guest User at login allows someone to get online as a guest, but prevents the guest user from accessing your data.

So what's the point of the Guest User account? This account plays a role in the macOS **Find My iPhone** feature by allowing someone who stole your Mac to get online so your Mac can be located. Therefore it is recommended that you keep the Guest User account enabled so your Mac can be located if it is stolen.

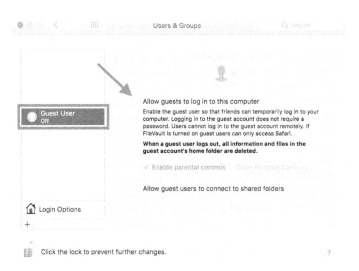

If you still want to disable the Guest User account, open the **Users & Groups** preference pane in the System Preferences application. Click the lock in the lower left corner to make changes. Enter your password when prompted.

Select the **Guest User** from the left column. Uncheck the box next to **Allow guests to log in to this computer.** Close the Users & Groups preference pane when finished. Checking this checkbox will re-enable the Guest User account.

Switch to a Standard User Account

The account created when you first set up your Mac is, by default, an administrator account. Using your Mac for day-to-day work as an administrator poses a security risk. If your Mac becomes infected with malware while you are logged in as an administrator, the elevated privileges of the administrator account can allow malware easier access to system resources, applications, and other resources. Therefore, it is a safe computing best practice to perform day-to-day activities as a standard user and to reserve the administrator account for adjusting system settings and installing applications. If you are using your computer as a standard user and need to make a change that requires administrator access, you will be prompted for the administrator account credentials.

If you have a brand new Mac and have just set it up, creating separate administrator and user accounts is a breeze. By default, Setup Assistant creates the default administrator account. You can use the **Users & Groups** preference pane in System Preferences to create a new standard account for your day-to-day computing activities. However, if you been using your Mac for a while, creating a new standard account won't work for you as all of your settings, applications, and data will only be accessible from your old administrator account. The solution to this dilemma is to first create a new administrator account and then to downgrade your existing account to a standard user.

To create a new administrator account, open the **Users & Groups** preference pane in the System Preferences application. Click the lock in the lower left corner to make changes. Enter your password when prompted.

Click on the **+** at the bottom of the left column. A drop-down configuration sheet will appear. Choose **Administrator** from the drop-down list next to **New Account**. Enter the **Full Name**, **Account Name**, **Password**, and click **Create User** to finish. Log out and log back in with your new administrator account to see if it works properly and that you did not fat finger the password.

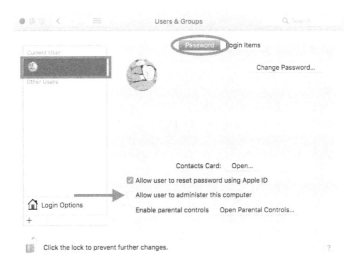

Using your new administrator account, launch the **Users & Groups** preference pane. Click the lock in the lower left corner to make changes, if the padlock is locked. Enter your password when prompted. Select your old administrator account, the one you want to downgrade to a standard user, from the left column. Uncheck the checkbox next to **Allow user to administer this computer**. Note the change in the left column to **Standard**. Close the Users & Groups preference pane when finished to save the change. Restart your computer for the change to take effect.

If you access financial sites like your bank, credit card, or broker, I suggest you create another standard user account to use exclusively for financial sites. Never browse the Internet or use email with your financial standard user account.

Create Strong Passwords with Keychain Access

 Keychain Access is the macOS application that handles certificates, stores passwords you create or those created by Safari, and allows you to store other data in an encrypted format. If you're unfamiliar with Keychain Access, it is probably because it is a little hard to find. Keychain Access is tucked away in the **Utilities** folder.

Keychain Access manages all of your login credentials, allowing you to create unique passwords for each website or application you access. This is a security best practice, ensuring that if one of your passwords is compromised, it cannot be used to break into all of the other sites where you have accounts. **Never reuse passwords among websites**. I recommend utilizing strong passwords and changing them every six months. Keychain

Access in combination with Safari can be used to automate the creation, storage, and retrieval of your passwords.

The advantage of using Keychain Access is that you can configure it to synchronize passwords over iCloud to make them available across all of your Apple devices. Although other third party password managers offer a similar feature. I'll show you a third party password manager later in this chapter that I believe does a better job of synchronizing passwords across Apple devices.

Keychain Access can be found in **Applications > Utilities** or by searching using **Launchpad** or **Spotlight**. To create a new password select **File > New Password Item**, enter ⌘N (command+N), or click the **+** button at the bottom of the Keychain Access window. Enter the **Keychain Item Name** and **Account Name**. Next, click the **Key** button to the far right of the **Password** field, which will launch **Password Assistant**.

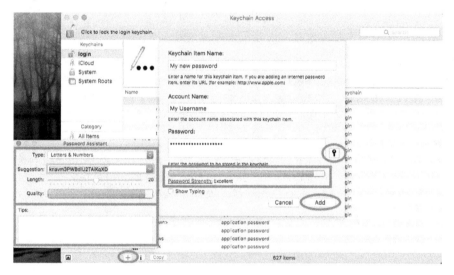

Password Assistant will launch in a separate window. Using the drop-down menu next to **Type**, select the type of password you would like to create. You have several choices: **Memorable**, **Letters & Numbers**, **Numbers Only**, **Random**, or **FIPS-181 compliant**. Password Assistant will suggest a password of 12 characters, which is too short for a strong password. I recommend using the longest password supported by the website or application. Use the **Length** slider to increase the number of characters. As the number of characters increase, you'll notice **Quality** turns to a darker green indicating a stronger password. If your chosen password has any problems, Password Assistant will tell you in the **Tips** box below **Quality**. If your password has a problem, select another password from the drop-down list next to **Suggestion**. When finished, click the red close window control in the upper left corner of the Password Assistant window. Your password is automatically placed in the password field of the new password item you just created. Click the **Add** button to save your new password to your keychain.

When you want to use your password, launch **Keychain Access** and search for the item by name using the search field in the upper right. Secondary click on the item and enter your password when prompted. Your password has been saved to the clipboard and you can paste it into the website or application.

When you are using Safari and enter a username and password on a website, you will be asked if you would like to save your username and password. Doing so avoids having to launch Keychain Access and search for your password each time you need it for that particular website.

If you a visiting a site for the first time and are creating a new account, Safari will suggest a strong password. To use the password suggested by Safari, click on **Use Safari suggested password,** which will appear below a website's password input field. Don't worry, you won't have to remember this monster. Passwords are automatically saved to the **Keychain Access** application and are recalled and populated into the password field the next time you log in to the website. And if you use iCloud Keychain, your Safari-generated passwords will be available on all of your Apple devices.

Apple's **iCloud Keychain** feature will save usernames and passwords in iCloud so your account credentials are available on all of your Apple devices.

Lock Your Mac

Locking your Mac helps protect your data and files from prying eyes and deters others from accessing your personal data. macOS lets you quickly lock your Mac. First you need to ensure macOS is configured to require a password and that automatic login is disabled.

To configure your Mac to require a password, open the **Security & Privacy** preference pane in System Preferences. If not already selected, click the **General** tab. If the padlock in the lower left corner is locked, click it and enter your password when prompted.

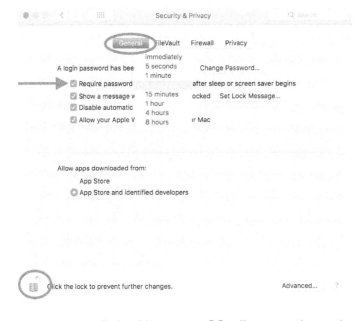

Check the **Require password** checkbox. macOS offers you the option of requiring a password **immediately** or after **5 seconds**, after **1, 5,** or **15 minutes**, or after **1, 4,** or **8 hours** after the display went to sleep or the screen saver began.

To lock your Mac immediately, use the keyboard shortcut ^⌘Q (control+command+Q) or select > **Lock Screen** from the Apple Menu. macOS is able to continue running background processes like a backup, uploading a video to YouTube or Facebook, or downloading a movie while your Mac is locked. Note that locking your Mac is different from putting your Mac to sleep. When your Mac is sleeping, it cannot run background processes.

Put Your Display to Sleep

Putting your Mac's display to sleep essentially does the same thing as locking your Mac. Background processes will continue to run and your Mac will be protected by your password once the **Require password** timer you set in the **Security & Privacy** preference pane expires. macOS does not have a native keyboard shortcut to put its display to sleep.

Once you have set the password and the require password timer in the **Security & Privacy** preference pane, you can put your display to sleep via. several different methods. Note that the timer controls the length of time you (or someone else) will be able to access your Mac without entering a password. For example, if you set this timer to 5 minutes, your Mac will not require a password for 5 minutes after you enter the lock keyboard shortcut.

You can lock your Mac by putting its display to sleep using the keyboard shortcut ⇧^**power** (shift+control+power). On an older Mac, the shortcut is ⇧^**eject** (shift+control+eject).

If you have a Macbook, Macbook Air, or Macbook Pro, you can close the lid to put your display to sleep.

Finally, you can configure a **Hot Corner** to put your display to sleep as described in the Desktop and Mission Control chapters.

Put Your Mac to Sleep

Another option to lock your Mac is to put it to sleep. This differs from locking or putting your display to sleep. When your Mac is asleep it cannot run background processes.

Your Mac will be protected by your password once the **Require password** timer you set in the **Security & Privacy** preference pane expires.

To put your Mac to sleep, use the keyboard shortcut ⌥⌘**power** (option+command+power). On an older Mac, the shortcut is ⌥⌘**eject** (option+command+eject).

You can also put your Mac to sleep by selecting > **Sleep** from the Apple Menu.

Log Out when Inactive

macOS can automatically log you out after a period of inactivity. This is a great feature in case you walk away and forget to log out, lock your Mac, or put your display or Mac to sleep. To set this inactivity timer, open the **Security & Privacy** preference pane in the System Preferences application.

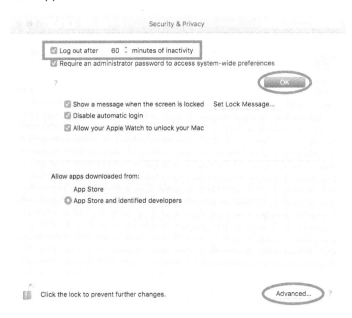

Click the **Advanced...** button in the lower right corner. Check the checkbox next to **Log out after** and enter the number of minutes of inactivity. Click **OK** and close the preference pane when done.

Show a Message When Locked

macOS lets you configure your Mac to show a message when the screen is locked. Open the **Security & Privacy** preference pane in the System Preferences application. If not already selected, click the **General** tab.

Check the checkbox next to **Show a message when the screen is locked**. Click the **Set Lock Message...** button. Enter your message in the configuration sheet that drops from the top of the pane and click **OK**.

Disable Automatic Login

With automatic login enabled anyone can access your Mac simply by restarting it. They will be automatically logged in as you with access to all of your files, Mail, Messages, etc. I highly recommend that you disable this feature.

To globally disable automatic login, open the **Security & Privacy** preference pane in the System Preferences application. Select the **General** tab. Next, check the box next to **Disable automatic login**. This change takes effect immediately and will also be reflected in the **Users & Groups** preference pane. Your Mac will ask for a user name and password when it starts.

Automatic login can be enabled for a specific user from the **Users & Groups** preference pane by clicking on **Login Options** at the bottom of the left column and turning on **Automatic login** from the drop-down menu. However, I do not recommend using automatic login for security reasons under any circumstances.

Unlock your Mac with your Apple Watch

You can unlock your Mac with your Apple Watch and the greatest thing about this feature is that you don't have to do anything. There are some caveats though, your Mac must be a mid-2013 or later model, your Watch must have watchOS3 installed, you must be signed into iCloud with the same Apple ID on both devices, and two-factor authentication must be enabled for your Apple ID.

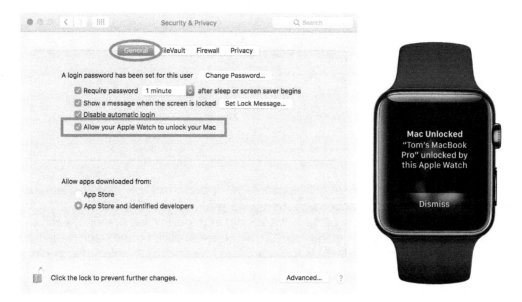

To enable Apple Watch Auto Unlock, launch the Security & Privacy preference pane in System Preferences and select the **General** tab.. Check the checkbox next to **Allow your Apple Watch to unlock you Mac**.

Wake your Mac from sleep by touching the Trackpad or the keyboard while wearing your Apple Watch. Your Mac will unlock and a message will appear on your Watch stating that it unlocked your Mac.

Require System Administrator Access to Change Settings

It's a good idea to require system administrator access in order to make changes to system settings in Systems Preferences, particularly if you have multiple people using your Mac. Even if you don't, you should do your day-to-day work as a standard user. Using an administrator account for day-to-day usage such as surfing the web or email poses a security risk. If your Mac becomes infected with malware while you are logged in as an administrator, the elevated privileges could allow malware easier access to system resources, applications, and other resources available only to the administrator.

To require system administrator access to change system-wide settings, launch the **Security & Privacy** preference pane. Click on **Advanced...** in the lower right corner of any of the tabs.

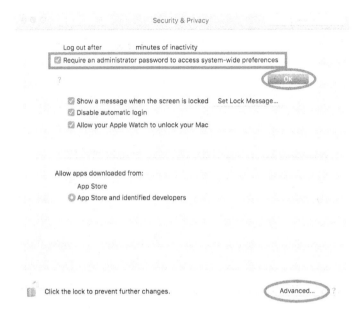

A drop-down configuration sheet will appear. Check the checkbox next to **Require an administrator password to access system-wide preferences**. Click **OK** when finished. When this feature is enabled, a padlock will appear in the lower left corner of each of the preference panes in System Preferences. You will have to click on the padlock and enter your system administrator credentials (username and password) to unlock the padlock in order to make changes.

Encrypt Time Machine Backups

 Hands down, Apple's **Time Machine** is the easiest backup application I have ever used. Its simple "set it and forget it" interface quietly backs up all of my critical data regularly without any intervention on my part. And the best part of Time Machine is how quickly and easily it can restore one file or your entire Mac.

Time Machine contains a copy of all of your files, including any data you would like to stay private. If you are concerned about unauthorized access, you can encrypt your Time Machine backup. Note that if you are only worried about encrypting your passwords in Keychain, your passwords are already encrypted when stored in the Keychain Access app, so it is not necessary to further encrypt them in Time Machine.

To encrypt your Time Machine backup, open the **Time Machine** preference pane in the System Preferences application. Next, click **Add or Remove Backup Disk...** to reveal a drop-down configuration sheet that will allow you to enable encryption on a new or existing Time Machine backup.

Select the disk drive you would like to encrypt under **Available Disks**. You can select an new drive for your Time Machine backup or select an existing one. Check the checkbox next to **Encrypt backups** to enable encryption. Click the **Use Disk** button. Enter a backup password and hint on the next configuration sheet. Click **Encrypt Disk** when finished.

Make Gatekeeper Less Restrictive

 Apple's App Store is the safest and most reliable place to download and install applications because Apple reviews each application before it's accepted, checking for malicious or junk software. If an application is later found to be malicious, Apple will remove it.

Gatekeeper makes your macOS computing experience safer by stopping applications that are not digitally signed with an Apple Developer ID from being installed. Gatekeeper protects your Mac from malicious software by ensuring it is from a trusted source, an Apple Developer, and by verifying the application hasn't been tampered with. Gatekeeper will block the installation of any application that is not signed by a valid Apple Developer ID.

Gatekeeper allows you to download applications from the App Store and from Apple Developers. You also have the option of making Gatekeeper more or less restrictive. Open the **Security & Privacy** preference pane in the System Preferences application. Click **General** if not already highlighted. Ensure the padlock in the lower left corner is unlocked. If not, click it and enter your password when prompted.

You have two available options: **App Store** and **App Store and identified developers**. You have the option of choosing the most secure setting, **Mac App Store**, which effectively means you cannot install applications unless they have been downloaded from

Apple's Mac App Store. The less restrictive setting, **Mac App Store and identified developers**, ensures that Gatekeeper will check that the application you downloaded is signed by a valid Apple Developer ID.

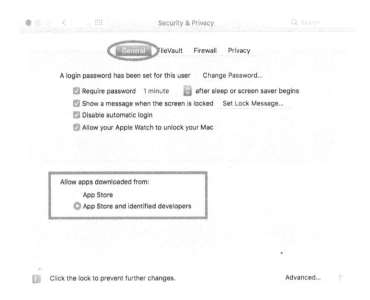

If you want to install unsigned software, macOS allows you to perform a manual override of Gatekeeper on a case-by-case basis. However, I recommend you only install applications that have been reviewed by a reputable publication. If you try to install an unsigned application, Gatekeeper will block it from being installed and display a warning dialog box. Clicking **OK** only acknowledges the warning.

To install an unsigned application after a Gatekeeper warning, you will need to unblock the installation by opening the **Security & Privacy** preference pane in the System Preferences application. You will see a message at the bottom of the **General** tab telling you why Gatekeeper blocked the install. If you want to continue the installation, click the **Open Anyway** and macOS will install the application.

Encrypt Your Drive

 Encrypting your disk drive protects your data in case your Mac is ever stolen. Encryption combined with the other security customization covered in this chapter makes it more difficult for a thief to access your data. **FileVault** will encrypt your entire drive.

Before enabling File Vault, there are a few things you need to consider. If you are in the habit of forgeting your password (or don't use a password to unlock your Mac) and lose your backup recovery key, your data is unrecoverable. This means your data is gone for good. FileVault's encryption is so strong, it's virtually impossible to break it and access your data. You can set up FileVault to use your iCloud password, so some risk is mitigated, but this will not help you if you forget your iCloud password or are temporarily without Internet access and need to get into your Mac.

FileVault could degrade the performance of some Macs, particularly older Macs with slower hard disk drives. You'll notice the performance degradation when opening large files. If your Mac is new and has a Solid State Drive (SSD), you will see little in the way of performance degradation.

If you want a truly secure system and have a new Mac with an SSD, FileVault is the way to go for the maximum level of security. To encrypt your entire drive with FileVault, open the **Security & Privacy** preference pane in the System Preferences application. If not already highlighted, click **FileVault**. Ensure the padlock in the lower left corner is unlocked. If not, click it and enter your password when prompted.

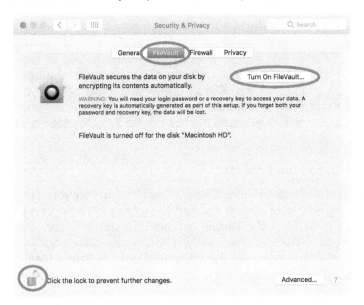

Click the **Turn On FileVault...** button. You'll be asked if you want to use your iCloud account to unlock your encrypted disk and reset your password if you forget it or use a recovery key instead of your iCloud account. If you choose the recovery code, you'll be presented with your 20-digit recovery code. **Make a copy of this code and store it in a safe place, not on the Mac your are encrypting**. If you lose both your password and the recovery key, you will not be able to access any of the data on your disk drive. It is a very bad idea to keep the copy of your recovery key on your Mac. If you forget your password you will not be able to access any of the data on your Mac including the recovery key. Store your recovery key in a safe, external location.

If there is more than one user account configured on your Mac, you'll be asked to identify the users who are allowed to unlock the encrypted drive. Each user is required to enter his or her password in order to have the ability to unlock FileVault. Click the **Continue** button to continue.

Finally, you will be asked to click **Restart** in the next dialog box to begin the encryption process. This is your last opportunity to change your mind. If you've changed your mind, press the **Cancel** button.

Clear Web Browsing History

Safari offers the capability to delete your browsing history, cookies, and other website data. **Safari** makes this task much easier to accomplish. In addition, you have control over the time period that you wish to delete.

To delete your web browsing history, cookies, and other website data, select **Clear History...** from the **Safari** menu. A dialog box will appear allowing you to choose to clear data from four different time periods: **the last hour**, **today**, **today and yesterday**, or **all history**. Click the **Clear History** button to clear your web browsing history.

Enable Find My Mac

If your Mac is ever stolen or lost you can use iCloud to lock or erase it to ensure your private data remains safe. To use this feature, **Find My Mac** must be enabled in the **iCloud** preference pane before your Mac is lost. Open the **iCloud** preference pane in the System Preferences application. Scroll to the bottom. Ensure the box next to **Find My Mac** is checked.

Remotely Lock or Erase Your Lost Mac

If your Mac is lost or stolen you can use iCloud to lock it to protect your personal data. To lock a stolen Mac, log into your iCloud account at www.icloud.com using your Apple ID and password. Launch the **Find My iPhone** app from iCloud. You can also use the **Find My iPhone** app on your iPhone or iPad. In the **My Devices** list, select your lost Mac. A window will appear offering 3 options: **Play Sound**, **Lock**, or **Erase Mac**. Note that your lost Mac must be found by iCloud before the Lock and Erase options appear.

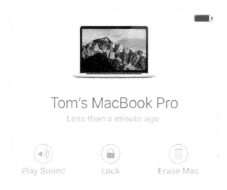

If you have simply misplaced your Mac, **Play Sound**, will cause your Mac to loudly play a sonar sound. Your Mac will make this sound even if the sound is turned off.

You can lock your Mac by selecting the **Lock** option. A window will appear confirming that you want to lock your Mac. Select **Lock** or **Cancel**. Create a PIN code in the next window and confirm it. Enter a message that you would like to display on your lost Mac. Locking your Mac will stop others from using it. Your lost Mac will reboot and will ask for the PIN to unlock it and will display your message. Note that once you lock your Mac, you are no longer able to erase it. If your Mac is returned to you, enter the PIN and your Mac will reboot and become usable once again.

The last option is **Erase Mac**. A window will appear confirming your desire to erase your Mac and stating that all content and settings will be erased and that it may take a day to complete. Select **Erase** or **Cancel**. Your Mac will be wiped and becomes essentially useless to the thief.

Create Strong Passwords with 1Password

 1Password is a third party, best-in-class application that allows you to create unique, strong passwords for every website or application you use. Passwords can be synchronized across all of your Apple devices using iCloud. And 1Password can even log you into a website with a single click. 1Password has won several awards including the Mac App Store Best of 2014, iMore 2014 Hall of Famer, Macworld Eddy Award, Macworld App Hall of Fame, and has a MacLife Editor's Choice "Awesome!" rating.

Using 1Password you can easily implement a security best practice – creating a unique, strong password for every website or application you use. You'll never forget a password again and your passwords are synchronized across all of your devices, even if they are Android or Microsoft devices. Your passwords are encrypted with 256-bit AES encryption and secured behind a single Master Password – the only password you have to remember. 1Password creates strong passwords for you with its Password Generator. Using unique, strong passwords ensures that your life won't be turned upside down if a data breach occurs at a website you frequent.

Companion applications for your iPhone and iPad are available and automatically synchronize your passwords and other secure data using iCloud.

1Password supports Safari and can log you into your favorite websites with a single click. A Menu Extra ensures that your passwords are always available, right from the Menu Bar. And 1Password protects more than just passwords. You can store your credit cards, bank account numbers, and create secure notes.

1Password's Security Audit features finds duplicate passwords, weak passwords, and passwords that are too old.

1Password is available for $64.99 (and is worth every penny) in the Mac App Store at: https://itunes.apple.com/us/app/1password-password-manager/id443987910?mt=12.

Enable Parental Controls

The Internet is a dangerous place and protecting your kids is a parent's full-time job. macOS makes protecting your kids a little easier by letting you control the applications your kids use, which websites they can visit, and how much time they spend online. To enable **Parental Controls** in macOS, open the **Users & Groups** preference pane in the System Preferences application. Click the lock in the lower left corner to make changes. Enter your password when prompted.

If your child doesn't already have an account on your Mac, click the **+** sign in the lower left to open the **New Account** configuration sheet. Select **Managed with Parental Controls** in the drop-down menu next to **New Account**. Select the **Age** from the drop-down list. You have a choice of **4+**, **9+**, **12+**, or **17+**. Create entries for the **Full Name**, **Account Name**, and choose a **Password**. Click the **Create User** button when finished. Enter your administrator password when prompted.

To configure parental controls, click on the child's account in the left-hand column in the **Users & Groups** preference pane. The checkbox next to **Enable parental controls** will be checked. Click the **Open Parental Controls...** button and enter your administrator password when prompted.

The **Parental Controls** preference pane will open. This preference pane contains a number of tabs to configure **Apps**, **Web**, **Stores**, **Time**, **Privacy**, and **Other**. The first tab we will open is the **Apps** tab. This tab allows you to configure options such as whether your child can use your Mac's camera and which applications your child is allowed to launch. You can set limits on **Game Center** activities and limit **Mail** to only allowed contacts that you have approved.

Clicking **Manage...** next to **Limit Mail to allowed contacts** lets you add allowed email addresses. The allowed contacts list prevents your child from sending or receiving mail from someone who is not on the allowed list. Check the box next to **Send requests to** and enter your email address. You will receive email whenever your child attempts to send or receive mail from anyone who is not in the allowed contacts list.

In the **Web** tab, you can implement **Browser Restrictions** so your child accesses only websites with content appropriate for his or her age. You can **Allow unrestricted access to websites**, **Try to limit access to adult websites**, or **Allow access to only these websites**. The last option allows you to whitelist websites and restrict your child's web browsing to only the sites on your allowed list. Click the **+** to add a website to the allowed list or the **−** to remove a website.

The **Stores** tab lets you disable access to the iTunes Store, iTunes U, and the iBooks store. You can also restrict music with explicit content, movies and TV shows to a particular rating, age appropriate apps, and books with explicit sexual content.

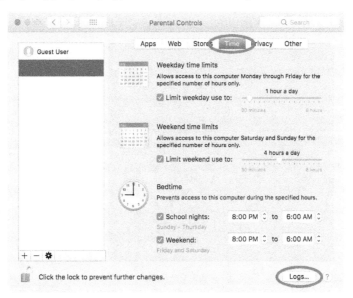

In the **Time** tab, you can set both weekday and weekend time limits, limiting the number of hours each day that your child can access your Mac. The **Bedtime** options ensure that your child cannot access your Mac during his or her bedtime on school nights and on the weekends.

The **Privacy** tab limits requests to location data, photos, contacts and other applications. From Privacy, you can control whether you will let new apps make changes to the Contacts, Calendars, Reminders, Twitter, Facebook, and Diagnostic apps. Unchecking the checkbox next to any app locks the current settings and prevents new apps from gaining access to them.

The **Other** tab enables or disables various macOS features including the ability to use Dictation, editing printers and scanners, burning CDs and DVDs, looking up explicit language in the Dictionary app, and modifying the Dock. For younger children, macOS provides a simplified view of Finder. Check or uncheck the desired options.

A **Logs...** button on each page allows you to review and clear a log your child's activity.

20

Bunch of Tricks, Tweaks, & Hacks

Create a Bootable High Sierra USB Flash Drive Installer

 If you own multiple Macs that you want to upgrade to High Sierra, you are facing a lot of downloading from the App Store. A better option is to create a bootable USB flash drive installer. You'll need a copy of the macOS High Sierra installer on your Mac and a USB flash drive with at least 8 GB capacity. Be sure there is nothing important on the USB drive as it will be erased as part of the creation of the installer.

Creating a bootable USB flash drive installer is a multi-step process.

1. Download macOS High Sierra from the **Mac App Store**.
2. While High Sierra is downloading, connect your USB flash drive to your Mac and launch **Disk Utility**.
3. Select your USB drive in the left-hand pane. Erase the USB drive. Disk Utility will pick the name **Untitled**. Don't bother naming it as it will be renamed automatically as part of creating the USB installer.
4. When macOS High Sierra finishes downloading, you will see the window below, which asks you to click continue to start the installation of macOS High Sierra. **STOP HERE!** Exit the installation by quitting.

5. Open Terminal and enter the following command. All four lines are a single command. **Do not** press the **return** key until you have entered the entire command. Because this command uses **sudo**, you will need to enter your root password when prompted. Don't worry if nothing appears in Terminal as you type your password. This is a security feature.

```
sudo /Applications/Install\ macOS\ High\
Sierra.app/Contents/Resources/createinstallmedia --volume
/Volumes/Untitled
```

6. Terminal will ask to erase your USB drive. Enter **Y** and press **return**.

```
Erasing Disk: 0%... 10%... 20%... 30%...100%...
Copying installer files to disk...
Copy complete.
Making disk bootable...
Copying boot files...
Copy complete.
Done.
```

7. You can quit Terminal when it is done creating the installer disk. Open Finder and check the Devices in the Sidebar. You should see a device called **Install macOS High Sierra**.
8. You are now finished with the creation of your macOS High Sierra USB flash drive installer.

To use your flash drive to install High Sierra, insert your USB drive into your Mac and hold down the ⌥ (option) key while restarting or starting. The startup disk menu will appear once your Mac has rebooted. Select your USB installer drive to continue booting your Mac directly into the macOS High Sierra installer. Follow the on-screen instructions. It should take about 45 minutes to an hour to complete the installation.

Tweak Background Updates

By default, High Sierra will automatically download and install updates in the background. If you would like to manually review the updates macOS plans to make to your Mac before they are installed, macOS offers a number of configuration options. To configure background updates, open the **App Store** preference pane in the System Preferences application.

When the checkbox next to **Automatically check for updates** is checked, your Mac will automatically check the App Store for updates. If you uncheck this box, macOS will no longer check or notify you of the availability of updates. You will have to manually check the App Store for updates.

When automatic updates are enabled, you can control how updates are downloaded and installed using the next 4 checkboxes. If you check the box next to **Download newly available updates in the background**, macOS will automatically download updates without asking your permission, however, you will be notified when updates are ready to be installed. Installation of updates is controlled via the next 3 checkboxes.

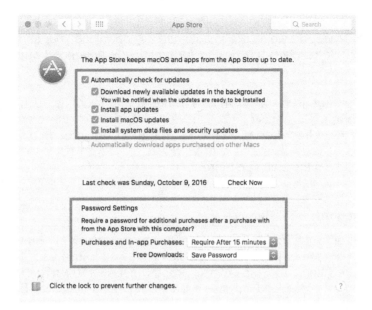

If the checkbox next to **Install app updates** is checked, macOS will automatically update applications without asking for permission. Uncheck it to disable automated application updates.

When the box next to **Install macOS updates** is checked, your Mac will install macOS updates automatically. Uncheck the checkbox to disable this feature.

If the box next to **Install system data files and security updates** is checked, macOS will automatically install system files and security updates without asking for permission. Uncheck the box to disable this feature.

Disabling any of the automatic installation options will require you to open the App Store app and review the list of updates and manually choose which ones to update.

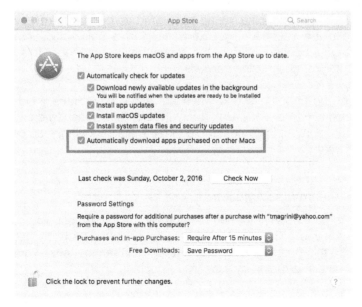

If you own multiple Macs and would like to automatically download your app purchases to all of your Macs, check the checkbox next to **Automatically download apps purchased on other Macs**.

The **Password Settings** section controls whether a password is required to make **Purchases and In-app Purchases**. You have two choices in the drop-down menu: **Always require** or **Require After 15 minutes**. For **Free Downloads**, you can always require a password or your password can be saved so you do not have to enter it to download a free app from the Mac App Store.

Control your Mac with BTT Remote

If you installed **BetterTouchTool** (see Chapter 2), you can use **BTT Remote** to control your Mac from your iPhone or iPad. BTT Remote allows you to use your iPhone or iPad as a trackpad or keyboard, run pre-defined actions in BetterTouchTool, access apps currently running on your Mac, and includes a file browser and launcher. BTT Remote is available for free in the App Store.

Precisely Adjust the Volume

Sometimes it seems you never can get the volume adjusted to your liking. One segment more is too much. One less is too little. Wouldn't it be awsome if you could adjust the volume in smaller increments? macOS has a solution for you!

Hold down the ⇧⌥ (shift+option) keys to adjust the volume in quarter-segment increments, allowing you to precisely adjust the volume exactly to your liking. This trick also works when adjusting the display brightness and the keyboard backlight.

Temporarily Quiet the Volume Adjustment

macOS makes an annoying popping sound each time you press the **F11** or **F12** key to decrease or increase the volume. If you're working in a quiet office environment the popping can disturb your concentration or the concentration of others. It is also annoying and loud when listening to music using earbuds.

To temporarily quiet the popping sound when adjusting the volume, hold down the ⇧ (shift) key while pressing **F11** or **F12**. Unfortunately, this trick doesn't work when adjusting the volume in quarter segment increments. To turn off this annoying, loud popping sound, check out the next tweak.

Permanently Quiet the Volume Adjustment

macOS allows you to permanently turn off the annoying and loud popping sound it makes when adjusting the volume. This is a blessing to anyone who routinely uses earbuds or headphones because this popping is so loud it is ear shattering. Also, your office mates will appreciate not being interrupted by your Mac's popping sounds.

To permanently turn off the annoying popping sound, open the **Sound** preference pane in System Preferences. Next, click **Sound Effects** if it is not already highlighted. Uncheck the checkbox next to **Play feedback when volume is changed**.

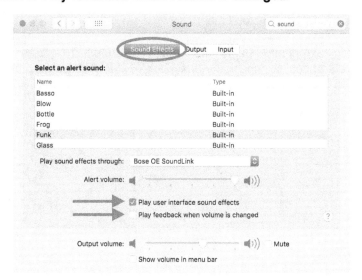

Disable User Interface Sounds

Your Mac will play various sound effects for certain actions like dragging and dropping an item into the trash. If you want to disable these sound effects, open the **Sounds** preference pane in System Preferences. Uncheck the checkbox next to **Play user interface sound effects**.

Make Help Center Behave

The macOS **Help Center** has a rather obnoxious habit. It refuses to act like other windows by stubbornly refusing to go to the background when it is not the active window. Help Center stays on top of all other windows whether it is active or not. This tweak changes this rather obnoxious behavior and forces Help Center to act like all other macOS windows.

First, close the Help Center window if open. Enter the following command in Terminal. This change takes effect immediately.

```
defaults write com.apple.helpviewer DevMode -bool TRUE
```

The next time you open Help Center you'll notice its more polite behavior. It no longer blocks other windows when it is not the active window.

To revert back to the Help Center's default obnoxious behavior, enter the following command in Terminal.

```
defaults delete com.apple.helpviewer DevMode
```

Save Changes Automatically When Closing Documents

By default, macOS will ask you if you want to save any unsaved changes when you close a document. You can turn off this behavior and have macOS automatically save unsaved changes to documents when you close them.

To enable automatic save of documents when closing them, open the **General** preference pane in System Preferences. Uncheck the checkbox next to **Ask to keep changes when closing documents**.

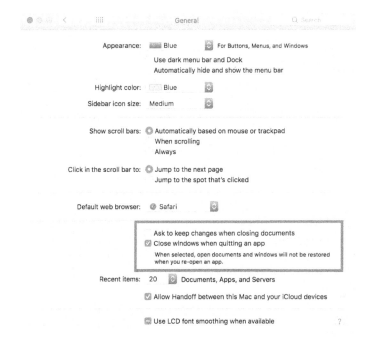

Stop Closed Windows from Reopening

Some more obnoxious behavior you may have noticed is that macOS will reopen files that were open the last time you quit an app. While this is occasionally useful if you're working on a single document over a long period of time, it is annoying most of the time because you have to close the old document to continue your new work. Those switching from a Windows PC may find this behavior particularly annoying since Windows does not exhibit this odd quirk.

This behavior is easy to correct. Open the **General** preference pane in the System Preferences application. Check the box next to **Close windows when quitting an application** and macOS will stop opening old documents when you launch an application.

Change the Highlight Color

The default highlight color when highlighting text in a document is blue. If you prefer another color, you can change the highlight color in the **General** preference pane in System Preferences. You have the choice of red, orange, yellow, green, blue, purple, pink, brown, or graphite. Choosing **Other...** displays a color wheel where you can select your own custom highlight color.

Enable the Expanded Save Dialog

macOS offers a small list of folders in its default save dialog. If you prefer to navigate the folder hierarchy to find the exact location where you want to save, you can enable the expanded save dialog as the default. The expanded save dialog displays the Finder Sidebar and allows you to navigate to your chosen destination folder. To switch between the minimalist and expanded views, click the little triangle at the end of the **Save As** field.

To enable the expanded save dialog as the default, quit all open applications. Launch Terminal and enter the following command.

```
defaults write –g NSNavPanelExpandedStateForSaveMode –bool TRUE
```

To revert to the macOS default, quit all open applications and enter this command.

```
defaults write –g NSNavPanelExpandedStateForSaveMode –bool FALSE
```

Enable a Wake & Sleep Schedule

You can create a schedule to start up or wake your Mac and to have it go to sleep, restart or shutdown. To enable a wake and sleep schedule, launch the **Energy Saver** preference pane in System Preferences. Next, click **Schedule...** in the lower right to reveal the drop-down configuration sheet shown below.

Check the checkbox next to **Start up or wake**, select a time of day and choose on which days your Mac will start up or wake. You have the choice of **Weekdays**, **Weekends**, **Every Day**, or you can choose a specific day of the week. Whether your Mac starts or wakes depends on how you configure the next attribute. Check the checkbox next to

Sleep and choose whether you want your Mac to **Sleep**, **Restart**, or **Shutdown**. Schedule the days and time using the drop-down list and time fields.

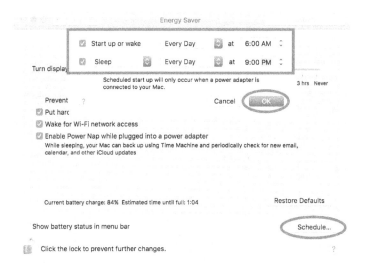

This feature offers a convenient way to "put your Mac to bed" each night and wake it up at a specific time each day. In the example above, my Mac goes to sleep each night at 9:00 PM and wakes at 6:00 AM daily. Similarly, you can schedule a specific date and time to restart your Mac each week.

Use Multiple Libraries in Photos & iTunes

  Photos stores all of your photos in a single photo library. If you have a large volume of photos, management of them becomes increasingly difficult as the photo library grows in size over the years. Creating photo libraries offers an option for better management than utilizing a single, gigantic Photos library.

To create a new photo library, quit Photos if it is currently open. Hold down the ⌥ (option) key while launching Photos. A dialog box will appear asking which photo library you want Photos to use.

Click the **Create New...** button and enter a name for the new photo library when prompted. If you want to save your new photo library in a location other than the **Pictures** folder, select a new location from the drop-down list next to **Where**. Click the **Save** button when finished and Photos will open your new library. To create additional Photos libraries, simply lather, rinse, and repeat.

Note that once you have multiple photo libraries, Photos will consider the last one you opened as the default. That means the library you last used will open automatically when you launch Photos. If you want to open another photo library, you will need to hold down the ⌥ (option) key while launching Photos. A dialog box will appear asking you which photo library you want Photos to use. Select the appropriate library and click **Choose**.

This trick also works for **iTunes**, allowing you to create multiple music libraries.

Add ½ Star Ratings to iTunes

 iTunes allows you to rate songs from 1 to 5 stars. If you need more precise ratings, you can enable ½ star ratings. I find this feature very useful when a song is not quite 5 stars, but it's better than 4 stars. 4½ perfect! To enable ½ star ratings in iTunes, first quit iTunes if it is open and then enter the following commands in Terminal.

```
defaults write com.apple.iTunes allow-half-stars -bool TRUE
```

To use the ½ star rating, simply drag your pointer left or right to change the rating in ½ star increments.

To revert back to the default of full star ratings, into the following command into Terminal. Be sure to quit iTunes first if it is open.

```
defaults delete com.apple.iTunes allow-half-stars
```

Synchronize External Calendar Sources

 The **Calendar** application is able to synchronize calendars between a number of email services and Facebook. It only takes a couple of steps to configure Calendar to synchronize with an external source. Launch the Calendar application.

Select **Calendar > Add Account...** to reveal a drop-down. Click the radio button next to the desired source and enter your login credentials when prompted.

To change how often Calendar synchronizes with external sources, select **Calendar > Preferences...** or enter ⌘, (command+,) to launch the Calendar preference pane. Select **Accounts** at the top of the pane if not already highlighted. Select the account in the left-hand pane. You have the choice of synchronizing every 1, 5, 15, or 30 minutes, every hour, or manually. For iCloud, you have the additional choice of **Push**, which updates your calendar immediately a change is made. Close the Calendar preference pane when finished.

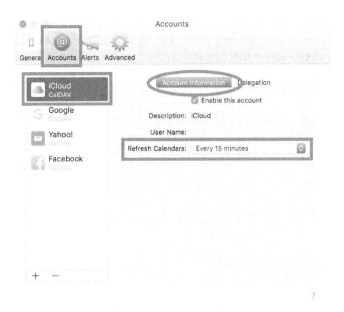

Subscribe to a Calendar Feed

 iCalendar, often referred to simply as iCal, is a standard Internet calendar format that allows you to share calendars. Apple's **Calendar** application utilizes the iCal format. By default, Calendar does not have holidays preloaded. You have to subscribe to an iCal feed to add holidays to your calendar. You can subscribe to Apple's U.S. Holidays calendar at:
webcal://files.apple.com/calendars/US32Holidays.ics.

Many calendars are available on the Internet for holidays in other countries. Additionally, you can subscribe to sports schedules, religious holidays, and academic schedules, to name a few examples. All you need is a direct calendar download link. You can subscribe to almost any iCal calendars you stumble upon on the Internet. Some good sources of calendars in iCal format are:
https://www.mozilla.org/en-US/projects/calendar/holidays/
http://icalshare.com/
http://calendarlabs.com

There are two methods to add an iCal file to the Calendar, subscribing or importing. To subscribe, the website must allow you to directly access the iCal file. The URL will begin with **webcal://** for you to subscribe. Some websites have a **Subscribe** button to make subscribing quick and easy. After clicking subscribe, a dialog box will appear with the URL of the calendar feed populated in the **Calendar URL** field. Click **Subscribe**.

If the website doesn't provide a subscribe button and only allows downloading of the .ics file, secondary click on the download link and select **Copy Link**. Next, launch the Calendar application if it is not already open. Choose **File > New Calendar Subscription** or enter ⌥⌘S (option+command+S). Paste the URL to the calendar file you just copied into the dialog box and click **Subscribe**. Next, you'll be presented with a dialog box to configure options such as event color, alerts, attachments, and how often to automatically refresh the calendar. If you plan to synchronize this calendar with your iPhone, iPad, or other Macs, select **iCloud** as the location.

Another method is to import a calendar by downloading the .ics file. I do not recommend this method. Subscribing is the preferable option as calendars to which you are subscribed are automatically updated and can be easily removed.

To change subscription settings, color, or to remove a calendar to which you are subscribed, click the **Calendar** button at the top of the Calendar window to reveal the sidebar. All calendars to which you are subscribed will be listed. A subscription will have an icon that looks something like a Wi-Fi icon. Secondary click on a calendar. You can access the subscription settings, change the color, or **Delete** the subscription using this contextual menu.

Add Favorite Locations to the PDF Drop-Down Menu

When you select the PDF drop-down menu from the lower left corner of the Print dialog box, did you notice **Add PDF to iBooks**, **Mail PDF**, **Save PDF to Web Receipts Folder**, or **Send PDF via Messages**? These are pre-configured printing workflows that allow you to send or save your PDF.

macOS allows you to add your own favorite locations to this drop-down menu as a printing workflow. To add your own favorite locations to the **Save as PDF** drop-down menu, select **Edit Menu...**, located at the bottom of the menu, to reveal the **Printing Workflows** dialog box. Click on the **+** and navigate to the location you wish to add. Continue clicking the **+** until you have added all of your favorite locations. Your favorite locations will appear on the Save as PDF drop-down menu below **Send PDF via Messages**.

Open in Preview
Save as PDF
Save as PostScript

Add to iBooks
Send in Mail
Send via Messages
Save to iCloud Drive
Save to Web Receipts

Edit Menu...

To remove a favorite location, first highlight the location and then click the **–** button.

Another Way to Add Favorite Locations

While the **Edit Menu...** feature works well, the limitation is that your favorite locations appear at the end of the menu regardless of where they should appear alphabetically. Additionally, you may have absolutely no need for one or more of the existing printing workflows and want to delete them.

A better way to customize the printing workflows shown in the Save as PDF drop-down menu is to add or remove them from the **PDF Services** folder in the **Library**. To open the PDF Services folder, launch **Finder** and enter ⇧⌘G (shift+command+G) to open the **Go to the folder** dialog box. Enter the following path and click **Go**.

`/Library/PDF Services/`

You will find the four printing workflows listed on the Save as PDF drop-down menu in the **PDF Services** folder. If you have no need for one or more of the workflows, drag them to the Trash. If you think you may need them later, drag them to another folder in your Home directory. Any change to the PDF Services folder requires you to authenticate using your administrator password.

To add a favorite location, enter ⌘T (command+T) to open another Finder tab. Navigate to the folder containing the folder you wish to add. Create an alias of the folder you want to add as a favorite by secondary clicking on it and selecting **Make Alias**. Rename the alias by adding "**Save PDF to**" or "**Send PDF to**" at the beginning of the alias name. Drag your alias into the PDF Services folder and enter your administrator password when prompted. macOS will order the contents of the PDF Service folder alphabetically, which is the reason why I suggested prepending the alias with "**Save PDF to**" or "**Send PDF to**."

To remove a printing workflow from the PDF Services folder, simply drag it to the Trash. Enter your administrator password when prompted.

Talk to Your Mac with Dictation

Done

Dictation is my favorite feature of macOS. Dictation is extremely useful, allowing you to quickly turn your thoughts into large blocks of text whether you're writing a term paper, a report, an email, posting to Facebook, or tweeting your followers.

Dictation is system-wide. You can dictate in any application anywhere text can be entered. This includes not only the usual suspects like Microsoft Office, Apple Pages or Mail, but other time savers like the address bar in Safari, the search box in Google.com or at Amazon.com, or in a web form. macOS lets you dictate text anywhere you are able to type it. Dictation is perfect for when you need to pull an all nighter to finish a term paper or project for work while avoiding getting grease from your extra pepperoni pizza on your keyboard.

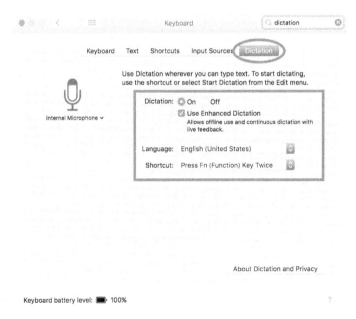

To turn Dictation on, open the **Keyboard** preference pane in System Preferences. Click on the **Dictation** tab if not already highlighted.

Click the **On** radio button next to **Dictation** to enable. The default shortcut to start dictation is to press the **fn** key twice. Press the **fn** key once to finish. You can change this using the drop-down menu next to **Shortcut**.

Check the box next to **Use Enhanced Dictation** so that you are not dependent upon an Internet connection for Dictation to work. When Enhanced Dictation is enabled, text will appear while you are speaking. When first selected, you will be prompted to select and download a language. Without Enhanced Dictation, your text will appear after you have finished dictating. This is due to the fact your speech has to be sent to Apple to be analyzed.

Hit the **fn** key twice to start dictating (unless you changed the keyboard shortcut in the Dictation & Speech preference pane). Your Mac will beep and the Dictation icon will appear to let you know macOS is ready to listen.

It's cool to see your text appear immediately with Enhanced Dictation. You can also edit your text live without having to stop dictating. Move your pointer or highlight the text you want to correct and dictate your corrections or use the keyboard. Press the **fn** key again to finish dictating.

Tell Your Mac to Talk to You

macOS includes a number of voices for text to speech applications, such as reading an iBook. The default voice is a male voice named Alex. macOS allows you to change the voice, download new voices, and change the rate of speech in the **Accessibility** preference pane.

To change the voice macOS uses for text to speech, open the **Accessibility** preference pane. Select **Speech** in the left column.

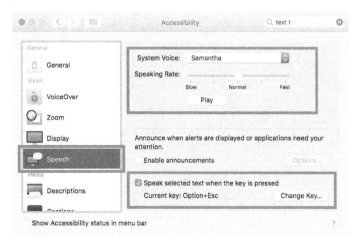

Use the drop down menu next to **System Voice:** to change the voice or select **Customize...** to download other voices. For iPhone and iPad users who like Siri's voice, choose **Customize...** from the drop-down menu and download Samantha's voice. Change the **Speaking Rate** using the slider. You can hear a sample by pressing the **Play** button.

The voice you selected will be utilized when your Mac reads to you. If you check the box next to **Speak selected text when the key is pressed**, you will be able to highlight any text and have it read to you by pressing ⌥**esc** (option+escape), which is the default. You can change this keyboard shortcut by clicking the **Change Key...** button.

Change Your Profile Picture

It's easy to change your profile picture and you can use any picture for your profile. Apple provides a number of default pictures you can utilize, but if you don't like the defaults you can choose a picture from iCloud, Photos, a folder on your Mac, or you can take a picture using your Mac's camera.

To change your profile picture, open the **Users & Groups** preference pane in the System Preferences application. Click the **Password** tab if it is not already highlighted. Click on your user name in the left-hand column. You'll see your current profile picture at the top of the right-hand pane.

To use a picture located in a folder on your Mac, open Finder, find the picture, and drag it onto your current profile picture in the **Users & Groups** preference pane.

Put Disk Drives to Sleep Faster

If you own an older MacBook with a hard disk drive, you can conserve battery power by putting your hard drive to sleep when not in use. For example, if you are simply browsing the Internet with your Mac, your hard drive is wasting precious battery power while spinning. macOS allows you to put your hard drive to sleep when it has been idle for a period of time.

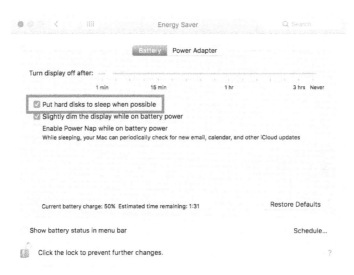

To put your hard drive to sleep to save power, open the **Energy Saver** preference pane in the System Preferences application. Check the checkbox next to **Put hard disks to sleep when possible**. macOS will put your disk drive to sleep if it has been idle for 10 minutes.

The idle time can be adjusted to be more aggressive in order to save more battery power. To shorten the idle time, open Terminal and enter the following command. Enter your admin password when prompted. This command will put your disk drives to sleep if they have been idle for 5 minutes.

```
sudo systemsetup -setharddisksleep 5
```

To revert back to the macOS default, enter the following command. Enter your admin password when prompted.

```
sudo systemsetup -setharddisksleep 10
```

Enable Sticky Keys

If you have trouble holding down two or more modifier keys simultaneously, the **Sticky Keys** feature allows modifier keys to be set without having to press all of them concurrently. The following modifier keys can be enabled as sticky: ⇧ ^ ⌥ ⌘ **fn** (shift, control, option, command, function). When the Sticky Keys feature is enabled, pressing a modifier key will stick it. The "stuck" key will display in the upper right of the screen to let you know it was pressed. To "unstick" the key, press it again.

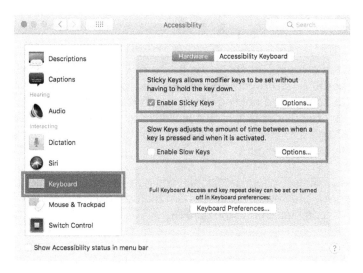

To enable Sticky Keys, open the **Accessibility** preference pane in the System Preferences application. Select **Keyboard** in the left column and check the box next to **Enable Sticky Keys**.

Click the **Options...** button to configure sound and display options. By default, macOS will beep and display the key in the top right of the screen when a modifier key is stuck.

You can select where you want the sticky keys to display with choices of the upper right (the default), upper left, bottom right, or bottom left of the display.

macOS allows you to configure the amount of time you have to hold down a sticky key, called the **Acceptance Delay**, before it is accepted. To enable this feature, click the checkbox next to **Enable Slow Keys** in the Accessibility preference pane. Click **Options** to reveal a slider that will allow you to adjust the Acceptance Delay.

Zoom the Entire Display

macOS allows you to zoom the display using a keyboard shortcut or scroll gesture. To enable the display zoom feature, open the **Accessibility** preference pane in the System Preferences application.

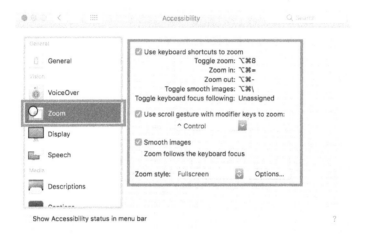

Select **Zoom** in the left column and check the boxes next to **Use keyboard shortcuts to zoom** and/or **Use scroll gesture with modifier keys to zoom**. The scroll gesture is a two finger drag up to zoom while holding down the chosen modifier key, ^ ⌥ ⌘ (control, option, or command). Two finger drag down while holding down the chosen modifier key to zoom back out. Be sure to check the checkbox next to **Smooth images** so the images won't pixelate as they become larger.

The **More Options...** button offers additional settings to configure the maximum and minimum zoom, show a preview rectangle when zoomed out, and to control the screen image as you move the pointer around the screen.

Set Visual Alerts

Sometimes you have to quiet your Mac. If you're working in a quiet office environment the cool alert sound you found may not be appreciated by your office mates. However, you still want to be alerted when a new message or email arrives. Instead of using an audible alert, macOS can flash the screen to alert you.

To turn on visual alerts, open the **Accessibility** preference pane in the System Preferences application. Select **Audio** in the left column and check the checkbox next to

Flash the screen when an alert sound occurs. You can click the **Test Screen Flash** button to preview a visual alert.

Kill the Spinning Rainbow Pinwheel of Death

Occasionally Finder will crash or get hung and you will experience Apple's spinning rainbow pinwheel of death. Finder will become completely unresponsive as the rainbow pinwheel defiantly spins and mocks you as you twiddle your thumbs hoping it disappears. Sometimes you just have to kill the darn thing.

To kill the pinwheel, relaunch Finder by holding down the ⌥ (option) key and secondary clicking on the Finder icon in the Dock. A contextual menu will appear with the option to **Relaunch** Finder. Sometimes Finder becomes so hosed that you will have to switch to another desktop space to make this command work.

An alternate method is to select > **Force Quit...** and choose Finder from the list of applications. Click the **Relaunch** button to kill the spinning pinwheel. You can also display the Force Quit dialog by entering ⌥⌘**esc** (option+command+escape).

Die rainbow pinwheel, die!

Force Quit Applications

If an app doesn't respond for a while, select its name and click Force Quit.

- Evernote
- Mail
- Microsoft Excel
- Microsoft Word
- Photos
- Safari
- Finder

You can open this window by pressing Command-Option-Escape.

Force Quit

Uninstall Unwanted Apps

In macOS you can uninstall an application by dragging it from the **Applications** folder to the Trash. You also can uninstall apps in Launchpad by clicking and holding until the apps begin to shake and an **X** appears in the upper left corner of the app's icon. Clicking the **X** deletes the app. Compared the process to uninstall an application on a Windows PC, this almost sounds too good to be true. And it is. Applications distribute many files throughout your system. Often applications will leave their detritus scattered across your hard drive or SSD after they are deleted using the above two methods.

AppCleaner is a small application that will thoroughly uninstall unwanted apps, hunting down their associated files and safely deleting the detritus. To delete an app with AppCleaner, launch AppCleaner and then drag the unwanted app from the Applications folder and drop it into the AppCleaner window. AppCleaner will find all files associated with the unwanted app. Delete the app by clicking AppCleaner's **Delete** button.

AppCleaner is free to download from the following website:
http://www.freemacsoft.net/appcleaner/

Restore a Previous Version of a Document

In macOS many applications will automatically save versions of documents as you are working on them. This safety feature lets you restore a previous version of a document if needed. macOS allows you to browse through various document versions and restore and older version. Versions are typically saved every hour, when you open, save, duplicate, rename, or revert to an earlier version of the document. If you are actively making changes to your document, macOS will save it more frequently.

To restore a previous version of a document, open the document if it is not already open. Select **File > Revert To > Browse All Versions...** to see which versions are available. Browse through the available versions and click the **Restore** button to restore the previous version you selected. You also have the option to revert back to the last saved version, which is timestamped by macOS, by selecting **File > Revert To > Previous Save**.

This feature may not be available in third party applications, most notably the Microsoft Office 2016 productivity suite.

Enable the Hidden macOS Power Chime

When you connect your iPhone or iPad to their chargers, they emit a chime to let you know they are charging. By default, your Mac does not sound a power chime when you connect it to its power connector. This hidden tweak will configure macOS to sound a chime when you connect your Mac to AC power.

To enable the hidden power chime, first disconnect your Mac's power connector. Launch Terminal and enter the following commands.

```
defaults write com.apple.PowerChime ChimeOnAllHardware -bool TRUE

open /System/Library/CoreServices/PowerChime.app
```

Now reattach the power connector and your Mac will emit an iOS-like chime to indicate it is charging. Be sure the sound is not muted and is turned up so you can hear the chime.

To disable the hidden power chime, enter the following commands in Terminal.

```
defaults write com.apple.PowerChime ChimeOnAllHardware -bool FALSE

killall PowerChime
```

Disable Message Read Receipts

 Read receipts let the sender know when you have read their message. If you want to turn off read receipts, they can be disabled globally in the **Messages** preference pane. To turn off read receipts for all senders, launch the Messages app and open its preference pane by selecting **Messages > Preferences...** or enter ⌘, (command+,). Click on the **Accounts** tab and uncheck the checkbox next to **Send read receipts**.

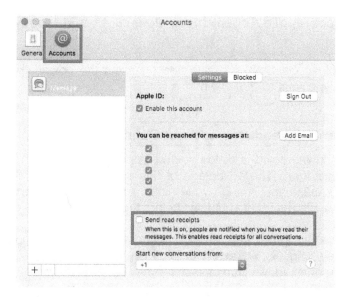

Note that read receipts are only available if you are communicating with someone using an iOS device or a Mac. If the other person is using an Android device, the read receipt feature is not available.

Enable or Disable Read Receipts for a Contact

 If you want to enable or disable read receipts for a contact with whom you are chatting, you can do so from the Messages window. If you have disabled sending read receipts globally using the last tweak, you can enable read receipts on a per conversation basis.

Click on the conversation in Messages and then click **Details** located in the upper right corner of the window. A configuration sheet will appear with several options including read receipts. Check the checkbox next to **Send Read Receipts** to enable read receipts for the selected conversation.

Similarly, if the read receipt feature is enabled globally, you could disable sending read receipts on a per conversation basis by unchecking the checkbox.

Note that this configuration sheet has additional options to turn on **Do Not Disturb** and to view the **Photos** and **Files** sent by the selected contact.

Disable Power Button Sleep

You can put your Mac to sleep immediately by pressing and releasing its power button. macOS allows you to disable this feature if you have no need for it.

To disable power button sleep, launch Terminal and enter the following command. Do not press the **return** key until you have entered the entire command. Log out and log in for this change to take effect.

```
defaults write com.apple.loginwindow PowerButtonSleepsSystem -bool
FALSE
```

With power button sleep disabled, pressing and releasing the power button will cause macOS to verify that you want to shut down.

Restart or Shut Down Immediately without Confirmation

When restarting or shutting down, a dialog box will appear confirming whether you really want to restart or shutdown. The advantage of this dialog box is that it gives you 60 seconds to **Cancel** in case you change your mind. Clicking the **Restart** or **Shutdown** button causes your Mac to restart or shutdown before the 60-second timer expires.

If you want to skip this dialog box and restart or shutdown immediately, hold down the ⌥ (option) key while selecting ⌘ > **Restart** or ⌘ > **Shut Down**. Your Mac will skip the dialog box and restart or shutdown immediately.

If you have an older Mac with an optical drive, you can hold down the ⌃⌥⌘ keys (control+option+command) while pressing the **eject** button to force your Mac to shutdown immediately.

About the Author

Tom Magrini has written 7 books about computers and technology. He has written six editions of the best-selling *Customizing macOS* series to help Mac users completely customize their macOS user experience with hundreds of tweaks, hacks, secret commands, and hidden features. Tom is also the author of *Cut the Cord: How to Cut Your Cable or Satellite TV Cord & Save Big Bucks*, which helps readers to save money by ditching expensive cable and satellite TV for streaming video over the Internet.

Tom is an information technology professional with over 30 years experience as an engineer, manager, and IT director. He has worked with Macs since 1984 and still fondly remembers his first Apple Macintosh computer with its 8 MHz Motorola 68000 processor, 9-inch 512 x 342 pixel black-and-white screen, 128 kB of RAM, and built-in 400 kB 3½-inch floppy drive. Tom has also worked with NeXT computers and the NeXTStep operating system, the forerunner to Apple's macOS. And yes, he has even crossed over to the dark side and has worked extensively with Windows PCs.

During the work week, Tom is a busy IT director, leading a team of IT professionals who maintain two data centers and the network, telephony, Wi-Fi, Office 365 messaging, server, storage, operating systems, security infrastructure, fiber optic cable infrastructure, and public safety radio system for a large municipality. Tom has taught programming, operating systems, Cisco Networking Academy, and wireless technology courses as a Computer Information Systems professor at two colleges. He has worked for numerous technology companies including SynOptics Communications, Bay Networks, FORE Systems, 3Com, and Cisco Systems, Inc. Tom is also a certified ITIL® Expert and holds a GIAC Security Leadership Certification (GSLC).

When Tom isn't working on his MacBook Pro or hanging out with his family and dogs, he enjoys reading, movies, writing, and the beautiful Arizona weather with its 300+ days of sunshine.

Please subscribe to Tom's Flipboard magazines, *Apple macOS + iOS*, where he keeps you up-to-date on the latest macOS, iOS, and Apple news, features, tips, and tricks.

Books by Tom Magrini

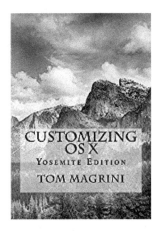

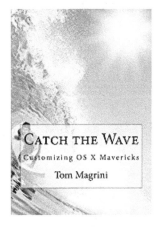

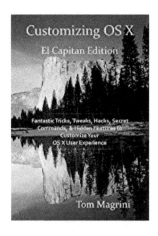

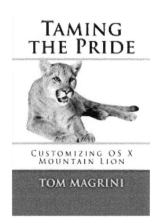